WALK TILL THE DOGS GET MEAN

WALK TILL THE DOGS GET MEAN

MEDITATIONS ON THE FORBIDDEN FROM CONTEMPORARY APPALACHIA

Edited by Adrian Blevins and
Karen Salyer McElmurray

OHIO UNIVERSITY PRESS
ATHENS

Ohio University Press, Athens, Ohio 45701
ohioswallow.com
© 2015 by Ohio University Press

To obtain permission to quote, reprint, or otherwise reproduce or distribute material from Ohio University Press publications, please contact our rights and permissions department at
(740) 593-1154 or (740) 593-4536 (fax).

Printed in the United States of America
Ohio University Press books are printed on acid-free paper ⊚ ™

25 24 23 22 21 20 19 18 17 16 15   5 4 3 2 1

Library of Congress Cataloging-in-Publication Data
Walk till the dogs get mean : meditations on the forbidden from contemporary appalachia / edited by Adrian Blevins, Karen Salyer McElmurray.
    pages cm
 Summary: "In *Walk Till the Dogs Get Mean,* Adrian Blevins and Karen Salyer McElmurray collect essays from today's finest established and emerging writers with roots in Appalachia. Together, these essays take the theme of silencing in Appalachian culture, whether the details of that theme revolve around faith, class, work, or family legacies. In essays that take wide-ranging forms—making this an ideal volume for creative nonfiction classes—contributors write about families left behind, hard-earned educations, selves transformed, identities chosen, and risks taken. They consider the courage required for the inheritances they carry. Toughness and generosity alike characterize works by Dorothy Allison, bell hooks, Silas House, and others. These writers travel far away from the boundaries of a traditional Appalachia, and then circle back—always—to the mountains that made each of them the distinctive thinking and feeling people they ultimately became. The essays in *Walk Till the Dogs Get Mean* are an individual and collective act of courage. Contributors: Dorothy Allison, Rob Amberg, Pinckney Benedict, Kathryn Stripling Byer, Sheldon Lee Compton, Michael Croley, Richard Currey, Joyce Dyer, Sarah Einstein, Connie May Fowler, RJ Gibson, Mary Crockett Hill, bell hooks, Silas House, Jason Howard, David Huddle, Tennessee Jones, Lisa Lewis, Jeff Mann, Chris Offutt, Ann Pancake, Jayne Anne Phillips, Melissa Range, Carter Sickels, Aaron Smith, Jane Springer, Ida Stewart, Jacinda Townsend, Jessie van Eerden, Julia Watts, Charles Dodd White, and Crystal Wilkinson"— Provided by publisher.
 ISBN 978-0-8214-2167-3 (hardback) — ISBN 978-0-8214-2168-0 (pb) — ISBN 978-0-8214-4531-0 (pdf)
 1. American literature—Appalachian Region. 2. Appalachian Region—Literary collections. I. Blevins, Adrian, 1964– II. McElmurray, Karen Salyer, 1956–
 PS537.W35 2015
 810.8'0974—dc23
                               2015026455

For those who came before
and for those who will follow

Homage to Hazel Dickens

Neither the house nor the barn can keep me, now I'm moving on.
Whether I go or stay the pain will be the same, so now I'm picking up

My suitcase with the leather handle that my Uncle Brack brought
home from France, and now I'm waving to you all.

After this nothing can ever hurt me because my heart is wrung
like a wet towel here, and my lips are swollen and red.

By way of Gerrit's Gap and then by way of Deep Creek Road
I've come to the turning, and turning away from air

fog-soaked and shining, away from the suckhole in the river.
The sewing factory closes and I've got to have a paycheck.

Since I was twelve I knew I'd have to turn my back
on the smoky kitchen, on the tow-headed boys fighting at the well,

on my mother's peaceable face. The faces I will meet later
will never measure up, you know that. Nothing will.

Both me and you have got to go sometime. Come on, let's tear
the heartstrings loose and head for the station.

Whether we go or stay, we've lost it.
The porch, the cold crocks of cream in the cellar,

the redbone hound in the yard, the wild azalea all orange
and sweet, we've lost it standing here looking at it

this way. So we should turn our faces outward
from this place, string our guitars, and go.

       —Irene McKinney

The writer is a secret criminal.

       —Hélène Cixous

Contents

HALFALACHIAN

OUTLAW HEART

Preface

When five women came together a few years back with a proposal for a panel for a national conference for writers, we began with questions about silence. All of us had roots in southern Appalachia and planned to talk about how our heritage was both a strength and a source of enormous expectation—from our workplaces, families, and the culture at large—to remain silent. We quoted short story writer Tillie Olson, who speaks of "times dark with silence . . . silences hidden . . . not natural silences." Our proposal considered silence as necessary renewal for ourselves as artists, but also as an unfortunate and even dangerous act of submission. Most importantly, we planned to discuss the power inherent in finding our voices as women and as writers.

The following spring, these ideas reshaped themselves for a second conference for the Appalachian Studies Association in Boone, North Carolina. This time two of us moved deeper into our questions, focusing our ideas on place and experience. What did silence have to do with our own heritage? How does the act of silencing relate to the place called Appalachia? And wasn't the lack of sanction by American mainstream literary culture a kind of silencing? How did that form us as writers? Did it teach us what we should and should not say? In first world definitions, we are often considered quaint—hillbillies and banjo pickers, primitive mountaineers, idealized in the effort to make us fit in to a larger paradigm. But *whose* larger paradigm? And was our place as writers within it or outside it? Wishful thinking on someone's part? Folklore? Tradition? And what happens to outsiders who break established codes and norms?

At that conference, at the invitation of Gillian Berchowitz and Ohio University Press, our proposal ideas became the beginning concept for a book. Soon, Tillie Olson's silence transformed itself as a subject, becoming the silence of family, geography, love, birth, death, religion, and sex—all of our most profound troubles and triumphs as individuals. We became more and more interested in work from a "new Appalachia"—one concerned with a fierce need for an environmental, familial, intimate, and cultural language powerful enough to break our traditional culture's need for compliance and acquiescence. The word "forbidden" entered our conversation.

One of us grew up in Eastern Kentucky, first in Harlan County, then in Johnson and Floyd. There, forbidden things abounded. Dancing and playing cards. Questions about Our Lord and Savior. The chance to go here, there, yonder, see all those foreign places. Getting above your raising with anything from books to desire to fierce determination. Power wasn't exactly forbidden, especially for women, but the rules for women involved particular circumspection. What one could or could not do when it came to the backseats of Plymouth Valiants on a Saturday night. Bathing during menses. The unlikely necessity of an education, when marriage and children and ensuring the generations ahead was the most likely future. This one of us read everything she could get her hands on. She read Melville, Hawthorne, Emerson. She traveled worlds belonging to men: Dostoevsky, Mann, Kazantzakis. And somewhere, somehow, years passed and she discovered the voices of her own hills. Agee, Still, Haun. *Mildred Haun*. A woman, writing about what could have been, should have been known. The voices of other women reached out to that one of us until she dreamed big, longed aplenty. The enormity of the Whole Wide World was not an easy prospect for a young woman who was raised to be humble. No voyage out seemed quite right except for the stories and essays that finally began to find their way onto her own pages.

The other one of us grew up with a different take on forbidden things. As the daughter of bohemian intellectuals whose own parents had left the farms of mountain North Carolina for left-leaning, artsy jobs in southwest Virginia, she spent years learning how to break the supercilious language codes of respectability and decorum imposed upon her by that generations-old class leap—one should never say *fuck* in a book preface, for example, she knew, or make nonessential references to the genitals of either gender. Far more seriously, though, it was Appalachia itself that was outlawed and banned. Appalachian literature was especially forbidden—too folksy and nostalgic by half, the intellectuals said. Not edgy enough. Not modern. Not cool. But weren't they—weren't *we ourselves*—full-blown Appalachians? Born and bred in the hollows just like our mothers before us and their mothers too? And had not all these women and men been educated in Appalachia? And taught school there—many of them—and read Philip Roth and William Faulkner and Eudora Welty under the tree in the green valley there below the Blue Ridge? Why were we excluding our own selves from our own canon? And could we really write like sex-crazed hipsters from Newark, New Jersey, or men in white suits from the hot, old Mississippi Delta that we'd never even laid eyes on? And what would be the cost to us if we tried?

Originally titled *Writing into the Forbidden: On Cultivating the Courage to Speak,* the essays we have gathered over the past two years consider a myriad of challenges to voices new and established in contemporary Appalachian poetry and prose. The writers we have worked with during these months understand the power of forbidden things and have taught us incalculable truths about the courage it takes to challenge silence and to speak.

In our collection, now titled *Walk Till the Dogs Get Mean: Meditations on the Forbidden from Contemporary Appalachia,* both established and emerging poets and prose writers with roots in Appalachia write about families left behind, hard-earned educations, selves transformed, identities chosen, and risks taken. The writers in these pages consider the courage required for any number of inheritances—faith, poverty, woundedness. They explore what it means to be tough, both in memory and in language, as well as what it means to be generous, to reach out beyond the confines of place as well as inward to the gift of language. These writers travel far away from the boundaries of traditional Appalachia, and then circle back—always—to the mountains that made each of them the distinctive thinking and feeling people they ultimately became. The essays in *Walk Till the Dogs Get Mean* are an individual and collective act of courage we are proud to have gathered together—one we hope will inspire new writers from the mountains and beyond for years to come.

Adrian Blevins
Karen Salyer McElmurray

FORBIDDEN GODS

SILAS HOUSE
The Forbidden Gods

MY FIRST MEMORY is of my mother being slain in the spirit.

I was six, maybe seven, and I had been sleeping under the hard wooden pews of the Lily Holiness Church on the poinsettia-red plush carpet, which had left an imprint on my cheek. Church services sometimes lasted three or four hours and at some point the children in the congregation faded away, lulled to sleep by chant-like prayers and the curling, staccato rhythms of the Holy Ghost.

But the music was moving through the church-house like a train again and the crash of cymbals, or the deep *thunk thunk thunk* of the bass drum, or the clinking, pounding piano keys, or perhaps the high squall of a beehive-haired woman crying out to God had awakened me.

I crawled out from under the pews, aware that the familiar panty-hosed legs of my mother were not nearby (so many times I watched her getting ready for church: her stockings produced from a plastic egg she bought at the Ben Franklin store on Main Street, the one that still had a COLORED fountain—the word stamped into the silver bowl—even though it was the late '70s; her hands, roughened by constant bleach and dishwater and mop-water, often snagging on the nylon material and causing small tears she repaired with dabs of clear nail polish, which she only bought for this purpose since wearing makeup of any kind was forbidden at our church) and scanned the sanctuary for my mother.

Most everyone was standing. Eyes closed, holy languages chewing at their lips, prayers eating their ways through the ceiling, arms swaying, palms open, fingers spread wide as if light would shoot out of their polishless tips. Some of them couldn't quite control their bodies: heads lolled about on their necks, or shot back and forth in a quick rhythm like the head-bangers I would see much, much later, once I had laid down my own religion and went to concerts where people did things like head-bang and smoke dope and drink out of boot flasks. Quite a few danced: this one shuffling in place with a gentle lift of his feet; this one running up and down the aisles like a chicken with its head cut off; this one twirling round and round like a woman showing off her bell-shaped skirt at a square dance.

Then there were the ones up front, at the altar. The holiest ones of all. Speaking the holiest of tongues, a low hum that could not so much be heard as seen in the occasional convulsions that electrified them, God sizzling up and down their bodies so that they had been knocked to the floor and lay there.

Being slain, they called it. Or: *Slain in the spirit.* Pentcostal

And this is what most everyone wanted. This was the highest form of worship. This was only accomplished by those who lived "right," who were the best people, the most holy, the most revered, the ones without blemish.

Cleaning

Always there were one or two—always women—who somehow were not affected by the spirit so they could attend to the slain. The sole purpose of these keepers was to pluck a white towel from the stack kept on the front pew and spread it over the legs of any woman who had become slain and might betray her modesty while she lay splayed out on the floor. The towel was spread over my mother's nyloned legs and denim skirt. This night the towel had been laid or knocked crooked and one of my mother's feet protruded. There was a hole in the stocking at her big toe, torn through because she had most likely kicked off her shoes and danced about the church before the Holy Ghost puts its Hand on her forehead and knocked her to the floor at the altar.

My first reaction was to be afraid. My mother was lying on the floor, after all, seemingly unconscious and in the midst of a fit that lightninged through her body, her lip trembling and the muscle in her jaw jerking as if her face had been overtaken by tremors.

But then: I knew. *She's just slain,* I thought. Already I knew the language of my people, of my culture. Already I had the lingo down pat. Other words that we said that didn't mean the same thing to us as they did to Normal People: "shouting" (to us this meant to be overtaken by the Spirit, which sometimes resulted in silent dancing, sometimes in the speaking of tongues, and sometimes in outright yelling, as the name would imply), "Having Church" (this did not mean the act of actually holding a church service; instead this was the moniker for church really getting in the swing of things: the spirit had zoomed into the room and overtaken the music and the bodies of the people; the Holy Ghost had been present), "anointed" (while most people would think of this as a verb defining the action of putting oil on someone, to us this meant that you had been chosen by God or that you lived such a clean life that you were worthy of God's richest blessings).

Just slain, I thought. Slain. *O ver taken by the spirit*

I was proud of her because this meant she was one of the holiest ones. One of The Chosen.

And I believed and believed and believed.

Until one day, I didn't any more. And then I spent the next several years trying my best to believe again.

YEARS LATER I am in my thirties and have only recently been hired at a small Southern university. I am a bit of a pariah without knowing why. Maybe I am just unlikable. Maybe I don't know how to play the social game of academia properly. But maybe it goes deeper than that. Perhaps because of my thick rural accent, which has always caused some people—especially academics—to not take me as seriously as others. A whole lot of Americans have bought into the media's portrayal of the rural dialect to equate to ignorance, racism, homophobia, misogyny, outright stupidity. Perhaps, even, because they have heard I was raised Holiness.

Stereotipe

Language and religion are both political, and the most liberal among us might claim to not judge others on their skin or gender but will openly make fun of people because of their ruralness or their religiosity, so long as that religion falls into the camp that the academic elites have deemed foolish. To be Muslim or Arab or Jewish is okay—at least the elites say this *out loud*—but to be Christian is somewhat suspect, and they might be suspect as well if they don't loudly voice their opinion on the stupid Christians among us.

And to have been raised a fundamentalist Christian? Laughable. Not just laughable, but laughable-to-one's-face.

Somehow I have been invited to this faculty party although I normally am left out.

Urbane - courteous and refined

A Virginia Woolf scholar is suddenly near me. She holds her glass of wine very high, leaning it against her collarbone where I can see red lipstick lining the entire rim, as if she turns the glass every time she takes a drink. She seems to have the idea that the drinking of wine makes one decidedly more urbane, more monied, more sophisticated. Her pearls—real—are magnified and distorted through the empty part of the glass.

"I wonder what you think of these students we have who speak in such a thick Appalachian accent," she slurs. Her eyes are very dark and nearly all pupil, as if her eyes have been dilated and never went back to their normal size.

"I think that if they speak in correct grammar their accent doesn't matter."

"But to speak Appalachian is to speak bad grammar."

"That's not true," I say, edging each word with politeness. "I speak Appalachian but I have always gone out of my way to have excellent grammar."

She acts as if I haven't spoken at all. "I tell them if they want to be taken seriously they should lose those awful accents."

"Would you have told that to Virginia Woolf?" I try to smile, even laugh a little when I say this. I want to be friendly. "Woolf certainly had an accent."

She takes a long drink of her Merlot, keeps her eyes on me. They are magnified and distorted through the glass.

I can see that she is chewing over my question and she already knows the same thing I do: of course she wouldn't have corrected her accent because to her ears the British accent Woolf would have possessed was one that sounded urbane, monied, sophisticated.

"Where are you from?" she asks, instead of answering me.

I tell her. (Christians that believe that they are above
"Aren't there a lot of holy rollers there?" My part of the world is well known for the number of Pentecostal, Holiness, and Old Time Baptists who live there.

"Yes. I was raised in the Holiness church. My parents still go there."

"Jesus, how did you escape it?" This from another English professor who has suddenly materialized beside her. He is not her husband but he puts his hand on the small of the woman's back as if to steady her. So far he has been very friendly to me at the couple of faculty meetings we've attended together.

"So you handled snakes?" the woman asks, looking into my eyes as if I am a very exotic creature so I realize she doesn't even mean to be offensive. She honestly just doesn't know any better.

"No, very few Holiness people actually do that."

"That's not what I've read," she says.

"You must still be getting over it!" the man says.

"It wasn't easy," I say, because this is true.

"Those people are crazy," the woman slurs. *gill*

I glance down at my glass of Tanqueray and tonic: the universal way to get out of a conversation with two assholes at a party. "Excuse me," I say. "I'm going to grab another drink."

I walked away because I had had this conversation with so many others before. I wanted to tell them how wrong they were. I wanted to say to them that my mother wasn't crazy, and neither were the other people with whom I went to church. I wanted to say how they had loved me, and I had loved them. I wanted to tell them about the culture the church provided for me, the family.

If only I had had time to tell them about the big suppers we all had together in the fellowship hall.

The baptisms that happened in the river or the pond at the mouth of Sweet Holler, the women in their fluttering dresses singing "There Is Power in the Blood" or the shimmering silver sound of tambourining as we made our way back up the bank belting out "I Know God Is God."

The evenings our youth group would all wear matching shirts—HOLY ROLLERS—when we went to the roller rink for Gospel Only Night.

Or the way we'd sing together in the church van on our way to Mammoth Cave, where the preacher would make a special request of the tour guide for us to turn out all lights so he could lead us in a special prayer way down there in the depths of the earth.

The smell of crayons and chalk in the Sunday School basement.

The comforting bosom of Gannie Morgan as I sat on her lap as a little boy after she had given me a stick of Fruit Stripe gum. I still connect that faux-grape smell to her.

The music and the safety and the books of the Bible, Matthew Mark Luke and John, the pride of standing before the congregation and reciting all of them correctly, the applause, the blue ribbon they had bought at the Christian bookstore.

The brown paper bags handed out at the annual Christmas play. Always inside: a Milky Way, an orange, an apple, a pack of Double-mint gum, and a scattering of peppermints. The play itself: towels used as head coverings, bathrobes as shepherds' clothes, a Cabbage Patch doll standing in for the Christ-child.

I look into my gin and tonic and remember all those people I grew up with. I remember all those times we had together. I remember all the goodness, the way I used to feel God sizzling up and down the aisles of the church. I want to tell the snobby professors about all of that.

They know about the bad parts, the reasons I left the church—the racism, the homophobia, the misogyny. They know everything that resulted from the culture war of the 1980s, when the fundamentalist churches made a sharp right turn and were encouraged by their local elites and political leaders to stop the spread of the gays, and of AIDS, and of abortion, and of adulterers, a move that forever changed all of those little country churches, making God smaller and smaller until for folks like me it felt as if He didn't even show up anymore.

It is impossible to explain the complexities of religion and fundamentalism to two drunken and intolerant people at a faculty party, mainly because they will never understand that their intolerance is so closely aligned to the terrible parts of the Holiness church that I and others fled, an inability to accept anyone who is different due to fear that has been fostered by our political leaders and the media for decades now.

MOST PEOPLE raised in fundamentalist Christian churches come to an important moment when they are about sixteen or seventeen years old. It is then that we must decide to either fully embrace the church or reject it. To either become a full-on card-carrying recruiter for Jesus or to rebel.

I chose to leave. And I went wild.

Since I had been taught that everything was a sin I figured if I was going to sin the least little bit I might as well do it all. So I did everything I could think of, which in retrospect wasn't much since I was so innocent. To me, drinking beers and going dancing was sinning at its most hardcore. At seventeen I was still shocked to hear people curse. I never touched any kind of drug until I was out of college. I did have a series of affairs with a variety of people, but I felt guilty after every *affair*

tryst. I prayed for forgiveness, crying large beseeching tears like the ones Christ had shed in the Garden of Gethsemane.

I spent years and years wandering in the wilderness, trying everything to find the God of My Own Understanding. Trying to not lose my belief. I needed to hang onto that, no matter how many people made fun of me or anyone else for possessing it.

I tried churches and dope and whiskey and sex and devoting my life solely to my children.

All the while, I was struggling to make sense of those two opposing things in my childhood: the brutal intolerance of the church that had given me the only acceptance I had ever known and the knowledge that a church should provide acceptance for everyone. I couldn't find a church like that. I searched and searched. So eventually I decided that I could make my own church in the wildwood. I would find God in trees and the sky and books and poems. I would find God in everyone I encountered. But most of all I would find God in the chattering keys of my laptop, in the blank spaces between the lines of the novel I was trying to finish. I would worship through creating art.

And then I realized that words are what had always offered me salvation, acceptance, love. Best of all, I came to understand that I could work out my own salvation in the pages of that first novel. That I could come to some understanding with my Holiness upbringing by writing about it in all of its complexities. I would write the truth that I could not tell to others over cocktails. I'd write about the good and the bad and the in-between of growing up in the House of God.

The truth.

That's all we can ever really hope to achieve in a piece of writing. Even in a piece of fiction: beautiful fiction must always rely on the essential truth the author is trying to illuminate.

For me, to write about growing up in the Holiness church and revealing any of that ugliness was a tantalizing danger. Would I be able to cut into that complex thing like a succulent watermelon, draw the knife through the red meat and sit the two halves side by side on the page for the reader to dig in and eat with their bare hands? I had to try.

Once my first novel was published I had many conversations with people who took the religious aspects of the book in a variety of ways. Some thought I had perpetuated stereotypes about the Holiness church, or about fundamentalist Christians. To them I said that I had only told my own truth. Others—mostly those who had left similar churches or were still active members of the Holiness church—felt I had gotten it just right. "I was only telling my own truth," I said, and I felt good about that.

For now are the days of the sound bite. Now are the days of the black and white. These are times when we must be one way or the other, Republican or Democrat, churchgoer or sinner, conservative or liberal, ally or homophobe, smart or ignorant. That's the way the politicians and the media want us to be. Because then we are easily contained.

Now are the days when it is forbidden to be too complex, to be too diverse in our ways of thinking and belief. We must either believe that this thing is totally wrong or that thing is totally right. I believe that the essential truth is that there is more grayness in the world than black or white. I believe that there is good and bad in all of us: in fundamentalists, in inclusives, in believers, in nonbelievers, in artists and those who consciously choose ignorance.

I FINALLY found a church that believes in all of the above, and I try to attend every Sunday that I am not on the road. I love the people. They are generous and kind. They love to cook big meals and do things as a church community, but also as members of the larger community and world. Every Sunday I am thankful for the congregation I've found there. But part of me is always thinking of the little church I grew up in, the one that stands about an hour down south from where I now live. Sometimes I think about driving down there early on a Sunday morning and sitting in the parking lot—I wouldn't go in; I *couldn't* go in, not now—just so I can hear the singing. Maybe I will glimpse through the window and see some of them shouting, waving their hands in the air. From my place in my little truck I would not be able to see those who are being slain in the spirit at the front of the church. But I would know they are there.

I've never done that, though. Instead, after leaving my good congregation I usually go home and find solace in the God I have there: the love of my life, my little dogs, my daughters, music, poetry, books, and always, always: the moment when I sit down and put my fingers to the keyboard and begin to write.

BELL HOOKS

A Constant Mourning

SUBLIME SILENCE SURROUNDS me. I have walked to the top of the hill, plopped myself down to watch the world around me. I have no fear here, in this world of trees, weeds, and growing things. This is the world I was born into: a world of wild things. In it the wilderness in me speaks. I am wild. I hear my elders caution mama, telling her that she is making a mistake, letting me "run wild," letting me run with my brother as though no gender separates us. We are making our childhood together in the Kentucky hills, experiencing the freedom that comes from living away from civilization. Even as a child I knew that to be raised in the country, to come from the backwoods, left one without meaning or presence. Growing up we did not use terms like "hillbilly." Country folk lived on isolated farms away from the city; backwoods folks lived in remote areas, in the hills and hollers.

To be from the backwoods was to be part of the wild. Where we lived, black folks were as much a part of the wild, living in a natural way on the earth, as white folks. All backwoods folks were poor by material standards; they knew how to make do. They were not wanting to tame the wilderness, in themselves or nature. Living in the Kentucky hills was where I first learned the importance of being wild.

Later, attending college on the West Coast, I would come to associate the passion for freedom and the wilderness I had experienced as a child with anarchy, with the belief in the power of the individual to be self-determining. Writing about the connection between environments, nature, and creativity in the introduction to *A Place in Space,* Gary Snyder states: "Ethics and aesthetics are deeply intertwined. Art, beauty, and craft have always drawn on the self-organizing 'wild' side of language and mind. Human ideas of place and space, our contemporary focus on watersheds, become both models and metaphors. Our hope would be to see the interacting realms, learn where we are, and thereby move towards a style of planetary and ecological cosmopolitanism." Snyder calls this approach the "practice of the wild," urging us to live "in the self-disciplined elegance of 'wild' mind." By their own practice of living in harmony with nature, with simple abundance, Kentucky black folks who lived in the backwoods were deeply engaged with an ecological cosmopolitanism. They fished; hunted; raised chickens; planted what we would now call organic gardens; made homemade spirits, wine, and whiskey; and grew flowers. Their religion was interior and private. Mama's mama, Baba, refused to attend church after someone made fun of the clothes she was wearing. She reminded us that God could be worshipped every day, anywhere. No matter that they lived according to Appalachian values, they did not talk about themselves coming from Appalachia. They did not divide Kentucky into East and West. They saw themselves as renegades and rebels, folks who did not want to be hemmed in by rules and laws, folks that wanted to remain independent. Even when circumstances forced them out of the country into the city, they were still wanting to live free.

As there were individual black folks who explored the regions of this nation before slavery, the first black Appalachians being fully engaged with the Cherokee, the lives of most early black Kentuckians were shaped by a mixture of free sensibility and slave mentality. When slavery ended in Kentucky, life was hard for the vast majority of black people as white supremacy and racist domination did not end. But those folks who managed to own land, especially land in isolated country sites or hills (sometimes inherited from white folks for whom they had worked for generations, or sometimes purchased), were content to be self-defining and self-determining even if it meant living with less. No distinctions were made between those of us who dwelled in the hills of eastern or western Kentucky. Our relatives from eastern Kentucky did not talk about themselves as Appalachians, and in western Kentucky we did not use the term; even if one lived in the hills where the close neighbors were white and hillbilly, black people did not see themselves as united with these folk, even though our habits of being and ways of thinking were more like these strangers than those of other black folks who lived in the city—especially black folks who had money and urban ways. In small cities and towns, the life of a black coal miner in western Kentucky was more similar to the life of an Eastern counterpart than different. Just as the lives of hillbilly black folks were the same whether they lived in the hills of eastern or western Kentucky.

In the Kentucky black subcultures, folks were united with our extended kin, and our identities were more defined by labels like "country" and "backwoods." It was not until I went away to college that I was questioned about Appalachia, about hillbilly culture, and it was always assumed by these faraway outsiders that only poor white people lived in the backwoods and the hills. No wonder then that black folks who cherish our past, the independence that characterized our backwoods ancestors, seek to recover and restore their history, their legacy. Early on in my life I learned from those Kentucky backwoods elders, the folks whom we might now label "Appalachian," a set of values rooted in the belief that above all else one must be self-determining. It is the foundation that is the root of my radical critical consciousness. Folks from the backwoods were certain about two things: that every human soul needed to be free and that the responsibility of being free required one to be a person of integrity, a person who lived in such a way that there would always be congruency between what one thinks, says, and does.

These ancestors had no interest in conforming to social norms and manners that made lying and cheating acceptable. More often than not, they believed themselves to be above the law whenever the rules of so-called civilized culture made no sense. They farmed, fished, hunted, and made their way in the world. Sentimental nostalgia does not call me to remember the worlds they invented. It is just a simple fact that without their early continued support for dissident thinking and living, I would not have been able to hold my own in college and beyond when conformity promised to provide me with a sense of safety and greater regard. Their "Appalachian values," imprinted on my consciousness as core truths I must live by, provided and continue to provide me with the tools I needed and need to survive whole in a postmodern world.

Living by those values, living with integrity, I am able to return to my native place, to an Appalachia that is no longer silent about its diversity or about the broad sweep of its influence. While I do not claim an identity as Appalachian, I do claim a solidarity, a sense of belonging, that makes me one with the Appalachian past of my ancestors: black, Native American, white, all "people of one blood" who made homeplace in isolated landscapes where they could invent themselves, where they could savor a taste of freedom.

In my latest collection of essays, *Writing Beyond Race,* I meditate for page after page on the issue of where it is black folk may go to be free of the category of race. Ironically, the segregated world of my Kentucky childhood was the place where I lived beyond race. Living my early childhood in the isolated hills of Kentucky, I made a place for myself in nature there—roaming the hills, walking the fields hidden in hollows where my sharecropper grandfather Daddy Gus planted neat rows of growing crops. Without evoking a naïve naturalism that would suggest a world of innocence, I deem it an act of counterhegemonic resistance for black folks to talk openly of our experience growing up in a southern world where we felt ourselves living in harmony with the natural world.

To be raised in a world where crops are grown by the hands of loved ones is to experience an intimacy with earth and home that is lost when everything is out there, somewhere away from home, waiting to be purchased. Since much sociological focus on black experience has centered on urban life—lives created in cities—little is shared about the agrarian lives of black folk. Until Isabel Wilkerson published her awesome book *The Warmth of Other Suns,* which documents the stories of black folks leaving agrarian lives to migrate to cities, there was little attention paid to the black experience of folks living on the land. Just as the work of the amazing naturalist George Washington Carver is often forgotten when lists are made of great black men. We forget our rural black folks, black farmers, folks who long ago made their homes in the hills of Appalachia.

All my people come from the hills, from the backwoods, even the ones who ran away from this heritage, refusing to look back. No one wanted to talk about the black farmers who lost land to white supremacist violence. No one wanted to talk about the extent to which that racialized terrorism created a turning point in the lives of black folks wherein nature, once seen as a freeing place, became a fearful place. That silence has kept us from knowing the ecohistories of black folks. It has kept folk from claiming an identity and a heritage that is so often forgotten or erased.

It is no wonder, then, that when I returned to my native state of Kentucky after more than thirty years of living elsewhere, memories of life in the hills flooded my mind and heart. And I could see the link between the desecration of the land as it was lived on by red and black folk and the current exploitation and shared destruction of our environment. Coming home to Kentucky hills was, for me, a way to declare allegiance to environment struggles aimed at restoring proper stewardship to the land. It has allowed me to give public expression to the ecofeminism that has been an organic part of my social action on behalf of peace and justice.

In *Longing for Running Water: Ecofeminism and Liberation,* theologian Ivone Gebara contends: "The ecofeminist movement does not look at the connection between the domination of women and of nature solely from the perspective of cultural ideology and social structures; it seeks to introduce new ways of thinking that are more at the service of ecojustice." In keeping with this intent, in the preface to *Belonging: A Culture of Place,* where I make a space for the ecofeminist within me to speak, I conclude with this statement: "I pay tribute to the past as a resource that can serve as foundation for us to revision and renew our commitment to the present, to making a world where all people can live fully and well, where everyone can belong."

The joyous sense of homecoming that I experience from living in Kentucky does not change the reality that it has been difficult for black rural Kentuckians to find voice, to speak our belonging. Most important, it has been difficult to speak about past exploitation and oppression of people and land, to give our sorrow words. Those of us who dare to talk about the pain inflicted on red and black folks in this country, connecting that historical reality to the pain inflicted on our natural world, are often no longer silenced; we are simply ignored. The recognition of that pain causes a constant mourning.

KATHRYN STRIPLING BYER
Water Wants to Know

how long beside this creek
will you sit?

How long watch the green
salamanders dart,

minnows flee
into the current?

How far
from your hearth-place

will you wander
before you turn back?

1.

Deep into the dying hemlocks she followed, down into the sink, as it is called. The earth hollowed out, caves on either side. Living trees glistened in the rain, her feet sliding over their wet roots, her hands reaching for their limbs to keep from falling onto the slippery trail.

At the end of the trail the earth opened, so she'd been told, water from above pouring down into a pit whose bottom she would never be able to see.

Whose edges she feared.

Around her the caves waited. Only small creatures could penetrate their openings now. And bats. Hundreds of bats. Had she forever lost the courage to crawl through such narrow cracks and tunnels? Had she once known how to find her way through crevices into what lay below?

Once women could enter stones. That she remembered. They could set up house there, deep within, when they needed to escape, but they could do so only if they wished never to return to the world outside. They would come to be known as the Women in the Rocks. Knock on the rock faces alongside a trail and those women would answer, their voices so faint you might not be able to hear them.

She had no desire to knock on their stone faces, to hear any voices that might rise from so deep within this passage, so she passed quickly on by the boulders that grew out of the vines like ancient dwellings, rocks swathed in lichens and dog hobble. Now and then a lady slipper pushed through the understory, but barely, as though fearful of testing the air through which she walked. Galax lay over the forest floor, as she knew it had once lain on the caskets of the dead.

The dead bodies of hemlock lay around her, amber-fleshed beneath peeling bark. On the needles of the ones still standing, she could see the white nests of larvae. *They will all die out,* she said aloud. Like the chestnut, the wolf, the panther, even the words that had once named these places. The native names. The first names.

Doomed as the women who stay too long inside their hearth-places.

By now her boots were soaked. She had been walking for days, although she knew it had only been hours. Time lumbered along with her, becoming substance, like magma about to become rock.

Indian time, she'd heard it called. When the clock hands stop. No matter how long one tries to start them up again, they never move. As she walked, she felt time had become something she could reach into like a spiderweb. Leaving its weavings on her fingers and bare arms.

Time had become something to sink into just as she was sinking into this place, the rain, the fog, the downward pull of the earth into itself.

Or herself?

Where was she? Who was that woman ahead of her on the trail, the rain-matted one, the one covered in mud, the one she'd been following? A woman alone in this forest, as she had been warned no woman was ever supposed to be.

The strange woman had been walking as long as she could remember toward the trail's end. The edge of the sink she feared and yet longed to stand beside. How she longed to look down into emptiness as if it held, not a secret, exactly, but a kindling from a time when the clocks had not yet been set ticking.

The rain-soaked woman moved with the vigor of greening out limbs in the wind, as if she had pushed herself up out of the earth. She kept a steady distance ahead, now and then vanishing, always reappearing in the fog. When she reached the edge of the dark mouth toward which they had both been walking, she stopped.

She waited. Water streamed down the edges of the rocks into the darkness below. Veils of fog tumbled endlessly into the pit. The strange woman's hair had itself become water. Her whole body seemed about to waver into some shimmering fabric of rain. As if she were a garment holding itself open to receive her.

Raiment.

That word came to her.

But to whom? The one who had followed?

Or the one who waited at the edge of the earth's open mouth?

2.

I know a woman whose neighbors once called her a witch, or so she has told me, and I believe her suspicions. I believe them because only a woman like her deserves such a description. A woman who once charmed herself into picking up the telephone to call a stranger, one whose face she had seen in the local newspaper, a stranger who wrote poetry about finding a way through the labyrinth of one's own life.

Nobody else's life.

No hand-me-down life, used up like dresses worn by generations of her kinswomen, pulled out of a cedar chest where they had lain waiting to be worn.

She picked up the telephone and dialed the number. Her hands trembled. When the stranger answered, her own voice quavered. Her fingers on the mouthpiece turned numb. But she spoke. She spoke her poems into the mouthpiece and the stranger listened. Soon her voice did not tremble, and when the stranger invited her to meet for coffee at the fast-food restaurant downhill from where she lived, she said she would come with her notebook full of handwritten poems. She would read them to the stranger who had said words were like touchstones, ways to cross over rapids, navigate beyond backwater.

I know this woman had not told anyone else that she wrote poetry. Why would she? She suspected her neighbors called her a witch because she roamed by herself on the ridge above her double-wide, hoping to catch a glimpse of bobcat or first wind of bear before the men tracked it down. If she had told anyone she wrote poetry, the news would have spread throughout the cove. She would have been considered a witch in earnest. Someone would no doubt have seen her charming a snake down from its coil. The raptors down from their thermals. There would have been no end to the stories.

And if they had found out that she met a stranger at the local Hardee's and read poetry to her, they would have said she was not only a witch but a woman who wanted to rise above her belonging-to place. Hadn't the old hymn warned, *We will not heed the voice of the stranger?*

"I do not trust my own voice," she said to the stranger, while the stranger, who was also a woman like herself, looked at the poems spread on the table.

The stranger-woman said to her, "You have a voice that rises up from the earth. I can hear the grass you walk upon. I can hear the river your father sits beside, waiting for you to cross over and join him in dreamtime."

"But I never finished high school," the woman whose neighbors believed to be a witch replied. "How can I claim these words? Nobody listened to me while I was growing up. My mama knew the boys chased me into the woods and had their way with me, but she never said a word. She never listened when I told her. I became afraid of telling anybody, even my father."

The stranger-woman said, "I can hear your voice in the grass stains left behind on your skin. The blood on your undergarments. I can hear your voice in the wind threading itself through the trees under which you lay."

The woman who had written the poems said, "I had a friend whose husband shot her down after he saw her talking to another man. He shot her outside the sewing plant where she worked."

The woman whose neighbors suspected her of witchery turned to the greasy window through which she could see the first green pushing out of the tulip poplars. "He had told her never to speak when she went into town, unless it was to family. He killed her because she spoke to another man, a stranger she saw in the parking lot. She smiled at him. Somebody told her husband."

The stranger-woman replied, "I can hear your voice in the blood spilling out of your friend's breast, how silently it pooled in the parking lot, until you spoke for it, just now, to me."

"But these words," the woman asked, pointing to the handwriting on the notebook pages, "am I using them the right way? Do I have the right to use them? I grew up on Shady Fork. I have never left home."

And the stranger-woman quickly looked up from the poems, her eyes kindling from brown to amber fire, and asked, "Why should you think I have more right to these words than you? Did ever you sign away your rights to your own words? Every word in our language belongs to you."

But the woman who suspected she had been called a witch replied, "My mama said I deserve what I get when I speak. She said a man ought not let his wife get out of their truck when they come to town of a Saturday. He ought not let her open her mouth to speak even a good morning. She must sit in the truck while he goes about his business, for he is afraid somebody might be waiting for her. Somebody she doesn't know yet. A stranger. My mama used to sing to me, "We will not heed the words of the stranger, for he would lead us into despair.""

The stranger-woman looked down at the words written into the pages and said, "I can hear your feet on the wet stones."

3.

Will I turn back?
Dare I keep straight ahead

across not enough rocks
for my bare feet to find?

Have I come to this
crossing too soon,

no one waiting
for me on the other side?

I know a woman who threw off her hand-me-down dress and
unlaced her shoes to cross over the creek to the other side. There
were dead branches to crawl over, slippery rocks for footholds. She
was afraid she had come too soon to this crossing, but the rocks kept
singing her over as her soles sought their footholds. An old song that
never grew tired of singing itself.

Herenow
Herenow
Herenow

physicality/time ,
Location   urgency

She could still hear voices behind her calling, "Come back." Other
voices whispered that they were glad she was gone, she never belonged
there anyway, she had become a stranger to them, she wanted to claim
her own words, she wanted, she wanted. She wanted too much.

But she sits on the banks of the other side where water wants to
know what she has found now that she has come to the crossing-over.
Water wants to know what she has found here. Now.

Slowly she begins to speak.

An armada of clouds riding the currents above me.
A kettling of buzzards.
A veil of midges through which I will walk.

She knows her words will themselves be lost in the passage of
time like the native words gone from these mountains, buried along
with the panther, the chestnut, the bison that once roamed the valleys, all of them folded into leaf meal, layer upon layer upon layer.

She also knows her bare feet are cold from the creek water, so she
pulls on her shoes and laces them tightly. The wet shimmy she wore

underneath her dress will dry soon enough. Deep in the woods she sees a clearing, small and bright as the eye of a needle. She knows she has always been able to guide each thread through the smallest of eyes. Why not this one, burning like kindling deep inside the dark falling over the trail?

She stands up. She begins walking.

JESSIE VAN EERDEN
Walk Till the Dogs Get Mean

A double movement of descent: to do again, out of love,
what gravity does. Is not the double movement of descent
the key to all art?

—*Simone Weil*

I WALK TILL the dogs get mean, far up the road through the little
houses in the black trees, past the trailers pinned with lattice and past
the cinder block ruins. The dogs come out of the shadows—part pit
bull, all mange, different color eyes, no collar, no chain—and they
can smell your skunky heart looking for something. When I get this
far up the road, I pick up a big stick, knowing I'll turn back, afraid,
but I listen to them first, snarling taut and grim. I watch them snort
around, daring me to take another step. Once I get a good look, I
walk back home, or toward home, and I do make it back to the house
itself, which is intact and discernible, but a house hollowed out.

I started walking when my marriage fell apart, three or four long
walks a day. I walked dazed and untethered, with no recognition of
my life and with most of the ache located in the throat. The freedom
was eerie, but the movement in my legs was good because I could
watch each step as a sturdy little fact, one foot then another foot, and
I lived in the Cascade Mountains of Oregon then and snow clung to
the spectacular Ponderosa Pines and sometimes the snow shivered
loose and fell to the ground and made the only other sound besides
my footsteps. I blinked like a mole at any and all light; I never changed
out of insulated flannel and jeans. Then I moved to my sister's in

Philadelphia for a few months, and I walked the cement path by the river, traffic screaming past on one side and college-boy crew teams gliding by on the other, and sometimes I sat on the rock wall and blinked at the ugly water and ached in my throat for Ponderosas and for him, my first love, my husband, my home, and at some arbitrary point I turned around and walked back the way I'd come, against the angry headlights.

Then I shambled my way back to West Virginia, to my childhood home for a time, blinking at the leafless silver trees and adding long underwear beneath flannel. Here too I walked, the roads I had once flown down on my bike, streamers spraying from the handlebars, curvy roads I learned to drive on. Out of habit from my youth, I would turn around when I reached the mean dogs that barked like crazy—Butch's coon dogs that barred the road like a posse; you never knew if they got fed. I'd head back home, but where was home? I'd crest the hill and see my parents' place, the house I grew up in, nestled there like a dollhouse, and feel a stranger there. I was a stranger in natty flannel watching my own life from outside. That house was where, long ago, I'd unconsciously made the doomed plans for how I would handle private disaster when it hit, and where I had begun a life more or less lived with all the appropriate words capitalized: God, Love, Marriage, Truth, Meaning, Art, and with words that turned into neat labels pinned to my shirt: Wife, Teacher, Writer. Losing home meant that all the words and labels went lowercase then scattered, and I was left with just me, very lowercase, which might be why I couldn't carry anything on these walks, except a branch, or a rock, when I was afraid.

I wasn't writing anything of consequence, just horrible repetitive lines about my mistakes and his, in flimsy notebooks that I hoped would blow away or burn, but one day I wrote on a scrap: *Walk till the dogs get mean.* I didn't know why I had written it. I took a job, found an apartment, bought a few blouses, but still could not say *I am here, this is my life now.* I was a shell, or I was a tunnel and the only real light showed up on the end looking backwards to the past: that's where the real life pulsed—in the life that was gone and the marriage I could not save. Present life was a paper joke, and I searched wildly for a way to get back, writing those compulsive pages of circular grief: *There has been some mistake, If I had only—If I had just—*.

One day, on another scrap, I wrote: *Walk till the dogs get mean then walk a little further.*

What was this about? Nothing literal now, since, in this new West Virginia college town, all the dogs were behind yard fences or on leashes. I was stymied in writing and loving and breath and prayer—all of it, and all of it connected—frozen in the liminal space between the past I longed for and the future I feared. I contracted, shrank, lost capacity for things requiring dimension, like joy, like forgiveness; I worked the longest hours I could work and watched TV and avoided the grocery store because there were aisles and aisles of life and light, too much to handle.

But this phrase about the dogs—it flickered—I scribbled a little more, tentative. The phrase transfixed me, and I would stare at the scraps of paper. Months went by; summer broke out; I wore a dress a time or two; as I scribbled I began to see that the only way *into* my life again was into the dogs, without going back: letting the path back give way to broomsage and brier, go wild. That's what the scraps seemed to add up to. I began to vaguely remember that I wanted to make art (the lowercase kind), I wanted to write (that *self* was still there), that the days could have a shape, and I felt a glimmer of possibility that I could say *I am here* and Here could mean Home and Home could be a fertile place again. Everything became bound up in this movement: *Walk till the dogs get mean then walk a little further.*

This metaphor is not a neat one. The dogs aren't neat symbols for things that terrify me and clamp me down; they simply begin to flesh out a living space of interior wreckage; they populate as they cower and rage; they're all part of me, what I'm capable of in cruelty, in mercy, in love, in hate, in anger, in calm, in creativity; they are shame and failure and fear and loneliness. And perhaps they are *surprise*. And they are the way forward: to face them, accept them, and get to know them as the inner hungers of my mistakes and losses. To face my demons, you could say, but I prefer to call them dogs because demons are abstract and dogs are more accurate to my idiom: these dogs involve porches and people and off-road vehicles, a kind of sparsely populated locale which seems a better, and maybe more generous, representation for the stuff found inside the busted-up self. Also because there has hung a scrim between me and the people in my life for a time, but it's not there between us, the dogs and me:

they come clear; their sounds are not muffled; their sharp teeth are, it seems, keen for me. They threaten to destroy me but offer to save me, to lead me into capacity again.

I'd like to write something useful for the wrecked heart, for others who have lived a portion of their lives frozen and bankrupt, unable to recognize themselves, because I know my loss is a commonplace kind. I don't know what will be useful to another, but the floating parallel metaphor, neat or not—the imagined inner space, where tarmac turns gravel turns dirt road—is useful to me as I try to say what it feels like these days to face up to my grief and shame and failure and to allow myself to be surprised by what I find inside of it. I'm not finding my way *back* but finding my way *into* an inviolable sense of home from which to live, create, love. I'm still finding my way.

And, of course, the reason I have always turned around at the barking frothy dogs is because I've been afraid.

ONE DAY, I walk a little further in, having awoken with my belabored head, opened the night shades, and left the house for good. Afraid or not, I am headlong for the pack. One dog's missing a leg, one a tail, one a piece of the chest as if gunshot. Their noses are dry and crusted black; one suffers a thorn in the paw. The dogs lure me and taunt me and eye me up for lunch—they are austere or near-rabid, some somnolent, others staring with wild eyes, unblinking, into the terrible light.

This time, I handle no rock or hickory branch white-knuckled, and I don't look back to the overgrown path gone to thicket. It no longer matters how I got here or where I've been: what matters is the very present snarl and snapping of teeth and that wild pus-filled eye staring me down.

They scruff the dirt; I can feel them circling.

First thing I notice among them is the basic truth the mean dogs know of the world: hunger and waves of animal hurt. It's hunger that makes them mean. That's no surprise, but when I get closer to the hunger beneath the meanness, I see there's even something beneath that, something inside hunger; it's like glimpsing the soft pink scar-skin where this one husky has lost its ear. I follow the husky to where he noses at the closed back door of a sinking trailer, howls a little. There's a mucked bowl that offered him table scraps once, long ago. I look in the window, feeling that I know who lives here, and I do: a shut-in on the bed, just lines of woman upon the sheets, bones, sadness, soreness. She's the pink skin beneath the husky's hunger, its inner dimension.

And then, I hear a pounding. The dog jumps, and so do I. A pounding again—on the front door, I think, and here too, I get an inkling of who this is:

A heavyset woman forces the latch loose, calling out to the one inside, then breaks down the door and busts into the dim room—I'm watching at the window—she's a Home Health aide in blue scrubs; she blusters around with her teased hair, cursing the mess. She picks up the overfull colostomy bag like it's a newborn, changes it, draws the old woman a bath and pulls out a new set of nightdress and under-wear, and all the while the aide's cursing and singing, then singing mostly, tenor like a man, big blue notes to match her scrubs, some song so familiar and old that it's new, and she has the kind of voice she can show off and nobody here minds that she does, even the husky gnawing at the scrap bowl's rim. The aide starts on the pile of dishes, then remembers, goes out to the car and comes back, to the back door where I'm peeping in. She has no time to fool with me; she just empties an Arby's paper bag into the bowl, roast beef and fries, and the husky tears in.

Back at the sink, the big woman sings the song, close and hot, and it becomes too much for me to bear, the fact of that song in the midst of all this. More unbearable than my fear of the dogs, than even the purpled pain of the bedsores, and I get skittish and fidgety, squirming at that window like a pinned bug, as eager to escape and as incapable. Once the aide leaves (her hand on the old woman's face, *See you soon*), I take off running through the woods, thinking this is a mistake, think-ing I'll head back, but that path is gone. I can only go deeper in.

IT'S ALMOST evening now. I am thin, onionskin, empty, nothing but homesick—but homesick for where? A pair of mutts ducks in and out of the trees alongside me and we're alone together; one foams through the teeth. Homesick for what? For something older than my-self, something ancient and inside hunger and inside sickbed loneli-ness and inside a tending and inside a song: home is inside-of and also holding it all.

More dogs slip like silverfish out from under porches.

Come at me, I say.

But then a diesel truck stutters into sight, bungling off-road. It scatters the pack. A bunch of boys stuff the cab, and another host of mean dogs pokes up from the truck bed. The boys' sighted guns hang out the window seeking antlers or anything that moves. Drunk as skunks, faces painted up like Green Berets behind enemy lines even though I can tell they never get out of the damned cab. Aerosmith on the radio scrapes up the silence. They don't have time to fool with me: here comes a doe rustling the leaves.

The truck jams to a stop; the music shuts off; the truck-bed dogs reorient snouts like compass needles and sniff her, and she likewise sniffs the fouled air and booze. This is the wretched kind of thing that happens back here, further in, and it's cruel. She is sleek and calm, stepping out of the brush, and one of the boys takes aim across the twenty yards through his stupid scope, fingering the trigger, the tapping of all time on his fingertips. I watch him, condemn him, but then I get an inkling, from somewhere unknown, that there's something underneath even cruelty. The kid raises his eyes from the scope and the gun goes slack; the doe bares her white throat to nibble a branch; he waves his brother to drive on.

They nod at me through diesel smell, like we're familiars, because we are.

Because home is inside-of yet holds it all: helplessness and eager cruelty abandoned last-minute, impossibly. It has to be all of this—I have an inkling—all of it belongs back here among the dogs, surprising and enraging. I walk on.

Night comes, and I walk.

Some oil-fur dog almost gets my leg, but I dodge it. Where am I going?

The night yields just a little to the morning, and they all slink away, strangely, snorting back to the underbrush.

THEN I see her. Coming out of the morning dark snarling, a black thing. It's imprudent to be defenseless, but my hands stay empty. No one now around for miles; no one else to give me permission, or to withhold it. She's the one I've been looking for without knowing it. I have sensed her but have never seen her before: she is everything, she is the forbidden thing, she is a force, a huge muscle-roiling bitch with swollen teats, keeping to the shadows till now, waiting for me. I come closer, she comes closer, a bitch with pups somewhere—the surprising thing—but I don't know where. I see the teats poofed out sore, like so many blisters of want. No pups around here—maybe taken or killed—and I say, *I am here, so come on, you, come at me,* nothing in my hands, her jaw frothy and wide but I don't care. I know it's only hunger that makes her mean, but that's not to say she won't devour me, her hulk and heft of full-blown shame. Ears magnetic toward me, eyes black slits, she may not let me go, but I need to find out what lies beyond her—that's where I've been going—beyond the pack, to the other side, a place I have an inkling of for the first time, as the morning dark lightens upon us. She and I go together, or neither of us goes.

She is so close now: her shoulders nearly knife up through her hide and fur, her underside was white once, our faces know each other and our breath is a fused fusty breath. *I am here,* I say. My throat aches, everything aches. *I am here.* I can say it. I trust her but I have no guarantee that she won't ravage me: trust is not control or certainty or some talisman against your destruction. She is hereness, she is surrender of what is lost, she is resistance to the clamoring fears of what's to come: *I am here.* We might look for her pups out there, beyond, each one in the litter a ball of quietness and fuzz so new, and I think maybe I could pick one up, a warmth cupped, the surprising blind face nuzzling itself into my open hand. I wonder if, for both of us, here beyond, there is a clearing of moss and green light we might make a run for, and something possible soaking there, like in a tub, so soft, if we can just get through, if we can survive this, if she doesn't eat me alive. There's nothing to do but to reach out my hand.

PINCKNEY BENEDICT

Orgo vs the Flatlanders

BY PINCKNEY BENEDICT

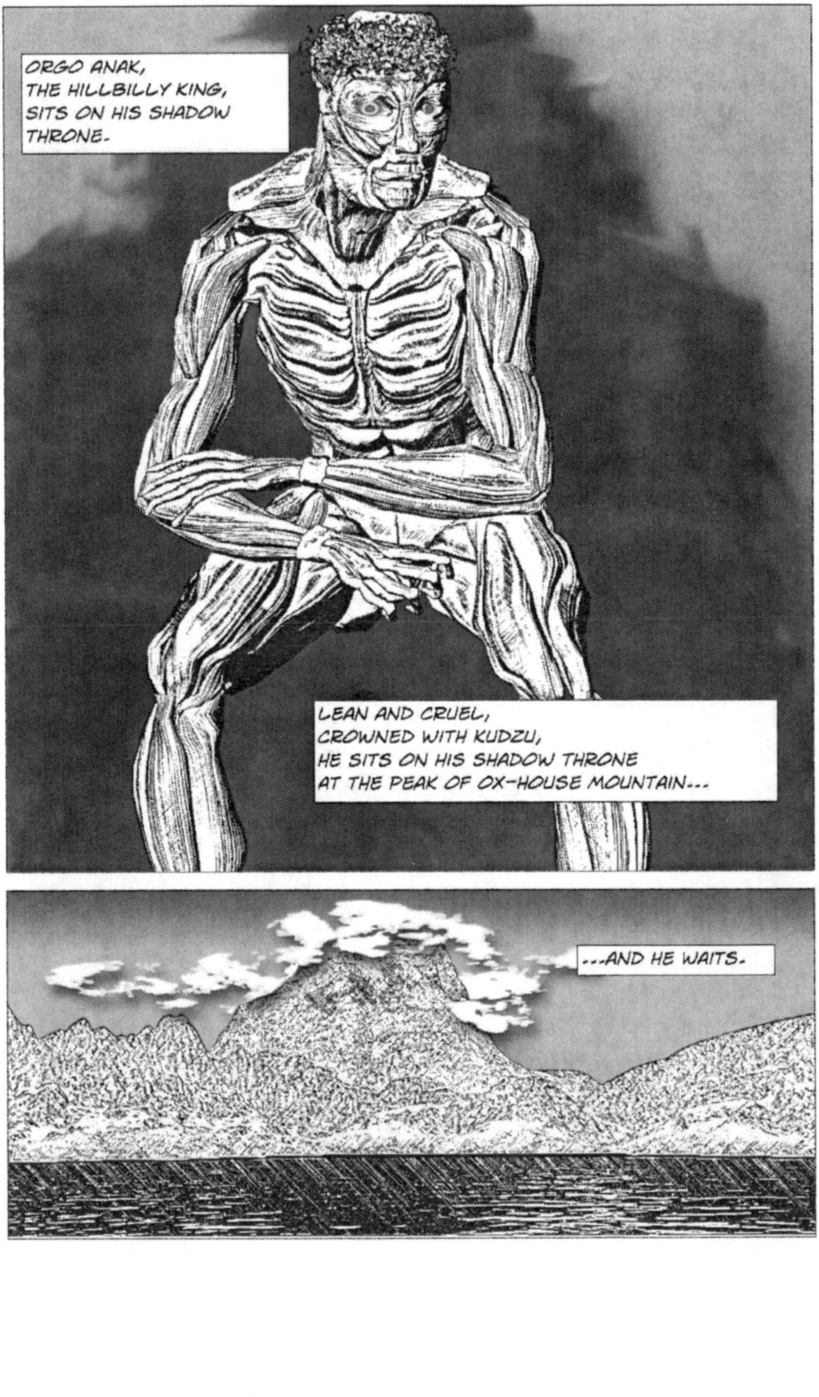

ORGO ANAK,
THE HILLBILLY KING,
SITS ON HIS SHADOW
THRONE.

LEAN AND CRUEL,
CROWNED WITH KUDZU,
HE SITS ON HIS SHADOW THRONE
AT THE PEAK OF OX–HOUSE MOUNTAIN...

...AND HE WAITS.

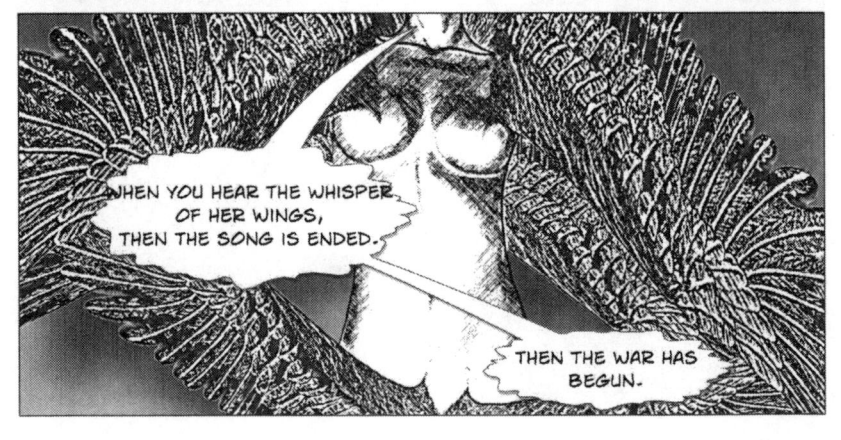

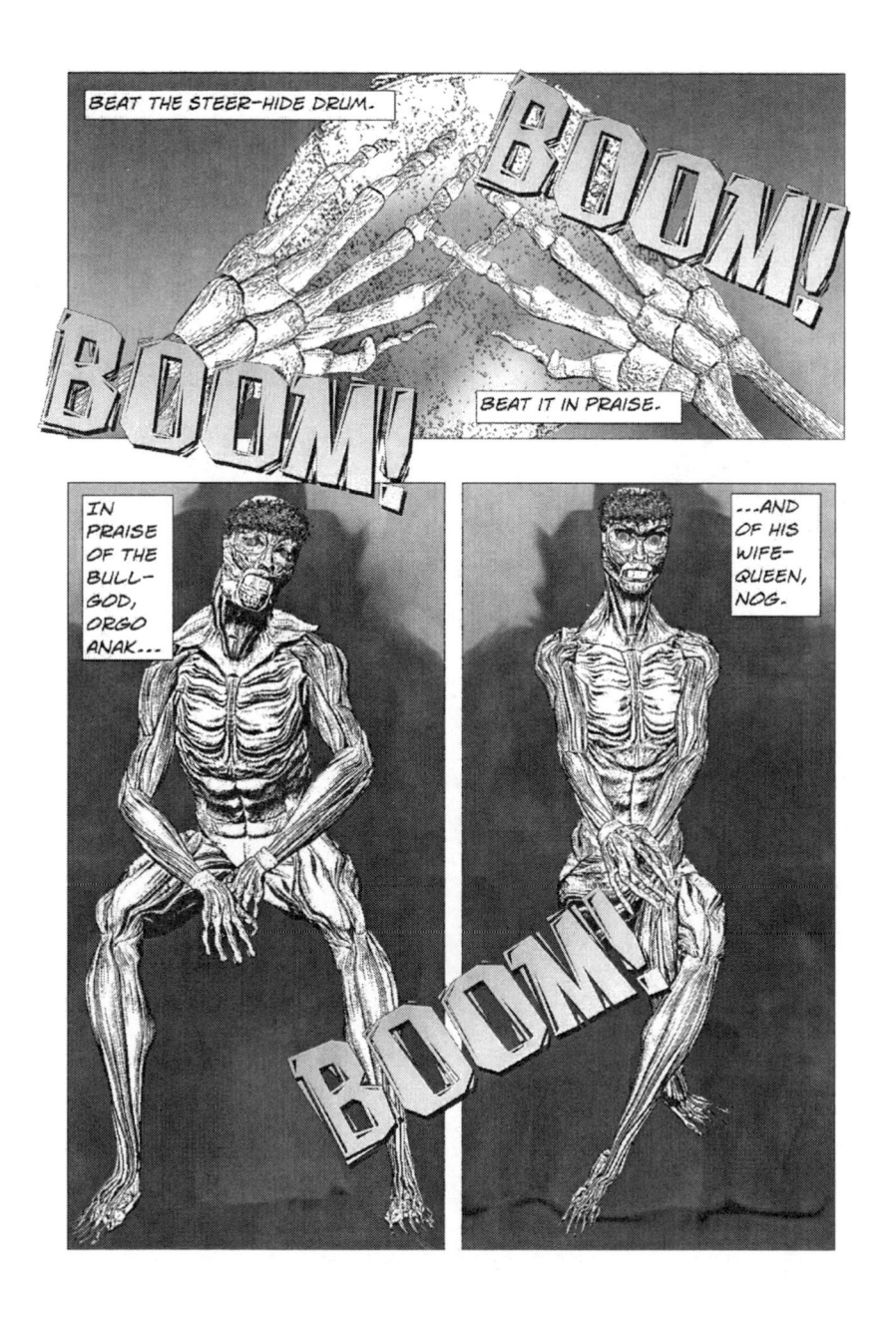

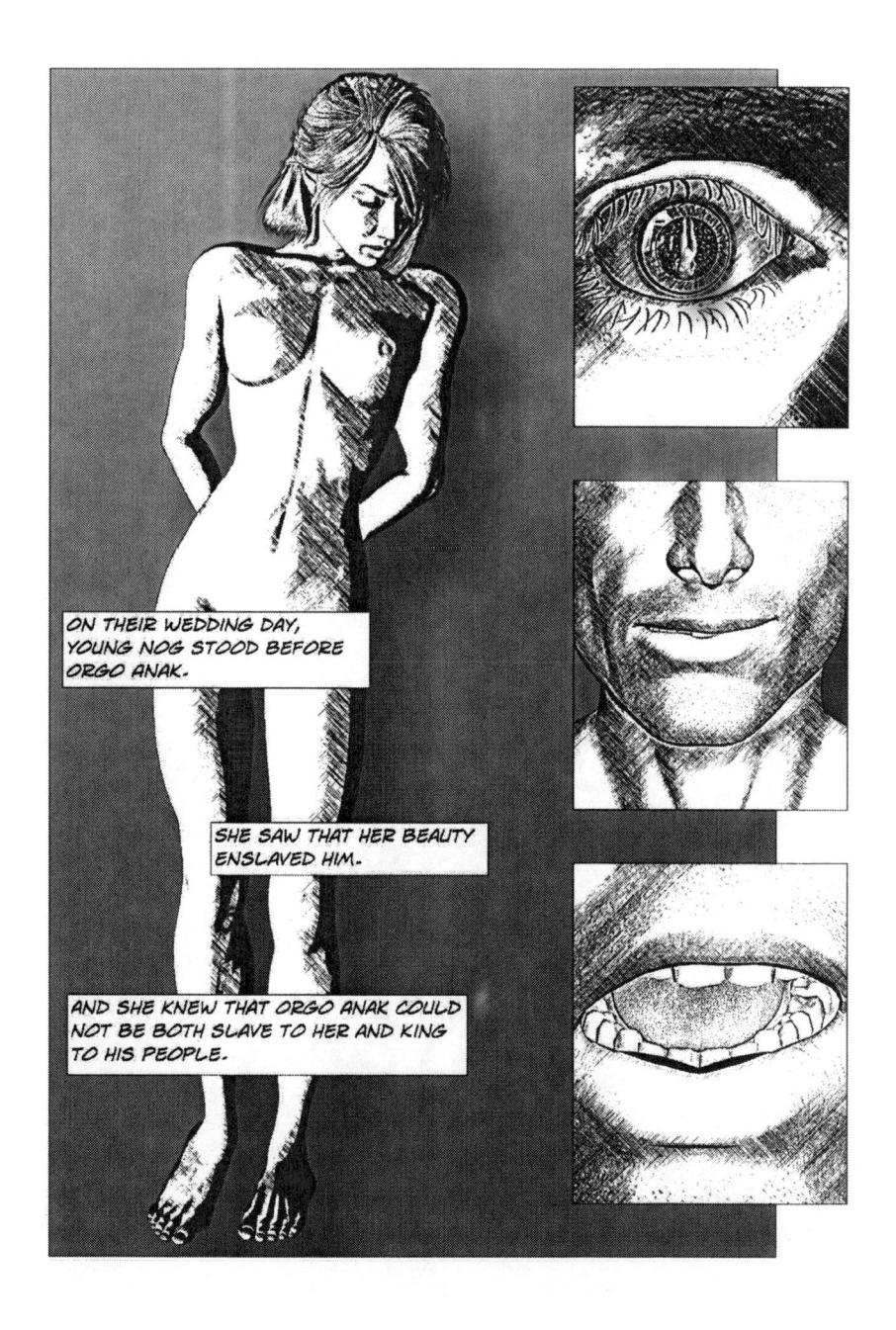

ON THEIR WEDDING DAY,
YOUNG NOG STOOD BEFORE
ORGO ANAK.

SHE SAW THAT HER BEAUTY
ENSLAVED HIM.

AND SHE KNEW THAT ORGO ANAK COULD
NOT BE BOTH SLAVE TO HER AND KING
TO HIS PEOPLE.

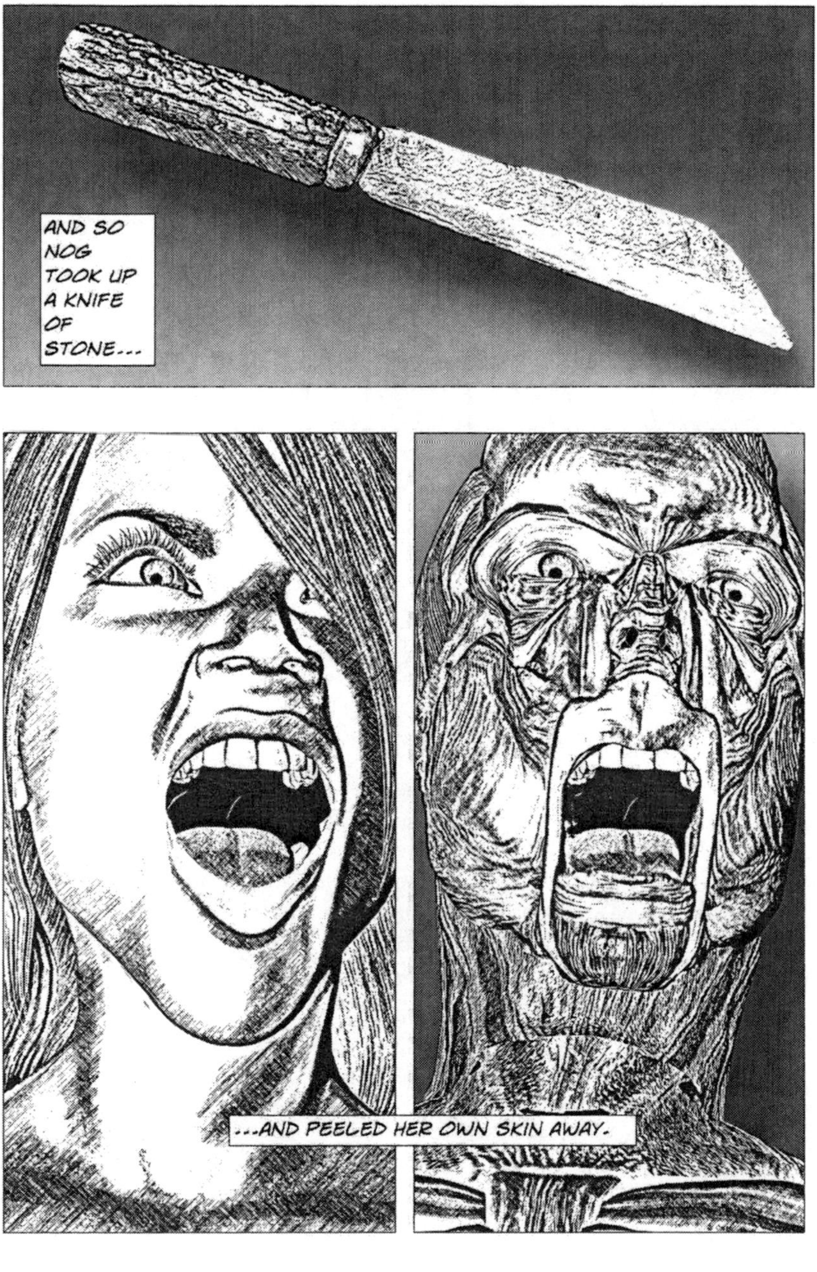

AND SO
NOG
TOOK UP
A KNIFE
OF
STONE...

...AND PEELED HER OWN SKIN AWAY.

THEY LEFT BEHIND THEM THEIR HOME
ON THE WINDSWEPT PLATEAU.

PINCKNEY BENEDICT

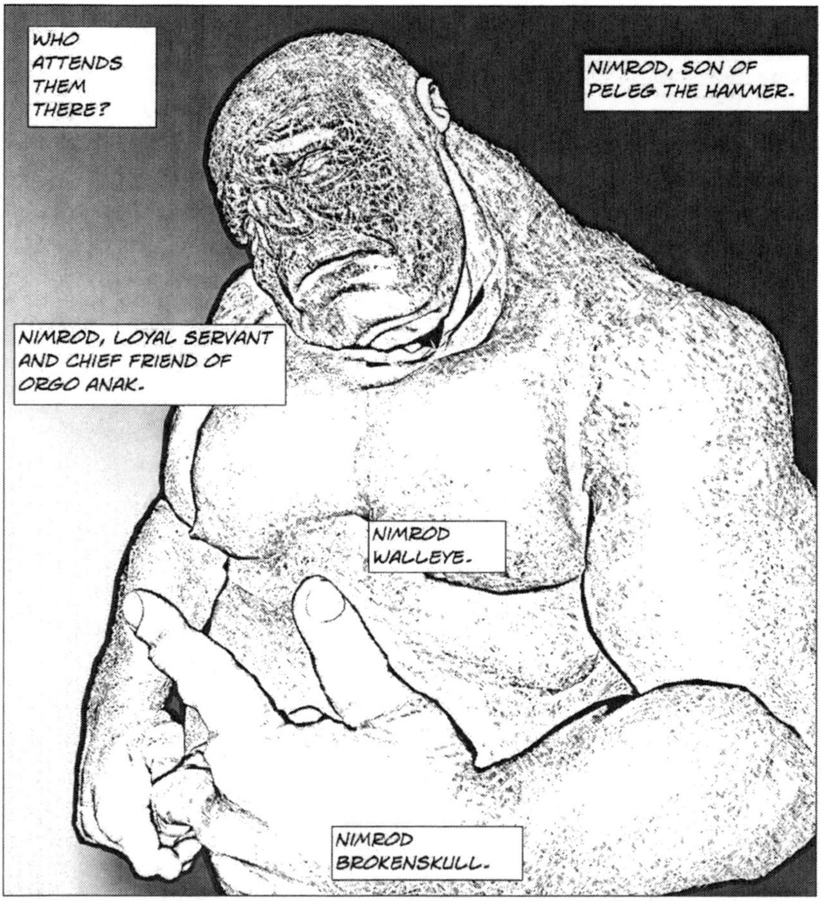

WHO
ATTENDS
THEM
THERE?

NIMROD, SON OF
PELEG THE HAMMER.

NIMROD, LOYAL SERVANT
AND CHIEF FRIEND OF
ORGO ANAK.

NIMROD
WALLEYE.

NIMROD
BROKENSKULL.

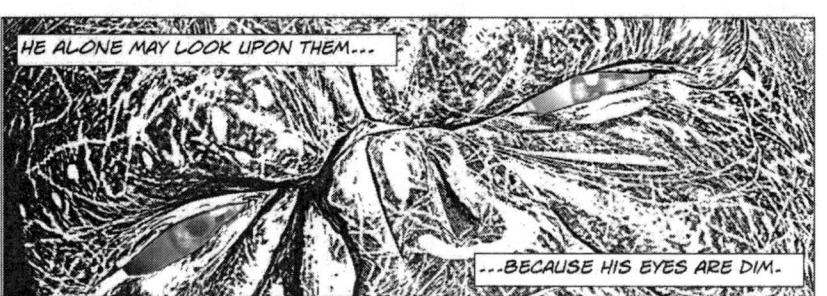

HE ALONE MAY LOOK UPON THEM...

...BECAUSE HIS EYES ARE DIM.

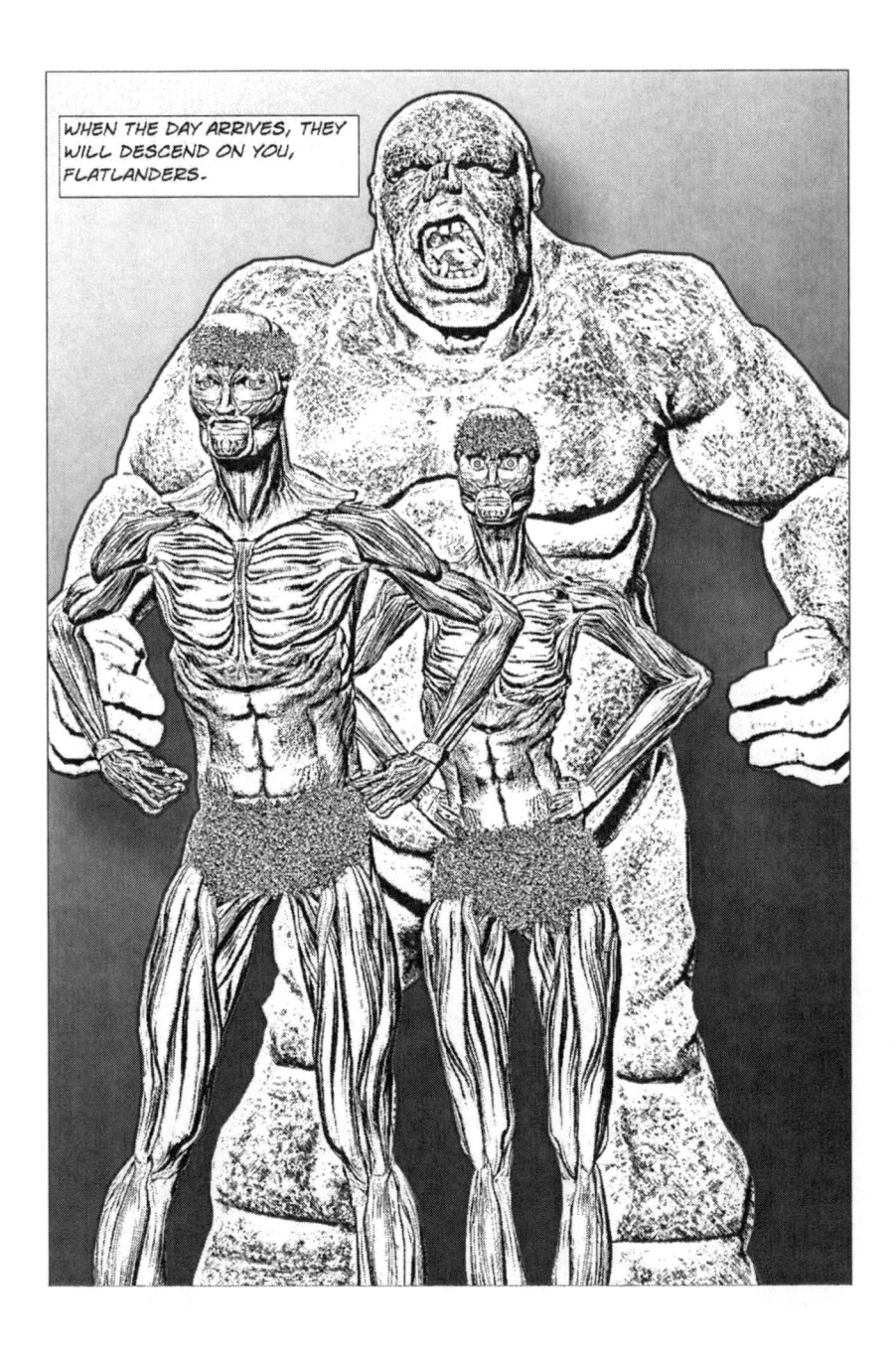

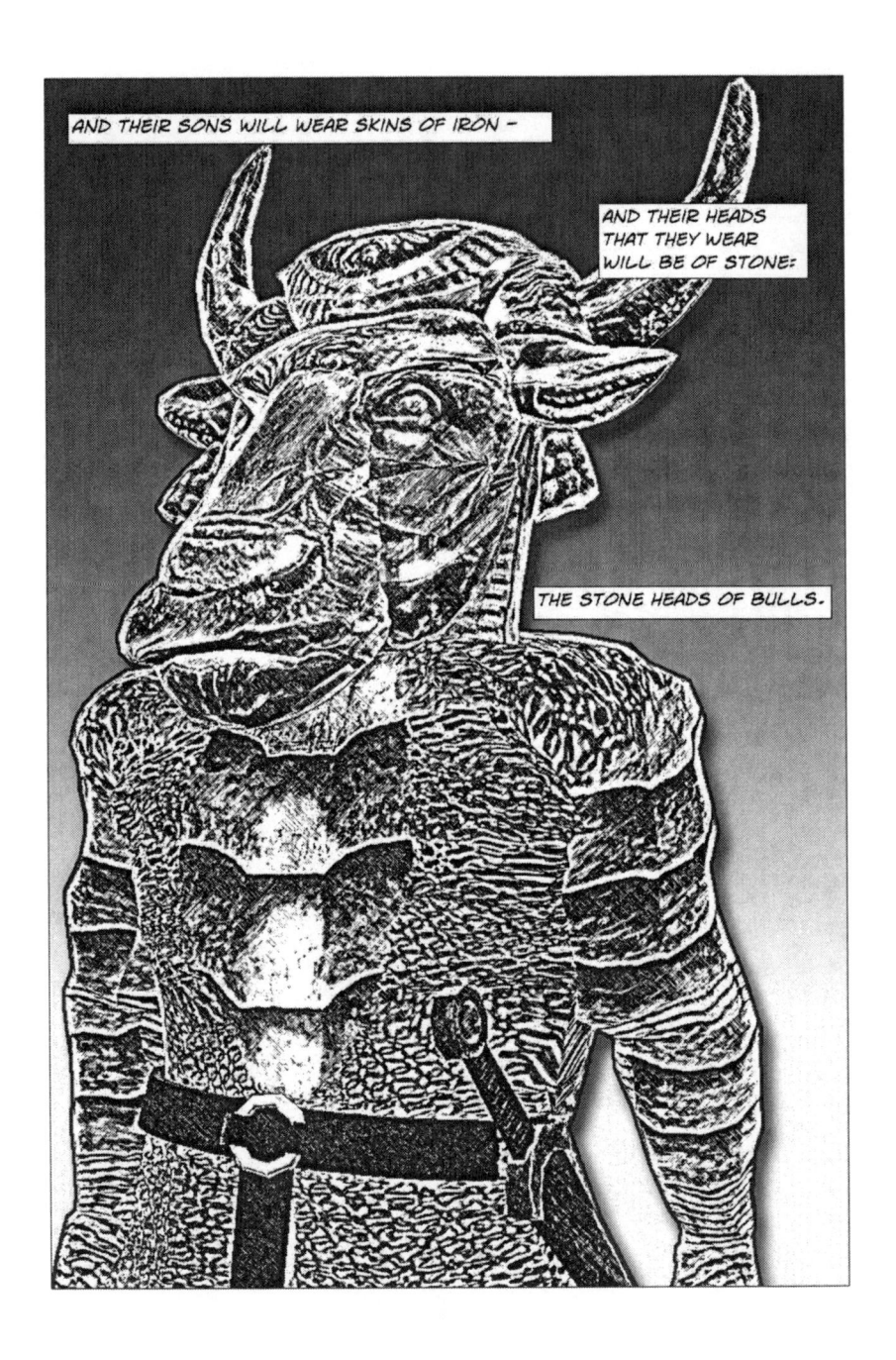

PINCKNEY BENEDICT

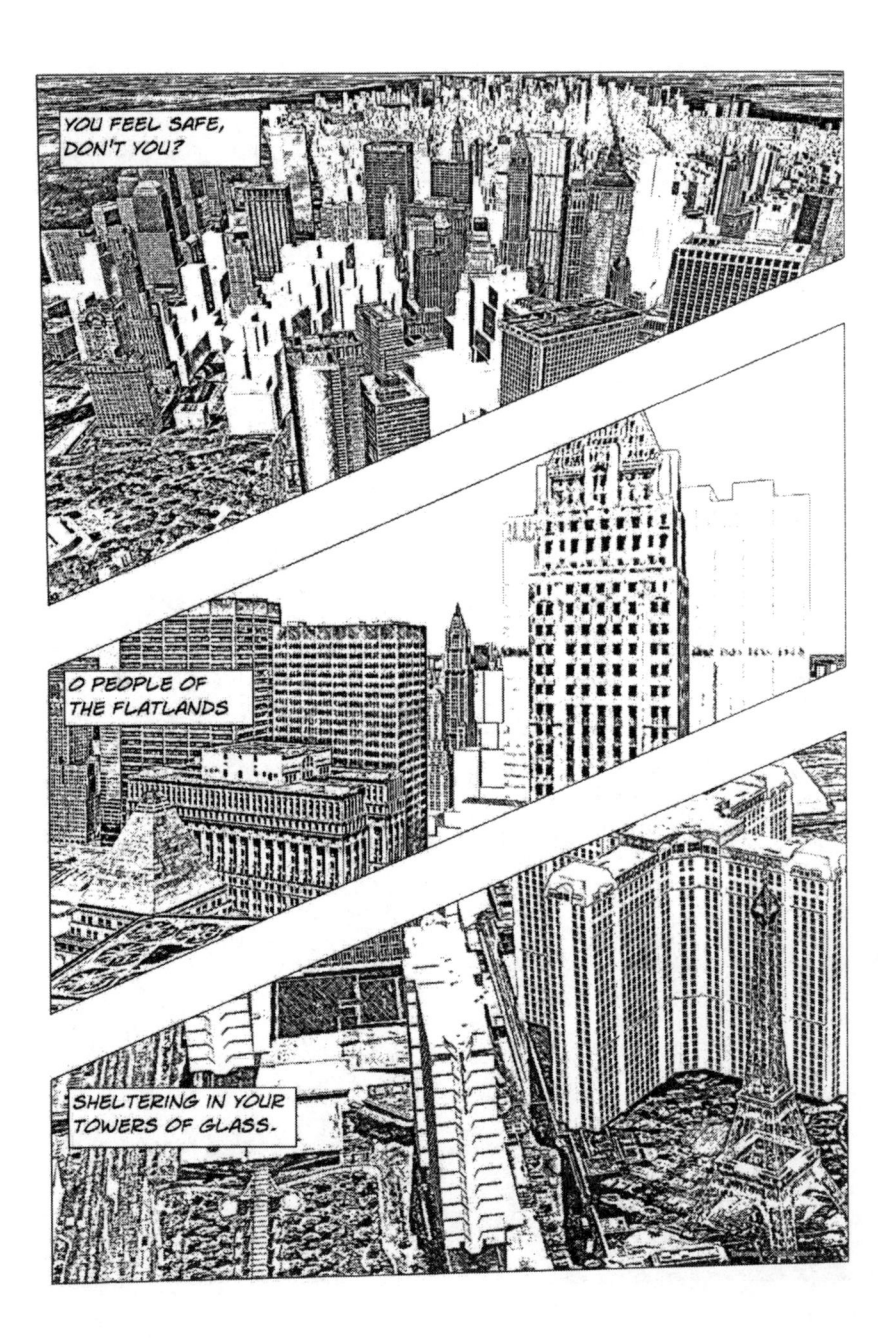

PINCKNEY BENEDICT

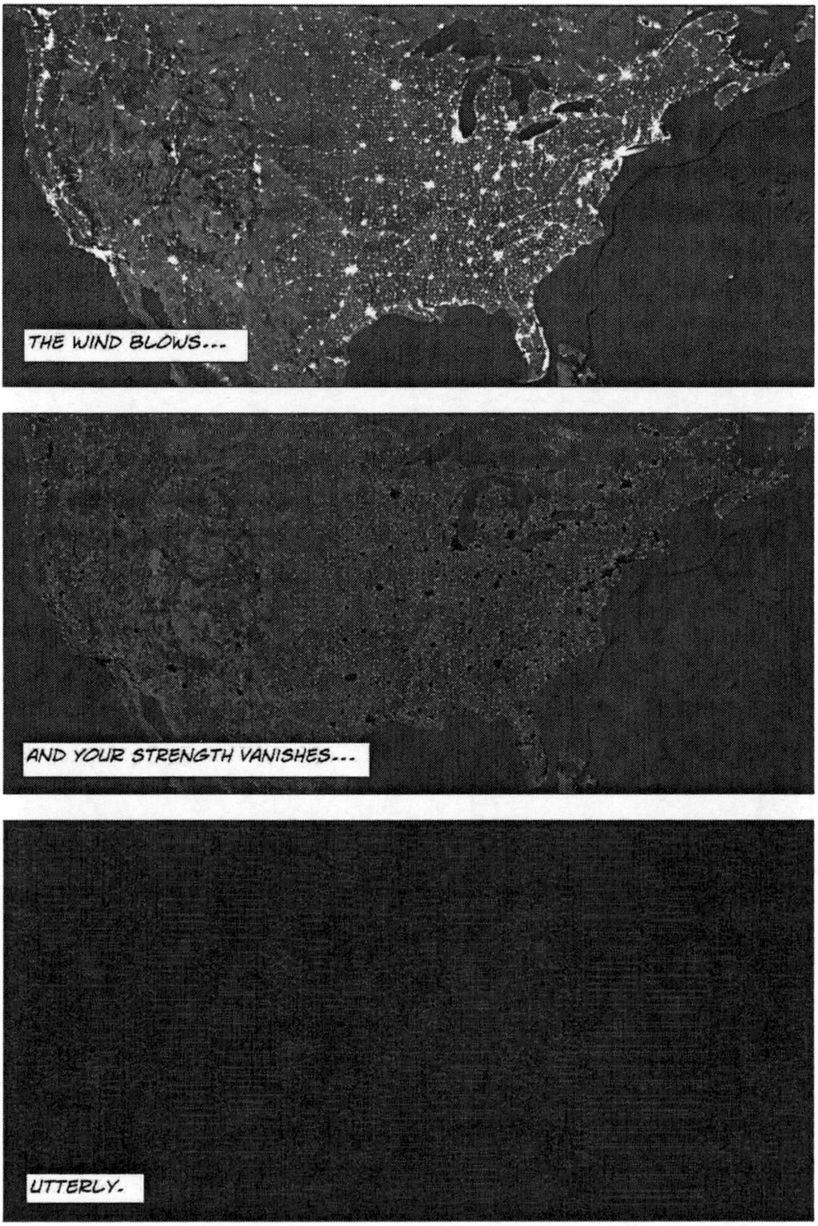

THE WIND BLOWS...

AND YOUR STRENGTH VANISHES...

UTTERLY.

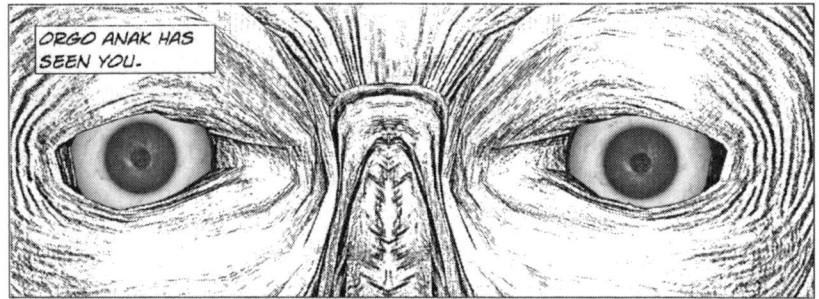

ORGO ANAK HAS SEEN YOU.

HE HAS SEEN YOUR TANGLED, INTOLERABLE CITIES.

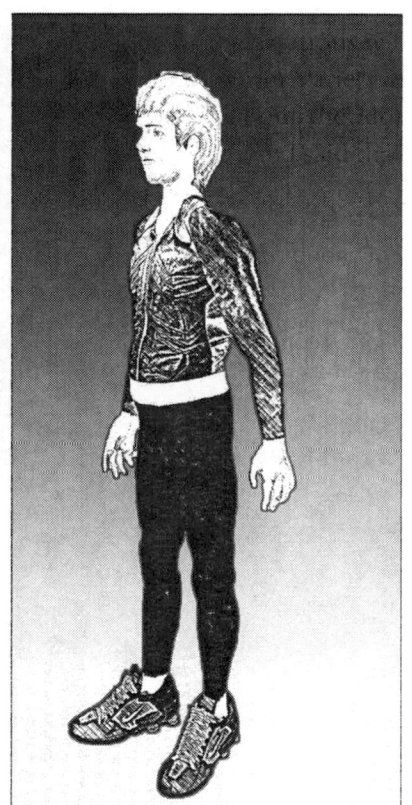

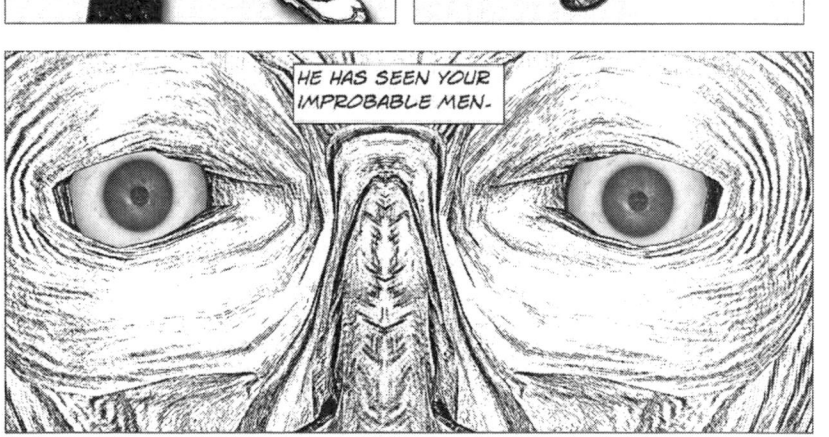

PINCKNEY BENEDICT

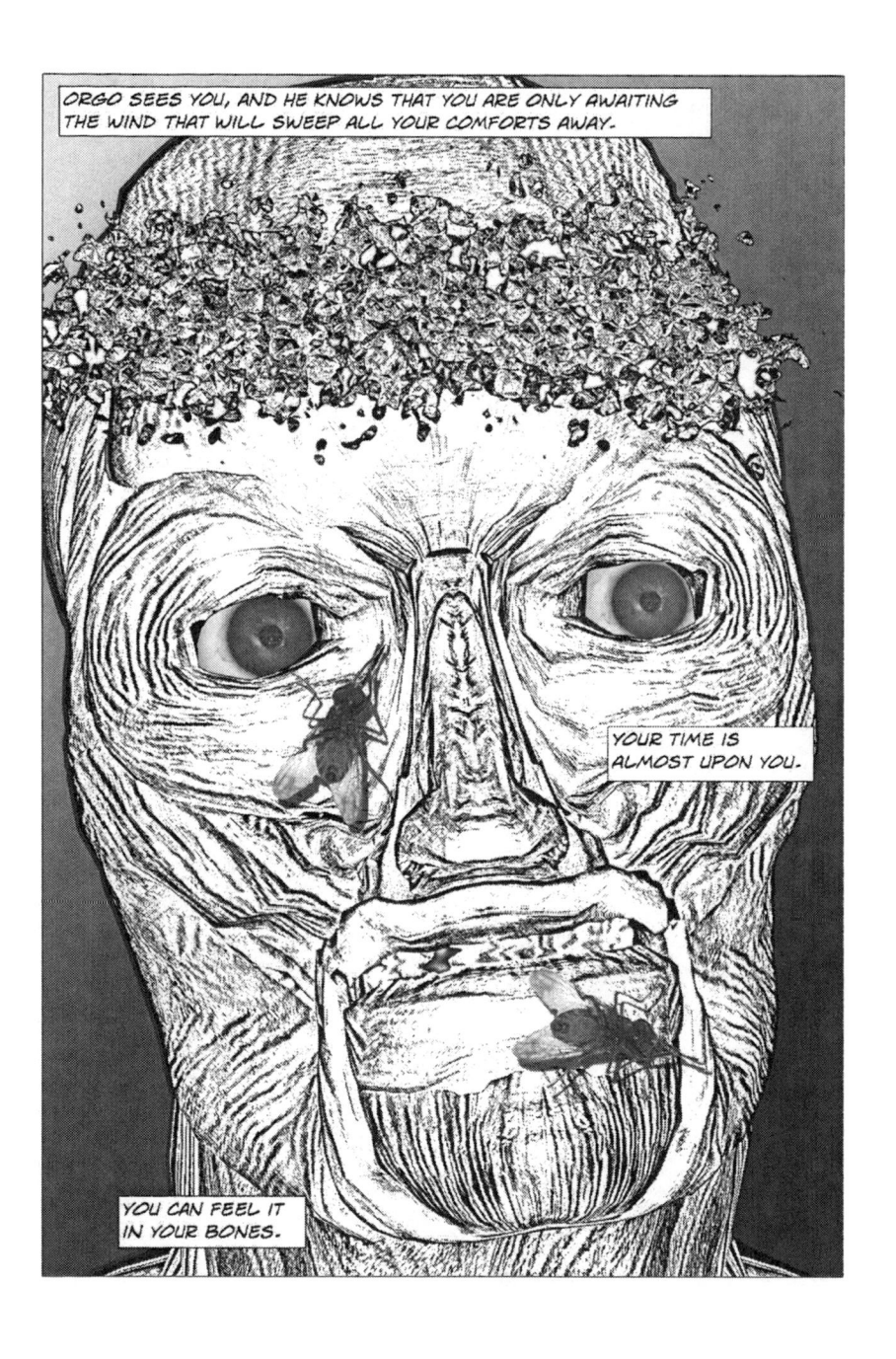

THE GEARS AND WHEELS THAT DRIVE THE FLATLANDS WILL GRIND TO A SLOW AND SHUDDERING HALT.

THE CLOCKS WILL CEASE TO KEEP TIME.

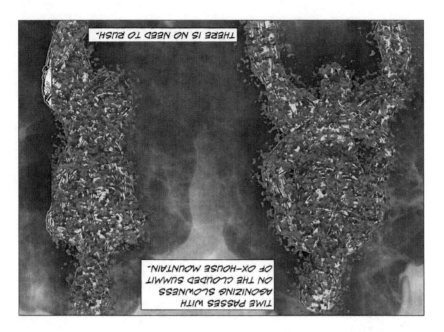

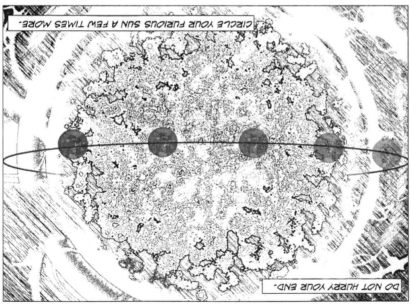

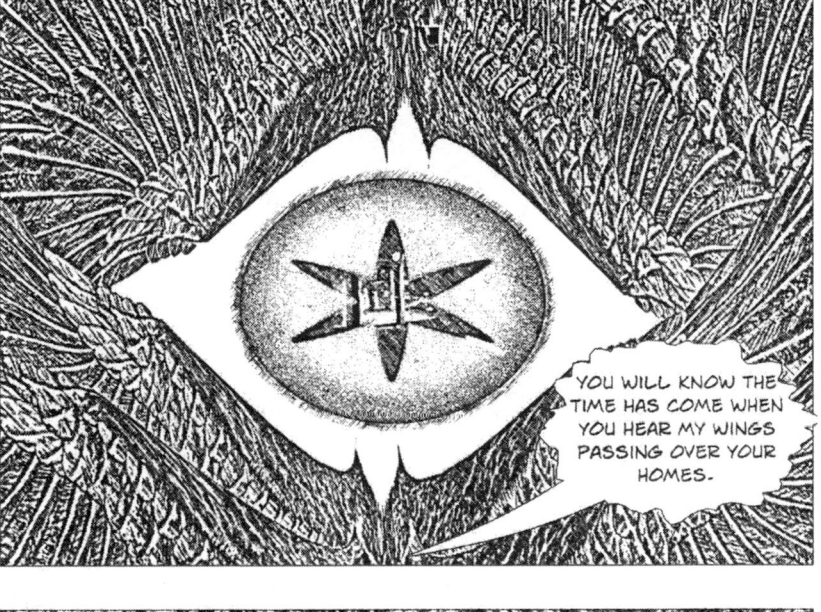

YOU WILL KNOW THE TIME HAS COME WHEN YOU HEAR MY WINGS PASSING OVER YOUR HOMES.

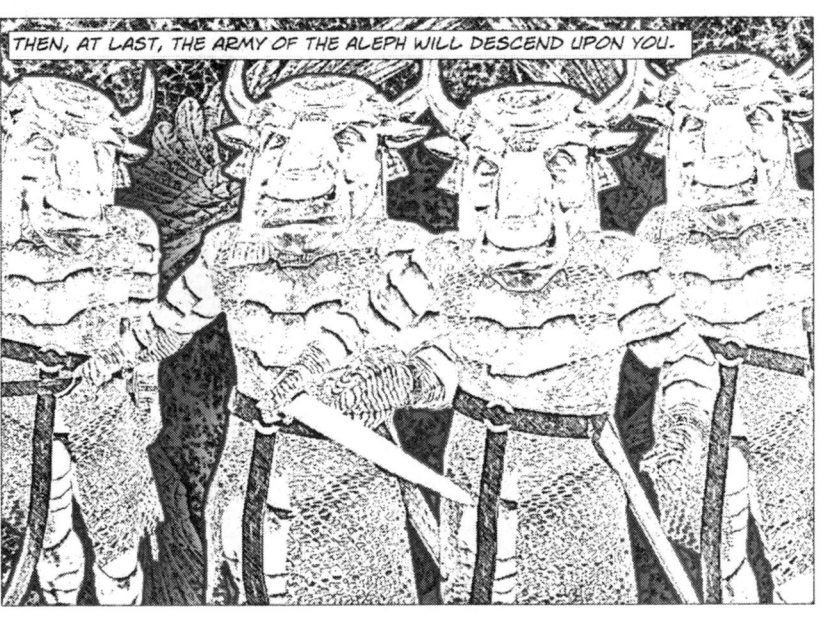

THEN, AT LAST, THE ARMY OF THE ALEPH WILL DESCEND UPON YOU.

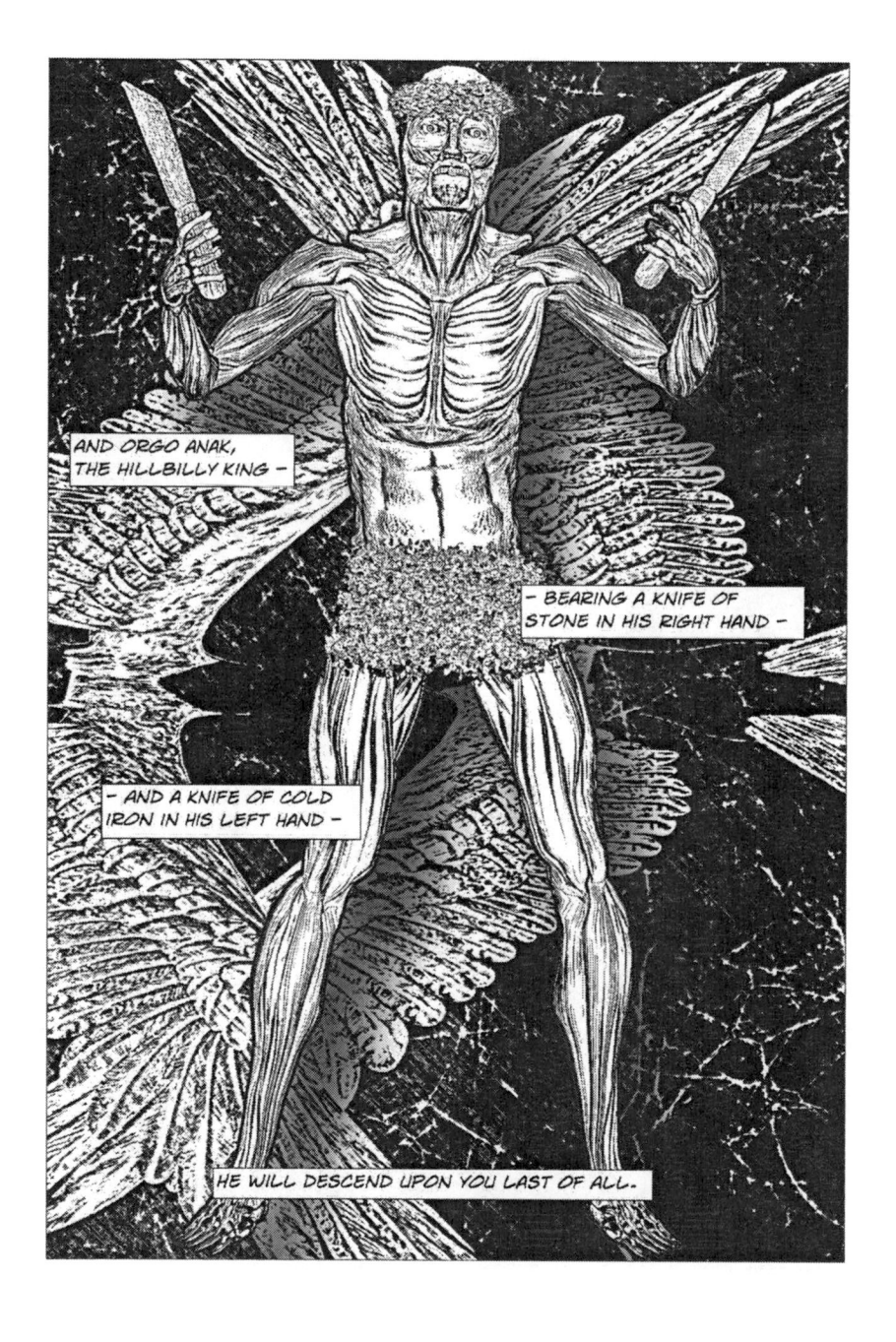

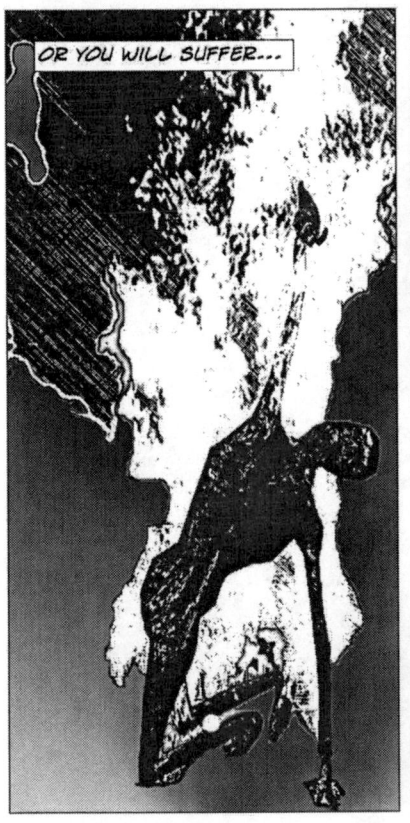

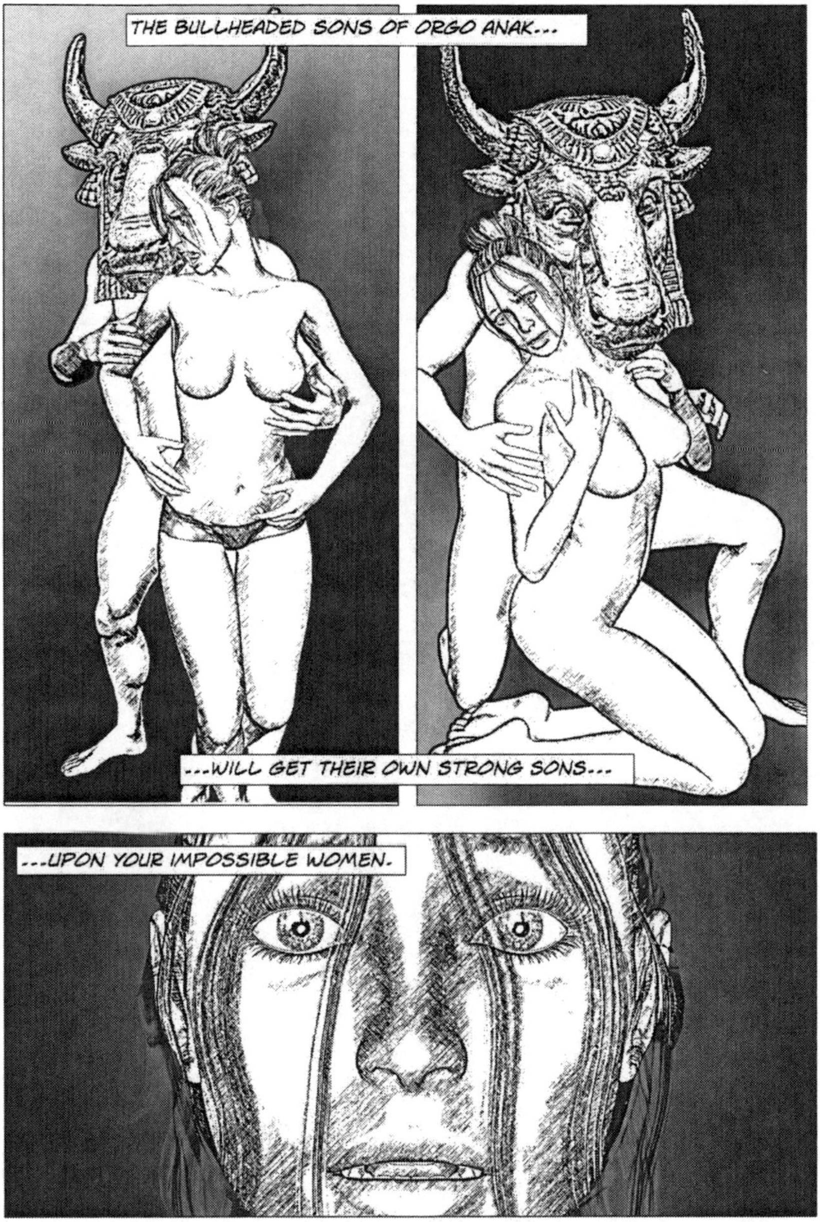

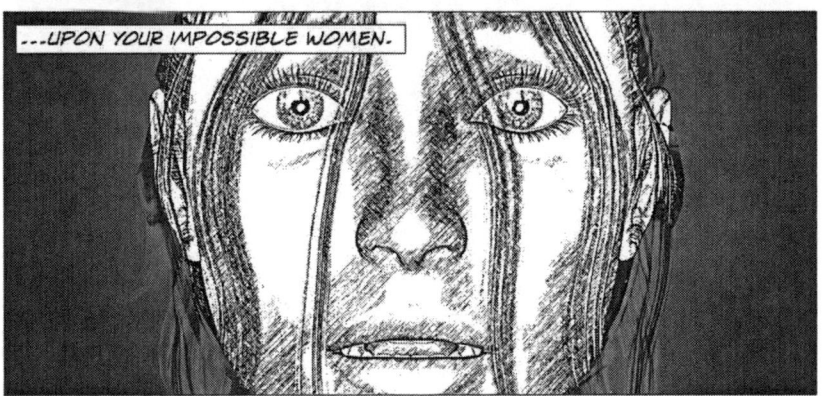

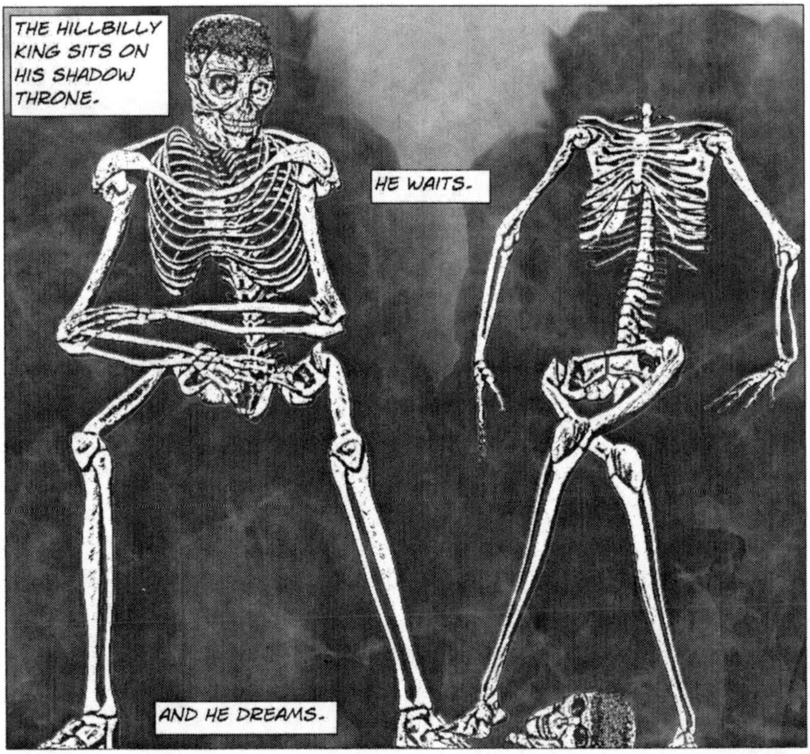

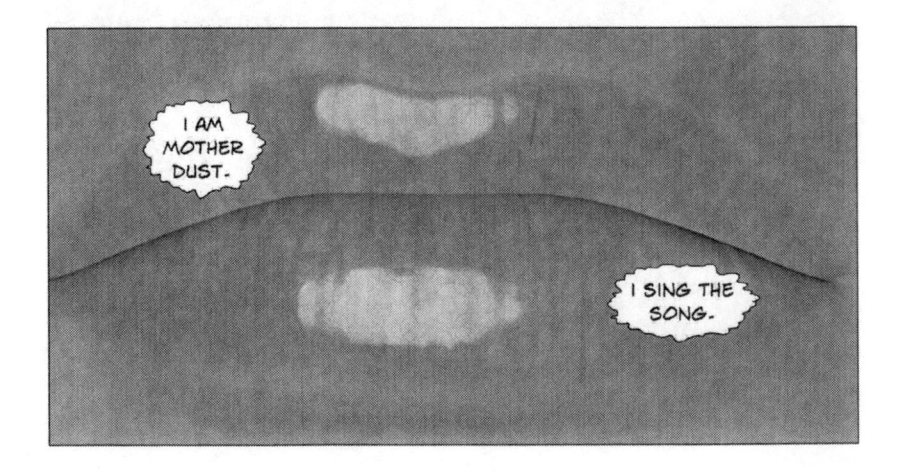

PINCKNEY BENEDICT

DOROTHY ALLISON
Deciding to Live

THERE WAS A day in my life when I decided to live. After my childhood, after all that long terrible struggle to simply survive, to escape my stepfather, uncles, speeding Pontiacs, broken glass, and rotten floorboards, or that inevitable death by misadventure that claimed so many of my cousins; after watching so many die around me, I had not imagined that I would ever need to make such a choice. I had imagined the hunger for life in me insatiable, endless, and unshakable.

I became an escapee—one of the ones others talked about. I became the one who got away, who got glasses from the Lions Club, a job from Lyndon Johnson's War on Poverty, and finally went away to college on scholarship. There I met the people I had always read about: girls whose fathers loved them—innocently; boys who drove cars they had not stolen; whole armies of the upper and middle classes I had not truly believed to be real; the children to whom I could not help but compare myself. I matched their innocence, their confidence, their capacity to trust, to love, to be generous against the bitterness, the rage, the pure and terrible hatred that consumed me. Like so many others who had gone before me, I began to dream longingly of my own death.

I began to court it. Cowardly, traditionally—that is, in the tradition of all those others like me, through drugs and drinking and stubbornly putting myself in the way of other people's violence. Even now, I cannot believe how it was that everything I survived became one more reason to want to die.

But one morning, I limped into my mama's kitchen and sat alone at her dining table. I was limping because I had pulled a muscle in my thigh and cracked two ribs in a fight with a woman I thought I loved.

I remember that morning in all its details, the scratches on my wrists from my lover's fingernails, the look on Mama's face as she got ready to go to work—how she tried not to fuss over me, and the way I could not meet her eyes. It was in my mama's face that I saw myself, in my mama's silence, for she behaved as if I were only remotely the daughter she had loved and prayed for. She treated me as if I were in a way already dead, or about to die—as unreachable, as dangerous as one of my uncles on a three-day toot. *That* was so humiliating it broke my pride. My mouth opened to cry out, but I shut it stubbornly. It was in that moment I made my decision—not actually the decision to live, but the decision not to die on her. I shut my mouth on my grief and my rage, and began to pretend as if I would live, as if there were reason enough to fight my way out of the trap I had made for myself—though I had not yet figured out what that reason was.

I limped around tight-lipped through the months it took me to find a job in another city and disappear. I took a bus to the city and spoke to no one, signed the papers that made me a low-level government clerk, and wound up sitting in a motel room eating peanut butter sandwiches so I could use the per diem to buy respectable skirts and blouses—the kind of clothes I had not worn since high school. Every evening I would walk the ten blocks from the training classes to the motel, where I could draw the heavy drapes around me, open the windows, and sit wrapped around by the tent of those drapes. There I would huddle and smoke my hoarded grass.

Part of me knew what I was doing, knew the decision I was making. A much greater part of me could not yet face it. I was trying to make solid my decision to live, but I did not know if I could. I had to change my life, take baby steps into a future I did not trust, and I began by looking first to the ground on which I stood, how I had become the woman I was. By day I played at being what the people who were training me thought I was—a college graduate and a serious worker, a woman settling down to a practical career with the Social Security Administration. I imagined that if I played at it long enough, it might become true, but I felt like an actress in the role for which she was truly not suited. It took all my concentration not to laugh at inappropriate moments and to keep my mouth shut when I did not know what to say at all.

There was only one thing I could do that helped me through those weeks. Every evening I sat down with a yellow legal-size pad, writing out the story of my life. I wrote it all: everything I could remember, all the stories I had ever been told, the names, places, images—how blood had arched up the wall one terrible night that recurred persistently in my dreams—the dreams themselves, the people in the dreams. My stepfather, my uncles and cousins, my desperate aunts and their more desperate daughters.

I wrote out my memories of the women. My terror and lust for my own kind; the shouts and arguments; the long, slow glances and slower approaches; the way my hands always shook when I would finally touch the flesh I could barely admit I wanted, the way I could never ask for what I wanted, never accept if they offered. I twisted my fingers and chewed my lips over the subtle and deliberate lies I had told myself and them, the hidden stories of my life that lay in disguise behind the mocking stories I did tell—all the stories of my family, my childhood, and the relentless, deadening poverty and shame I had always tried to hide because I knew no one would believe what I could tell them about it.

Writing it all down was purging. Putting those stories on paper took them out of the nightmare realm and made me almost love myself for being able to finally face them. More subtly, it gave me a way to love the people I wrote about—even the ones I had fought with or hated. In that city where I knew no one, I had no money and nothing to fill the evenings except washing out my clothes, reading cheap paperbacks, trying to understand how I had come to be in that place. I was not the kind of person who could imagine asking for help or talking about my personal business. Nor was I fool enough to think that could be done without risking what little I had gained. Still, though I knew the danger of revealing too much about my life, I did not imagine anyone reading my rambling, ranting stories. I was writing for myself, trying to shape my life outside my terrors and helplessness, to make it visible and real in a tangible way, in the way other people's seemed real—the lives I had read about in books. I had been a child who believed in books, but I had never found me or mine in print. My family was always made over into caricatures or flattened into saint-like stock characters. I never found my lovers in their strength and passion. Outside my mother's stubbornness and my own outraged arrogance, I had never found any reason to believe in myself. But I had the idea I could make it exist on those pages.

Days, I went to training sessions, memorized codes, section numbers, and memo formats. Nights, I wrote my stories. I would pull out scraps of paper at work to make notes about things I wanted to write about, though most of those scraps wound up tucked in my yellow pad. What poured out of me could not be planned or controlled; it came up like water under pressure at its own pace, pushing my fear ahead of it. By the end of the month, I'd taken to sitting on the motel roof—no longer stoned, but still writing. By then I was also writing letters to all the women I really didn't expect to see again, explaining the things that writing my stories had made real to me. I did not intend to mail those letters, and never did. The letters themselves were stories—mostly lies—self-justifying, awkward, and desperate.

I finished that month, got assigned to a distant city, put away my yellow papers, and moved—making sure no one who knew me from before could find me. I threw myself into the women's community, fell in love every third day, and started trying to be serious about writing—poems and essays and the beginnings of stories. I even helped edit a feminist magazine. Throughout that time I told stories—mostly me stories about myself and my family and my lovers in a drawl that made them all funnier than they were. Though that was mostly a good time for me, I wrote nothing that struck me as worth the trouble of actually keeping. I did not tuck those new stories away with the yellow pads I had sealed up in a blanket box of my mother's. I told myself the yellow pages were as raw and unworked as I felt myself to be, and the funny stories I was telling people were better, were the work of someone who was going to be a "real" writer. It was three years before I pulled out those old yellow sheets and read them, and saw how thin and self-serving my funny stories had become.

The stuff on those yellow pads was bitter. I could not recognize myself in that bitter whiny hateful voice telling over all those horrible violent memories. They were, oddly, the same stories I'd been telling for years, but somehow drastically different. Telling them out loud, I'd made them ironic and playful. The characters became eccentric, fascinating—not the cold-eyed, mean, and nasty bastards they were on the yellow pages, the frightened dangerous women and the more dangerous and just as frightened men. I could not stand it, neither the words on the page nor what they told me about myself. My neck and teeth began to ache, and I was not at all sure I really wanted to live with this stuff inside me. But holding on to them, reading them over again, became a part of the process of survival, of deciding once more to live—and clinging to that decision. For me those stories were not distraction or entertainment; they were the stuff of my life, and they were necessary in ways I could barely understand.

Still, I took those stories and wrote them again. I made some of them funny. I made some of them poems. I made the women beautiful, wounded but courageous, while the men disappeared into the background. I put hope in the children and passion in the landscape while my neck ached and tightened, and I wanted nothing so much as a glass of whiskey or a woman's anger to distract me. None of it was worth the pain it caused me. None of it made my people or me more understandable. None of it told the truth, and every lie I wrote proved to me I wasn't worth my mother's grief at what she thought was my wasted life, or my sister's cold fear of what I might tell other people about them.

I put it all away. I began to live my life as if nothing I did would survive the day in which I did it. I used my grief and hatred to wall off my childhood, my history, my sense of being part of anything greater than myself. I used women and liquor, constant righteous political work, and a series of grimly endured ordeals to convince myself that I had nothing to decide, that I needed nothing more than what other people considered important to sustain me. I worked on a feminist journal. I read political theory, history, psychology, and got a degree in anthropology as if that would quiet the roar in my own head. I watched other women love each other, war with each other, and take each other apart while never acknowledging the damage we all did to each other. I went through books and conferences, CR groups and study groups, organizing committees and pragmatic coalition fronts. I did things I did not understand for reasons I could not begin to explain just to be in motion, to be trying to do something, change something in a world I wanted desperately to make over but could not imagine for myself.

That was all part of deciding to live, though I didn't know it. Just as I did not know that what I needed had to come up from inside me, not be laid over the top of my head. The bitterness with which I had been born, that had been nurtured in me, could not be eased with a lover or a fight or any number of late-night meetings and clumsily written manifestos. It may never be eased. The decision to live when everything inside and out shouts death is not a matter of moments but years, and no one has ever told me how you know when it is accomplished.

But a night finally came when I woke up sweaty and angry and afraid I'd never go back to sleep again. All those stories were rising up my throat. Voices were echoing in my neck, laughter behind my ears, and I was terribly terribly afraid that I was finally as crazy as my kind was supposed to be. But the desire to live was desperate in my belly, and the stories I had hidden all those years were the blood and bone of it. To get it down, to tell it again, to make something—by God, just once to be real in the world, without lies or evasions or sweet-talking nonsense. I got up and wrote a story all the way through. It was one of the stories from the yellow pages, one of the ones I had rewritten, but it was different again. It wasn't truly me or my mama or my girl-friends, or really any of the people who'd been there, but it had the feel, the shit-kicking anger and grief of my life. It wasn't that whiny voice, but it had the drawl, and it had, too, the joy and pride I some-times felt in me and mine. It was not biography and yet not lies, and it resonated to the pulse of my sisters' ears and my desperate shame, and it ended with all the questions and decisions still waiting—most of all the decision to live.

It was a rough beginning—my own shout of life against death, of shape and substance against silence and confusion. It was most of all my deep, abiding desire to live fleshed and strengthened on the page, a way to tell the truth as a kind of magic not cheapened or distorted by a need to please any damn body at all. Without it, I cannot imag-ine my own life. Without it, I have no way to know who I am.

One time, twice, once in a while again, I get it right. Once in a while, I can make the world I know real on the page. I can make the women and men I love breathe out loud in an empty room, the dreams I dare not speak shape up in the smoky darkness of other people's imaginations. Writing these stories is the only way I know to make sure of my ongoing decision to live, to set moment to moment a small piece of stubbornness against an ocean of ignorance and obliteration.

I write stories. I write fiction. I put on the page a third look at what I've seen in life—the condensed and reinvented experience of a cross-eyed, working-class lesbian, addicted to violence, language, and hope, who has made the decision to live, on the page and on the street, for me and mine.

O RUINER OF HOLY THINGS

CARTER SICKELS

Bittersweet: On Transitioning
and Finding Home

EVER SINCE I was a kid, I've heard stories about southeastern Ohio, where most of my family was born and raised. My great-granddad used to eavesdrop on the neighbors' phone conversations back when there was something called the party line; Granddad's buddy Rooster Jenkins liked to *raise hell after he'd been in the sauce;* there was a great-great-uncle who was murdered; my father's childhood friend Bad Dog Perkins killed himself after he came back from Vietnam. They all had nicknames: Ears, Toothpick, Spider. It wasn't until years later that I started to think about these half-forgotten stories and names, overcome with a longing to return to my roots even as I moved further away from them.

Whenever we made the seventy-mile drive from Columbus, where the flat land is good for farming or building Walmarts and strip malls, to my grandparents' land in the foothills of the Appalachians, my father took the long way, past forgotten coal mining towns and forests and old strip sites and hillside farms, and down winding back roads, to point out landmarks and wax nostalgic: the "scenic route," my brother and I called it, both of us complaining from the backseat that we were carsick.

Visiting my grandparents meant going "down home" or to "the homeplace." Red beef cattle grazing in the field, a pair of black buzzards circling in the sky. My father's siblings and their kids would show up the same weekend and we'd crowd into my grandparents' small ranch house, the adults divvying up the extra bedrooms and the kids sprawled on the living room floor in a nest of sleeping bags and blankets, exhausted and elated from a day of exploring, the TV flickering over our faces. Sometimes Grandma, a night owl, stayed up with us and we watched Johnny Carson and David Letterman.

On the holidays, peals of women's laughter rang from the kitchen. Smells of roasting turkey and cigarette smoke. Cherry, pumpkin, pecan, blackberry pies cooling on the table. Sometimes, after he'd been drinking, Granddad would play "Orange Blossom Special" on his fiddle. He used to play in a bluegrass band called the Green Valley Boys. I never cared for that music as a kid—it wasn't until I left Ohio that I fell in love with the twang of Ralph Stanley, Bill Monroe, Earl Scruggs. After dinner my mother and I would go on a walk, oak leaves crunching under our feet. My mother cut vines of bittersweet to later braid into a wreath.

Once a year, usually at the end of summer, we'd have a "wienie roast." The adults would sit in lawn chairs on the front patio, telling stories and drinking Cokes and smoking cigarettes, while the kids played freeze tag and football and Wiffle ball in the pastures, whichever ones the cows weren't penned in. Grandma filled the ice cream maker with rock salt, eggs, cream, milk, ice, and sugar, and one of the men turned the hand crank until the ingredients blended into a concoction that wasn't anything like the ice cream at the store but a sweet, thin, delicious cream flecked with grains of ice, which we spooned over warm cherry pie. We roasted hotdogs and marshmallows on sticks that our fathers had sharpened for us, and played hide-and-go-seek under the starry sky. In the mornings, everyone crowded into the kitchen for a breakfast of eggs, bacon, stacks of buttered toast: when one person finished, someone else would take the free chair. Grandma, who always ate last, fried eggs perfectly: just one delicate touch with a toast corner would split the bright yellow yolk.

My grandparents lived just down the road from the old hillside farm where my grandfather was born and raised, a mix of pastures and forested land with high weeds entangling broken-down farm machinery, caves where the cows went to cool off in the summer, and a cattail-lined creek where we fished for bluegill and catfish and always threw them back. Granddad pointed out Indian mounds and the mile-long path he used to walk to school, a one-room building that was no longer there, and our fathers handed us buckeyes for good luck and told stories about when they were boys and their grandmother made apple pie and persimmon jelly. I'd go with my father, granddad, brother, uncles, and cousins, and we walked the land generations before us had walked. Most of the time I was the only girl. Back then, there was nothing to question. Later, things became murkier. As I grew up and moved closer to my true self, I became less recognizable to my family, and I distanced myself from the place that I love.

I WAS the only one in the family to leave Ohio. I moved away in 1995. After I left, I still visited regularly, but it took a few years before I really started to miss the family land. I began to long to go back to my roots. I didn't know this was where I came from until I left.

These visits back, from my early twenties to midthirties, were never free of tension or uneasiness. I did not fit in. I was a queer, anyone could see that, and no one talked about it. My hair was short; I dressed like a guy. No one ever asked me if I was dating anyone. Everyone ignored the awkward moments, like at my grandfather's funeral when one of my cousins' kids asked me if I was a boy or a girl.

Sometimes I didn't know what I was, except that I was queer. Back then, in those years before I transitioned from female to male, I identified as a lesbian out in the world, even though I knew there was something not quite right about this. Mostly, I tried to exist without being noticed. I felt uncomfortable in my own skin and terrified to face my true, and complicated, feelings.

The awkwardness felt even more intense around my family, where I didn't identify as anything. Around them, I had no present, only the history of the years I'd spent as a child, a girl. They asked no probing questions; I offered no telling details. My grandparents talked to me about the weather or asked about school. When I was in college, Grandma cut out the columns I wrote for the undergraduate paper, including one about safe sex and another about diversity, but never mentioned them. In the last stage of her life, when she was confined to a nursing home, the two of us shared a moment alone. She skipped the small talk and looked me right in the eye and asked if I was gay or straight, her gnarled fingers, hardening from the Parkinson's, heavy on my hand. She was the only one in the family who ever asked me that and the only one who ever told me she didn't care: she just wanted me to be happy.

WHEN I first began thinking about my novel *The Evening Hour*, I was living worlds away, in Harlem. I loved New York—the diversity and creativity, the dense layers of people and buildings and art—but I missed the hills and trees and smell of dirt, my home. One afternoon I came across an article about mountaintop removal coal mining. I had no idea what that was, and what I read stunned me. Coal companies were blowing up the Appalachian mountains, burying streams and flattening West Virginia, just across the Ohio River, a forty-minute drive from my grandparents'. I did more research. I read articles and books, watched documentaries, and pored over geographical survey maps. Eventually, I went to see for myself.

That first trip to West Virginia stirred up all my Appalachian memories. The forests were thick with the trees that my granddad had once taught me the names of: black walnut, hickory, pawpaw. There were mountains instead of hills, but from what I could tell, the places weren't that different, at least not culturally and socially. I met people who resembled my aunts and uncles and cousins and the characters from the stories my grandfather and father told. One woman said, *I was tickled pink,* and I heard the voice of my grandmother. They invited me into their homes decorated with porcelain knickknacks, pictures of the dead and Jesus, and American flags and big-screen TVs.

I met a Vietnam vet who drove me around the mountains; I spoke with grandmothers turned environmentalists; I followed a long-haired, pistol-packing woman into the woods; I listened to a tough, country man dressed in camouflage explain that he was worried about his granddaughter getting sick from the water, and as he talked, his eyes dimmed with tears. They could have been my relatives. They grew up believing in God and family and the coal company. If they voted, they voted Republican. But now their homeland was being taken away from them and they had changed. I saw the gray masses of what can only be called annihilation, the mountains bleeding from the wounds mining had inflicted. Poisoned water, destroyed homes. The Appalachian mountains and forests are some of the oldest in the world. Once they're gone, they're gone. And what about the people who live there, who call these rugged mountains home?

They were fighting for their lives, their way of life. Many of them lost their friends, their communities, even their families, because they stood up for what they believed, while most people in the towns ignored what was happening, or joined the Friends of Coal lobby. In a way, they were already used to being on the outside—they'd been stereotyped as ignorant hillbillies for hundreds of years, and had to fight to be seen and heard and recognized. Now they also had to stand up to people in their own community.

They inspired me. This place, these people, touched me, opened me up, settled under my skin, returned me to my roots. Life was short, they were telling me. Don't be afraid of who you are; don't back down.

EACH TIME I went to the mountains of West Virginia to do more research, I felt a sense of harmony. The collective memory of the place accompanied by my own memory pierced something deep inside me. The boarded-up stores, rundown homes, country churches, the way the hard sunlight hit the yellow maple leaves, a cardboard sign that said *Jesus Saves*. In my writing, I wanted to express my love for the place, but I also did not want to hide from the darker, harder parts: the claustrophobic web of religion, the stark closed-mindedness, the drug addiction and poverty and destroyed land and ruined waters.

I felt harmony when I went to West Virginia, but there was also discord. Just like when I went to Ohio, I didn't talk about my personal life, my queer identity. It didn't matter as much: I was there to ask questions about their lives, not explain my own. There wasn't the same kind of pain or loss I felt around my family; there wasn't the same level of shame—shame for hiding, and the shame that I knew I brought to them.

Still, I felt uneasy. Sometimes straight-up fear. I was looking more and more androgynous. Every time I stopped for gas or to use the bathroom, I worried someone would question, gay-bash, or kill me. I kept my head down, did not engage. The stories that all queers know but that rarely make the news stay close, hold fast. I drove down back roads, passing the occasional Rebel flag and pickups plastered with bumper stickers for Bush. On the highways, yellow and white crosses looked down on me from the hills, reminding me of where I was and who I was. Liberal. Outsider. Queer.

People don't think of queers living in Appalachia, but of course, they do and always have. When I was writing my novel, I remembered a guy I'd met, years ago, who lived in one of the forgotten coal mining towns in Ohio. He sometimes carried a purse and painted his nails. He got his eyebrows done and weekly manicures, and he also started fights and shot heroin. I always felt awed by him, how he survived in such a rural closed-minded community and called this place home.

I started wondering, what would it mean to come of age here, not as a girl, but as a boy? Could a man find love with another man? How did one cultivate a masculinity that embodied such maleness— the hunting, drinking, and fighting—with the sensitivity I'd witnessed, like my grandfather cutting a twig of sassafras and peeling back the bark with his pocketknife and handing it to me: "Tastes like root beer." This was the world of men, through which I was still finding my way both in my novel and in my life.

I HAVEN'T been back to the coalfields since I started transitioning. The next time I go, it will be easier to move through the world—I'll be myself, be read as male, there will be no confusion. But I'll also be read, correctly, as a gay male, which brings up its own set of worries about stopping for gas.

I also haven't gone back to my family's homeplace. My grandparents are dead, and I have not seen my extended family in years. The threads of our history grow thin. Fabric unravels.

Now I live in Portland, Oregon. I moved across the country to be free of my past, so I could live in a place where I could be the real me, where I could go by the name I chose for myself. Because how could I feel at home in a place where for so long I didn't feel at home even in my own body?

Everything out west is big. Magnificent and beautiful and grand. I go hiking, and sleep under cedar trees. And yet. I miss the scrappiness of the Appalachians, the particular way the golden autumn light looks on the trees you don't see out here, like the redbuds—delicate branches beaded with pink buds and heart-shaped leaves.

My experiences, so unlike those of my parents and grandparents, carried me away, and I left behind the identity they expected of me. I was the one who left, but now I want the family stories, to know where I come from. I still write about this place of dreams and nightmares, my yearning mixed with fear. I look for a home in words and language.

And, maybe that's okay. Maybe one day I'll go back to the homeplace as myself. Maybe home is fluid, just like identity, and sexuality and gender. It wasn't until I transitioned that I could finally feel at home in my body. At home with my name, at home with myself. Transitioning is like stepping into another country and yet a country that I already knew from some deep place inside me.

When my novel came out, I sent a copy to the Vietnam vet I'd met years ago in West Virginia who had become a friend. He'd become my main contact in the mountains, telling me stories, driving me around, and giving me a place to stay. But he knew me as someone else. I slipped a short note in the pages of the book, and told him about my transition. I kept it short, didn't try to explain. I signed my new name. I felt anxious, bringing these two parts of my life together, and I didn't know what to expect: maybe I'd never hear from him, or maybe he'd bombard me with questions, confusion, repulsion.

A few days later, I received an email. "Dear Carter," he began. His note was also short: "I'm happy that you have found your inner happiness and that you feel comfortable enough to share it with me. . . . I have absolutely no problem whatsoever with anyone's right to discover who they are and to live accordingly. I'm happy for you."

I read it several times. The phrase *right to discover* struck me. That's what all of this was—discovery and rediscovery—of myself, my family, my roots. Now I had my own name, my own stories. I had to go away to wade through all the fear and hurt and shame, to find the light, in order to maybe one day come back as a son, brother, nephew, or grandson. It took a long time to accept myself. I didn't know it at the time, but the people I met in West Virginia were teaching me something about courage. They were helping me find my way.

CHRIS OFFUTT
Someone Else

BY THE TIME I was fourteen, my parents were accustomed to my absences—wandering the woods, sleeping in town, eating at other people's homes. What mattered to my folks were academic grades, which I kept at all A's: not particularly difficult in the schools of Appalachia during the sixties and seventies. Of equal importance was granting utter obedience to Dad, and never causing my mother public embarrassment. With this veneer of civility thus attended to, I was free.

I don't remember how I met the fatman. I assume he approached me. He lived in town on the second floor of a small building, where he rented a single room with a bathroom in the hall. He was nice. He bought me candy bars and bottles of pop—which my parents never allowed me to have. I told him about my family life, spending days in the woods, and girls I liked. At four feet, eleven inches, I was the shortest kid in high school, reputed to be among the smartest, lousy at sports, and had long blond hair. He listened to me. He offered a kind of sympathy that was foreign, an attentiveness I needed. He accepted that I wanted to be an actor or a comic book artist when I grew up, and he believed such aspirations weren't incredulous. He didn't talk about himself much but implied that he'd experienced life beyond the confines of Rowan County, and that I would like it out there when I finally left.

I was vulnerable, I suppose, although not a dire misfit. I was open and friendly, having gone through eight years of grade school with the same small group of kids, then riding the bus each day to the only high school in the county. One by one, my classmates began losing the habit of attending school. It was not expected but certainly accepted, and of little concern. After all, we were from Haldeman, the community farthest from town, site of the main bootlegger, weekly drag strips, occasional shootings and arson. We were at the bottom of a pecking order that didn't start very high. In high school, for the first time, we all became aware of our status. Some of us responded by staying at home, by changing style of dress, or becoming withdrawn. I explored town.

The fatman's room was so small there was no space for a chair and we both had to sit on the bed. The whole time I pretended it was happening to someone else. Afterwards, the fatman said he liked me. He gave me money. I left the room and walked to the drugstore where my mother picked me up after shopping for groceries. I bought a lot of comic books at the drugstore. She didn't ask where I got the money.

I don't remember his name or what he looked like. I don't recall the print on the wallpaper or the color of the bedspread. What I do remember is the overhead light fixture, a plain bisected globe in a ceramic setting that emitted a dim yellowish light. Surrounding the globe and painted over many times were plaster rosettes with narrow leaves that curved in tiny flourishes. I remember the light because I spent all my time staring at it and waiting until I could leave.

When I returned, I climbed the steps slowly, trying not to make any noise because I didn't want to get the fatman in trouble. A clot of tension rose along my spine, vibrating like an embedded blade. I felt hollow—my heart pounding, sweat trickling down my sides, mouth dry, my stomach congealed to stone. The fatman opened the door and ushered me in. The bed sagged when he sat down. The money lay in sight on the bedside table. Time stopped as I slid away from my body to rove the air. I became my own spirit averting my eyes, imagining a life beyond the hills. I would be a movie actor. Beautiful women would throw themselves at me as I left French cafés. I departed the county in a limousine. I was the mayor's son, the governor's nephew. I was secretly adopted. I inherited a Lexington horse farm. I was anyone but a lonely kid feeling the dampness of fat fingers.

Just before I started being someone else, I decided my parents would be proud of my open-mindedness in such a small town. They considered themselves progressive. My mother wore miniskirts and my father had a beard. They traveled, leaving me in charge of my younger siblings for a few days at a time. They went to exotic locales for Science Fiction conventions—Cincinnati, Louisville, St. Louis, Nashville, once even Florida. I thought that what I was doing with the fatman made me similar to my parents. They wrote porn. They had affairs. If they knew about the fatman, they would respect me, maybe even like me.

The fatman took me to the movies. We stood in line but didn't have to buy tickets. The fatman looked at the owner, put his hand on my shoulder, and nodded once. The owner looked at me without changing expression and let us in free. I felt important.

The fatman bought a large buttered popcorn and gave it to me. This was the first time I ever ate buttered popcorn at a movie. I was not allowed to have popcorn at the movies because my father said it was too expensive. Occasionally Mom made popcorn at home, but she never put butter on it. We watched *The Godfather,* which affected me in a very powerful way. I'd never seen a movie that long or that slow. The world was utterly foreign but I understood its insular nature, the power dynamics, the violence and loyalties. After the movie, the fatman gave me a dime because I insisted on calling my father and telling him that if anything ever happened to him, I would avenge his death. I was crying into the phone. My father said little.

The fatman wanted me to touch him in his bed, but I refused. I explained that I liked girls, though I'd never been with one. I'd kissed three and touched one's bra strap, but never got any further. The fatman offered me two hundred dollars to help him make a movie. They'd shoot the whole thing in a hotel room nearby, but I'd have to touch a man, maybe another boy about my age. I told him that I really wanted to be with a girl, and suggested we make that kind of movie instead. He said if I made a movie with a man, afterwards he would provide me with a girl to be with, plus I'd get the money. I told him no. He told me to think about it, but I didn't. Instead I looked at the light fixture and went away in my mind. I'd developed the ability to go rapidly, to vanish from the circumstances, and enter a trancelike state in which I was a prince with a personal garrison at my command, a lavish kingdom to rule, and a harem of lovely women. I fell in love with a commoner and abandoned all my riches for her. We lived by the sea in Italy. We held hands always and forever. Our eyes never left each other. We were together throughout the ages, each era presenting its version of our love. Abruptly I was back in the dim room. My legs were bare and cold, my body tense. The fatman was breathing hard. I took the money and left.

The last time I went to the room, I encountered another boy on the steps. I'd seen him before, outside the building, but we never spoke about the fatman. We both pretended like we didn't see each other. He was my age with long blond hair, new to school, his mother divorced, a rarity at the time. He crouched on the steps and motioned me to be quiet. I joined him, moving silently. We were midway up the staircase so that our heads were level with the floor above. The bathroom was at the top of the stairs and the door was not fully closed. Through it we could see the fatman standing in the shower, his vast naked bulk exposed. He was vomiting and defecating simultaneously. It was a sickening sight, so repulsive that it was hard to stop staring. I realized the fatman was crying. Not just weeping but an uncontrollable sobbing that made his shoulders quake, his torso ripple. He leaned on the wall as if in surrender.

The other boy and I slipped down the stairs and laughed about what we'd seen. What else could we do? We didn't know the extent to which the fatman influenced the rest of our lives. We never talked about it and he soon quit school. It took me many years to wonder if the other boy made a movie at the motel. By then he was dead of an overdose. The fatman had once suggested I bring my brother to visit, and I got very angry. The only good that I can find in all this now is that I protected my brother. At least I did that.

The fatman left town as suddenly as he'd appeared. I didn't speak to anyone about him. Instead, I began to shoplift. Every time I entered a store I walked around as if browsing, while secretly examining lines of sight and avenues of getaway. I was a meticulous planner. The best technique was to set what I wanted to steal near the door, then buy something cheap that required a shopping bag. On my way out of the store, I'd browse a little bit, then surreptitiously slip the preset goods into the bag. I got very scared as I walked to the door, my body encased in the same adrenalized state as when climbing the steps to the fatman's room. I breathed slowly through my mouth, sweating inside my clothes. On the sidewalk outside, I felt the euphoria of relief at having gotten away. Stealing supplied an intensity to life that was absent otherwise. It later left me feeling bad about myself, which didn't matter, because by then that felt normal.

I skipped school and began spending all my time at the pool hall with older guys. I learned to shoot a good stick. I also learned to make marijuana pipes from an empty toilet paper tube, a Coke can, an apple, anything I could punch two holes in. Some college boys I thought were cool gave me acid. Next I tried Valium. I began taking amphetamines and breaking into cars. I never got caught. I never stole anything good. I dropped out of high school and joined the army, but they didn't want me. I went to college.

In a psychology class, I read an article that defined victims of sexual abuse. This made me feel uneasy because I knew the whole fatman business was my fault. I didn't like the idea of being a victim. Nobody forced me to enter that building and climb those stairs and push open the dark wooden door. I went there freely. I went there more than once. I felt special. I felt bad. I wondered if I was gay. I dropped the class and got stoned, then drunk, and stayed that way for a good long while.

Twenty-five years later I began talking about the fatman. I thought I might feel relieved, or unburdened, but I didn't. I told my wife. I told my parents and siblings in a group letter, which I suppose was cowardly, perhaps even cruel. It was shocking enough that no one knew how to respond. My father, surprisingly, called. He wanted to know if the man who'd abused me still lived in the county. In fact, Dad evoked *The Godfather*, saying that he would send Vito and Luigi to kill the man. I didn't have the heart to tell him how that particular movie figured into things so long ago.

After revealing my old secret, I mainly felt embarrassed. Worse things happened to people, and much worse things happened to women. I was never forced or hurt. I was passive and it was a long time ago. I understood the fatman had probably been abused as a child. I also knew that I should find it in myself to forgive him, an act which would ultimately benefit me. But I couldn't do it. I'd spent too many years hoping the fatman went to prison. I hoped every inmate spat on him in the corridors. I wanted them to fill his food with poison, smack him around in the yard, and ambush him in the shower. I wanted him to be scared and alone. I wanted his life to be so miserable that he spent every day wishing he was someone else. I wanted him to memorize the dim flat light fixture in his cell. I wanted him as dead as I felt, as dead as I still feel sometimes, as dead as the other boy I saw on the steps will always be.

JASON HOWARD

Bastards and Ghosts

IN UNION SQUARE, I lounge on the stone steps at the south end of the park. I take my partner's hand, lean in to kiss him. My heart is here in Manhattan, here in this moment, here on the arm of my man, far away from the scorn and disgust too often found in our native Kentucky, the memories of which bear down on me—a sign from a rally that reads *All Gays Will Burn In Hell,* a preacher mouthing the word *reprobate,* my mother's voice saying *I'm through with you.*

I push these words out of my thoughts. They do not matter. What counts is only this moment, this scene we have wandered into as we walked uptown after dinner. The traffic from 14th Street hums lightly by, background music to the action unfolding all around us. Although it is only an evening in late May, the city is baking, its oven of concrete and steel preheating for the coming summer. The faint scent of weed wafts through the park, mingling with the coarse smell of the subway that rattles beneath me.

Just below us a group of boys gather around an old-school boom box. Tape deck, volume knobs, bulking square speakers. One bends down, his ear touching the webbed metal of the speaker. "Ella," he whispers, a prayer, running his hand across the cool plastic casing of the stereo. He is stoned and beautiful, his ebony shoulders gleaming beneath the straps of his red tank top. He reclines on the steps, moving his lean arms up to cradle his head. He stares at the stars, which seem to mirror the scattered lights of Manhattan skyscrapers.

Ella Fitzgerald's velvety voice floats through the air, rising above the statue of Gandhi, above the magnolia trees clustered in this corner of the square, their waning blooms framing Mahatma's body like a starburst. This is a cinematic outtake from *Breakfast at Tiffany's* or *An Affair to Remember.* I imagine for a moment that we are being captured on celluloid, an out-of-body experience that allows me to become a camera on a boom, zooming in for a close-up of our faces. Silas, my partner, studies my profile with his blue eyes, lighting on the squared tip of my nose—*that strong English nose,* he calls it. I relax against his arm and sigh.

The beautiful boy below us offers a soliloquy to Ella, his face still turned toward the stars, mouthing the words to her "September Song." I clasp my love's hand tighter.

This is what matters: we're here together, joined at the marrow in Union Square. A unit, a union.

Gay men in exile. Appalachian refugees.

SINCE CHILDHOOD I have nurtured a secret fantasy world, one that runs parallel to wherever I find myself living. Sometimes, in my fantasies, I live in Hampton Court Palace just outside of London, reveling in the dramas of the court of Henry VIII and Anne Boleyn. I occasionally move through the world as Jacqueline Kennedy Onassis, wandering the streets of New York alone, my wraparound sunglasses a shield, allowing me to people-watch to my heart's content.

Growing up in Dorton Branch, a small hollow tucked away in the Cumberland Mountains of southeastern Kentucky, fifteen miles from the Tennessee-Virginia border, I often found myself a stranger. In some ways, I was a typical mountain boy, roaming through the woods, building tree houses and wading in creeks in search of crawdads, pedaling my neon green Huffy bicycle. I devoured soup beans and corn bread, developed a lasting affinity for classic country music, and sat at the feet of some great storytellers. In those moments, I became Huck Finn on the Mississippi, allowing the river to take me wherever it wanted.

But the rest of the culture seemed foreign. Once, when I eight and was staying all night with a friend, his uncle dropped by to see his father. "Hey, buddy," he hollered, his maroon Dingo cowboy boots thudding on the small rectangle of parquet at the sliding door. Slapping each other on the back, they settled down at the kitchen table, the flames from two Bics lighting their Marlboro Reds. My friend and I paused our Nintendo game, laying down the controls and creeping into the living room to listen.

"Did I tell you about the deer I killed last weekend?" my friend's dad asked. "Eight-pointer. Killed it from my tree stand. Buddy, it was a good shot, let me tell you."

"No kidding," the uncle replied, tapping the cigarette with his right index finger to dislodge an ash. "What did you do with it?"

"Took it over to Middlesboro to have it mounted. Freezing the meat. I'll send you some."

At this, my friend joined the men at the kitchen table. "I went too, Uncle Jamie. It was a real good shot. Next time I'm going to get me one. An eight-pointer."

"Sure you will, buddy," his uncle said, moving the cigarette to his mouth, before turning toward me in the living room. "How about you, little man? You hunt?"

The dreaded question. I had no interest in hunting, didn't want to shoot a squirrel or rabbit, let alone a deer. My father didn't even own a gun. The one time I had gone hunting, three years before with an older cousin, I had been reprimanded for talking, swatted on the behind for alerting the squirrels to our presence. The woods to me were for exploring, for admiring the way dead, orange-colored pine needles carpeted the ground, climbing giant rocks covered in moss and lichen, propping up under an old oak and opening a book.

"No," I replied, my eyes studying the seam in the floor where the burgundy carpet of the living room met the beige linoleum of the kitchen, a border that I didn't, couldn't, cross.

"You're missing out, buddy," he said, turning back to his nephew. "Hunting will make you a man."

But I was not a man by his definition. By middle school, I was watching classic films like the campy 1959 version of *Imitation of Life*, lip-synching to Barbra Streisand's "Gotta Move," writing fan letters to Diana and Fergie that received polite replies on their official stationery from ladies-in-waiting. *Faggot* was a word that I became acquainted with, hurled at me on occasion in the hallways between classes. And for good reason—I had a secret friend, a boy I kissed in empty classrooms during Science Olympiad practice in the afternoons. When the teasing and derision became too much, we broke up. He began dating a girl, and I turned my back on my Southern Baptist raising, joining a Pentecostal church where the congregation spoke in tongues and danced in the Spirit to the intoxicating beat of a piano, guitar, bass, drums, and tambourines.

In high school, I became a ghost of my true self, haunting the church on Saturday nights and Sunday mornings and evenings in search of peace. At the altar, I knelt on plum-colored carpet, praying for deliverance from my reprobate mind. During the week, I sometimes fasted, denying myself physical food in hopes of strengthening my spirit and resolve, all the while never, ever telling anyone that I was gay.

When I moved to Washington, D.C., to attend university, this image that I had carefully stitched together like an Appalachian quiltmaker began to fray, the pieces and seams of my denial unraveling like broken thread.

One spring afternoon, I sat in Dupont Circle reading Rainer Maria Rilke's *Letter to a Young Poet*. The circle was bursting—office workers in navy blue suits carrying briefcases in one hand and a Starbucks concoction in the other, mothers and nannies pushing strollers or playing in the grass with toddlers, homeless men playing a game of checkers on the stone tables—all framed by the flutter of leaves in the maples, birches, and ginkgos that ring the circle. High atop the bowl of the white marble Daniel Chester French fountain, a cluster of blackbirds and sparrows surveyed the park, their feet perched on the edge of the giant birdbath.

And then I saw them, two men in their sixties having tea on a nearby bench. In between bites of fat scones and sips from paper cups, they talked easily, their conversation drowned out by the symphony of falling water, laughter, and a twenty-something playing the guitar. When a sudden breeze stirred up a whirlwind of leaves and dirt, they reached to secure their stack of napkins. A piece of twig caught in the bushy, gray hair of one of the men. The other moved to retrieve it, and his companion caught his hand, bringing it instead to his mouth. There, in full view, lips met palm. Then they returned to their tea.

My eyes moistened at this open display of affection, an image that lingered as I returned to Rilke and his admonition to "be patient toward all that is unsolved in your heart." But that day, that moment, those two men became muses for my own coming-out process that began to unfold, coinciding with another revelation—a renewed sense of pride in my Appalachian roots.

Although I loved the city, I occasionally missed the music and food of home. I searched out recordings by the Carter Family and Dolly Parton, playing them alongside songs by Madonna and Destiny's

Child. I worked hard at perfecting a skillet of corn bread and a recipe for sweet tea, which I craved as much as my more recent loves of sushi and *pierogi*.

Then, after six years of living in D.C., I moved back to Kentucky to pursue my writing full-time. I did not return to the mountains, instead settling at first in a small town an hour away from my birthplace. I fell in love there with a fellow writer, surrounded myself with a chosen family—writers, musicians, and artists who lived the creative life and embraced progressive values. Yet in spite of this community, I was isolated in this conservative town where, in the words of Little Edie in the documentary *Grey Gardens,* "they can get you for wearing red shoes on a Thursday."

But then I moved to Berea, Kentucky, where I melded easily into its population of first-generation college students, skilled artisans, old-time musicians, aspiring writers, and aging hippies. My partner soon followed, and we bought a home, a two-story Arts and Crafts structure on a dead-end street that we call the "gayborhood." A lesbian couple has settled just a few doors down; they live next door to a gay couple, two nontraditional college students studying agriculture and natural resources. Across the wooded gully that meanders behind our house lives a gay man, a professor at the college.

In the prevailing political colors of the day, Berea is a shimmering blue oasis surrounded by a desert of red. Our small liberal arts college is famous for its egalitarian mission. Berea College was the first integrated and coeducational school in the South, having admitted blacks, whites, and women upon its founding in 1855. That social justice tradition continues—Berea has clung to one of the Appalachian frontier's remaining vestiges, a *live and let live* philosophy that much of the region has forsaken. The irony is that Berea is not an Appalachian town, at least not strictly in the geographic sense. Instead, it is a border town, nestled where the bluegrass region of Kentucky, with its rolling fields and prime horse countryside, meets the foothills of the Cumberland Mountains.

But a border town is also a place of conflicts, and Berea is no exception. For the last two years, the town has been embroiled in a heated debate over passing a fairness ordinance, which would extend protections in the areas of employment and public accommodations to anyone perceived to be lesbian, gay, bisexual, or transgender. While residents of the town proper are supportive of the proposed measure, those living in the conservative, rural areas where the city limits extend are staunchly opposed, showing up at city council meetings and spewing hateful rhetoric. The council has not taken up the ordinance, preferring instead to attempt to placate both sides, hoping the issue diffuses on its own. But it will not. My own family is proof enough.

One morning in Berea I was summoned by the incessant ringing of the bell, then someone pounding on the door. I peered through the frosted glass and saw my mother, lips pursed, face contorted in anger, before I opened the door.

"What is it?" I demanded, piecing together what the problem was before she even had a chance to speak. I had refused to answer her calls that morning, and she had made the ninety-minute drive from her house to mine in anger and frustration.

"I've called and called you," she hollered. "You are going to talk to me."

Curtains shifted in the front window of the house across the street. My next-door neighbor came out on her porch, watching nervously for a moment to make sure everything was all right.

"No, I don't have anything else to say," I replied, standing in the doorway, the metal sill marking a boundary between us that she demanded to cross.

"Let me in," she shouted. "You have to stop this. It's wrong."

I remembered how nervous I felt coming out to my parents over a year before. As an only child, raised in a fundamentalist household, I knew that my father would not accept it, but I had hope for my mother, whose sweet, compassionate disposition I had always admired. I told her first, in front of my aunt and cousin, and she accepted me, holding me as I cried, telling me she would always love me.

That changed just three days later when she told my father. She called and expressed her doubts, saying that my being gay was wrong, sinful. After months of being patient, trying to find common ground, hoping that she would come around, I had all but given up.

"This is how God made me, and you're not going to talk to me that way," I replied. "If you want to talk calmly and rationally, you're welcome to come inside."

She refused. I told her to leave, that no one, no matter who she was, blood kin or otherwise, was allowed to cause such a spectacle on my own front porch, a territory Southerners consider sacred, its edges denoting a borderline of peace, not conflict.

"If you do this, I'm through with you," she replied, marching to the car. I followed, asking her again to talk rationally. I watched as she backed out of the driveway, my arms limp at my sides.

SEVERAL YEARS ago, Silas and I made our first trip abroad. Five days in London, along with a brief excursion to Paris on the Eurostar. In the weeks before the holiday, I often took my virgin passport out of its place in my nightstand with anticipation, caressing the rough navy cover and tracing the gold letters with my index finger. I opened it and turned to the information page, lamenting my garish picture, which returned my gaze with a sneer. Moving to the right, I checked my vital information again for errors, any oversight that might create complications:

> Surname: HOWARD
> Given Name: JASON KYLE
> Nationality: UNITED STATES OF AMERICA
> Date of Birth: 01 MARCH 1981
> Place of Birth: KENTUCKY, USA

I visualized our trek through customs in hopes of conjuring up a speedy, effortless experience. But I quickly returned to the information, to my nationality and place of birth, switching them around in my mind. *Should these be reversed?* I asked myself.

> Nationality: KENTUCKY, USA
> Place of Birth: UNITED STATES OF AMERICA

I was jarred by this notion. While proud of my Appalachian roots, my study of history has made me rightfully wary of the dangers of provincialism. Of sectionalism. I have always considered myself first and foremost an American. So why does it feel as if I have lost my country, Appalachia?

In *Speak, Memory*, Vladimir Nabokov writes of being granted a "Nansen" passport from the League of Nations, a green-colored document given to Russian émigrés who had lost their citizenship following the October Revolution of 1917. Customs officials regarded the bearer with censure, he notes, viewing them "with the preposterous disapproval with which certain religious groups regard a child born out of wedlock."

I imagined myself calling the State Department and explaining my plight. "I am a refugee," I would insist to the Passport Office. "I want to apply for a Nansen passport."

They would not have understood. They would threaten to put me on a watch list. I would hang up in frustration.

My thoughts returned to *Speak, Memory*, to Nabokov: "Not all of us consented to be bastards and ghosts."

"ONE LAST question," I say to the man sitting across the table from me in a lawyer's office in Charleston, West Virginia. I study his ruggedly handsome face for a moment, glance at his large, gnarled hands, coated with a faint layer of coal dust that no amount of scrubbing can remove. One rests on the faux mahogany conference room table, the other clasping the hand of his husband.

Sam Hall is a twenty-eight-year-old openly gay coal miner who filed suit in December 2010 against his employer, a subsidiary of corporate outlaw Massey Energy, for sexual and gender discrimination and harassment due to his sexual orientation, and I am here to interview him for a national magazine. At his workplace he has faced a litany of homophobic slurs, a sign attached to his car that read *I like little boys,* someone vandalizing and removing the wheel weights from his car, his fellow miners shaking their dicks at him underground and in the bathhouse, a coworker muttering *I would like to see all faggots die.*

I say it again—*one last question*—and nudge my iPhone and time-worn microcassette recorder closer so I don't miss a word of his answer. "Why do you stay in West Virginia?"

I am asking for myself as much as for his response, which is immediate.

"This is where we're from, and I'm not going to be pushed away," he shakes his head. "I'm not going to be told, 'Well, if you go here it's going to be easier for you.' Life's not easy. When I want to live somewhere I'm not going to have somebody else push me out."

But this is his answer, not mine.

If I were honest with myself, I would respond that I'm not sure I want to be in Kentucky forever. That in many ways this is no longer my home, but where I'm from, and that I am also from all of the places that have shaped me—Dorton Branch, D.C., New York, London, Key West, Berea.

"I'M A writer," legendary journalist Jimmy Breslin announces at the beginning of Spike Lee's film *Summer of Sam.* "I write about New

York, the city of my birth, where I've lived and worked all my life. The city that I love and hate both equally." His delivery is straightforward, matter-of-fact. Framed by the chaos of Times Square, Breslin makes no apologies for his honesty or for the complexity of his statement.

I repeat his last sentence aloud as I work in my office on the second floor of our house. I pause, lifting my eyes from the computer screen. By instinct, I turn to my left and stare out the window, past our neighbor Eunice's home across the street and through a wild tangle of tree limbs. In the distance I see the first rise of the Appalachians, blots of indigo on the horizon. Beyond that border lies the region of my birth, where I can no longer live and work. The region that I love and hate both equally.

I cross this boundary only rarely these days, usually to travel to the occasional reading or to visit my nine-year-old niece. When I make the familiar trek to my native Bell County down I-75, exiting at London and following Highway 229, I know the hairpin turns by heart. I take them fast, wanting to get to Dorton Branch and back to Berea as quickly as possible, driving as if my life depended on it.

On these trips, I am scarcely able to inhale the beauty that surrounds me, the sight of redbuds and dogwoods and sarvis blooming on the mountainsides. As I grip the steering wheel, I consider how much my life has changed, how it was interrupted in middle school by a culture that does not understand who I am, how it took me ten more years to begin a process toward living openly, the opinions and judgment of the rest of the world be damned. How I, the ultimate Appalachian insider—born and bred here, carrying its accent on my tongue—have now become an outsider, unwelcomed by many in the land of my birth. My Mustang hugs the narrow road as I sing along with John Lennon: *Mother, you had me / But I never had you.*

I mimic his primal screams—*Mama don't go*—but mine is a cry of resignation, acceptance. Like Nabokov and the exiled artists who spoke of Mother Russia, I both celebrate and mourn this wondrous, cruel region, Mother Appalachia—for the casseroles friends and neighbors bring after a death, for the hateful looks I receive from shoppers when I wear my favorite tweed flat cap in the Dollar General. For the beauty of an old-time creek baptizing, for the venomous tirades of ignorant preachers.

The word *bastard* ricochets through my mind as I turn onto Highway 25-E, still singing along, my voice as thin as silt.

Daddy bear
~~JEFF MANN~~
Offensive Hillbilly Queer

RECENTLY, I WAS invited to speak to a local book club here in Pulaski County, Virginia. All of the ladies in attendance appeared interested; several responded enthusiastically; many said they would buy the book, for themselves or for relatives.

It was a pleasant experience—we authors do love an audience—though one aspect of the afternoon had me mildly off balance. I'd been asked to discuss not my own publications but my father's. I doubt that any of my ten books would have appealed to that audience of polite, well-dressed elderly ladies living in the mountains of southwest Virginia. Daddy's book did appeal, as I knew it would.

PERRY MANN'S *Mann and Nature: A Collection of Essays* (Delavan, Wisconsin: Kettle Moraine Publishing, 2011) contains thirty personal essays that focus on topics close to my own heart: country living, farming, Appalachian self-reliance, environmentalism, mountain landscapes, and the shifting beauties of the seasons. The collection has found favor with a wide range of folks. Daddy, as of this writing ninety-one years old, has always wanted to publish a book, and since its release, has proudly reported to me a slew of fan letters, hard-copy and e-mailed, and many an invitation to read at bookstores in our region. He has, in other words, achieved a modicum of what I never have: a mainstream audience.

I am honestly pleased at the positive reception of his book, at the same time that I'm admittedly envious. At age fifty-three, I regret my own lack of literary recognition. I'm as voracious as any writer for critical attention and ego-food, yet I have gotten little of both. (Or not enough: to a narcissist, no amount of affirmation is ever sufficient.) My work has been, to a great extent, neglected, passed over, and ignored, or so it feels to me. As a result, my bitterness is considerable, my envy of more successful authors acidic and intense.

Only the good Southern manners my mother bred in me allow me to hide these unattractive resentments on a day-to-day basis. That, and a few cautionary examples: other writers I've met who have expressed the same snarling envy. I've seen how ugly such behavior is, and so I refuse to reveal my bile in public. I admit to such feelings in this essay only because, for me, writing is about honesty, no matter how uncomfortable or unseemly.

It is that very honesty that has limited my audience. I am aware of that. Hoist with my own petard, that irresistible Shakespearean phrase. This awareness does not reduce my bitterness a whit.

My partner of fifteen years, understandably weary of my incessant complaints, often points to the controversial nature of what I publish and politely suggests that I have chosen my path and so should gracefully accept the consequences. Well, no! At the same time that I wouldn't do anything differently, given the chance, I also reserve the right to snarl. Simply put, articulating my welling acrimony makes me feel better. I'd rather spit acid than swallow it.

WHAT'S CONSIDERED controversial and what's considered acceptable depend on context. Had I been born somewhere other than Southern Appalachia, or if I had left my native region and made a life in some far-off liberal city, things might have been different. As it is, I was born in Clifton Forge, Virginia, and grew up in Covington, Virginia, and Hinton, West Virginia, both small mountain towns. I attended West Virginia University for undergraduate and graduate degrees, then taught there briefly. For the last twenty-three years, I've taught at Virginia Tech, living in both Blacksburg, a liberal university town, and Pulaski, Virginia, another small mountain town. I have stubbornly remained in a region in which I feel alternately anomalous and pretty much at home.

Today, as I contemplate my publications, it seems as if I've written nothing *but* the controversial. True, there are a few innocuous poems about Appalachian food and family ties, which should be palatable to mainstream folks. Other than that, almost everything I write is likely to offend someone somewhere. My preferred topics are those that my people—Southerners and Appalachians—would surely regard as inappropriate, even vulgar, a word my genteel mother used with matchless acerbity. The more devout would call my books perverse and satanic; at least one Amazon reviewer has used the word "vile."

And what are those topics? Like most writers, I am drawn to the problematic, to sources of tension and conflict. The first in the list is homosexuality.

With the help of lesbian friends, I realized I was gay when I was sixteen. Being LGBT in America is still difficult. Being gay in a small town in southern West Virginia in the 1970s was especially challenging. I have dealt with confusion, fear, anger, shame, desire, and hope of varying intensities ever since. During my WVU undergrad days, I began to explore the gay community, share erotic experiences with other men, and write poetry making sense of my (frequently unreciprocated) desires. To my pleasure, gay literary journals began accepting some of these pieces for publication in the early 1980s.

During my graduate school days in Morgantown, I wrote a collection of love poems as my creative thesis. One batch was inspired by a promiscuous bartender and another by a charming narcissist who compulsively bounced checks, neither of whom was particularly interested in me after the first few nights together. That didn't matter. I was young, ardent, and hungry as hell for sex and romance; their indifference and their good looks enflamed me, inspiring me to write a plethora of lovesick poems.

As if mere homosexuality weren't sufficiently taboo for whatever ornery muse goads me to write what I do, when I moved to Blacksburg to start a new job at Virginia Tech in 1989, it wasn't long before I was groin-deep in other controversial and forbidden topics: BDSM and adultery. Bondage had fascinated me since childhood—so many roped-up superheroes in comic books and hog-tied cowboys in Westerns. I'd begun to identify with the leather community as early as my sophomore year in college, when I read Patricia Nell Warren's novel *The Beauty Queen* and related powerfully to a butch gay couple that shared loving but sadomasochistic sex. I managed some dabbling with a few willing partners, serving as top for Steve, bottom for Jim.

Then I met The Mythical Thomas at Virginia Tech and fell passionately and catastrophically in love. I call Thomas mythical simply because I've already written about him so much elsewhere. He already had a partner; he and I conducted a secretive affair nonetheless, hot meetings rich with sweat, musk, body hair, ropes and gags. It was the most satisfying and profound erotic connection I've ever had; he was the submissive muscle-cub of my dreams. It ended very unpleasantly after just a few years, and its aftermath left me in agony. I've never gotten over it. That's good, I guess. Wounds can be an inexhaustible source of creative energy. My first book of poetry, *Bones Washed with Wine*, was entirely inspired by my feelings for Thomas, and much of my second collection, *On the Tongue*, was as well. Both volumes are quite frank about the emotional turmoil and ambivalence of adultery and the deliciously kinky sex we shared. Such verse has a long tradition: the European troubadours often wrote of their longings for other men's wives.

No, the elegant book-club ladies—or the mainstream audience I'm using them to represent—would not find such poetry appealing, I fear. Nor would they relish my other works, most of which explore gay sexuality and fetish to some extent. There are my many erotic short stories in assorted anthologies, several of them collected in *A History of Barbed Wire* and my vampire-themed volume, *Desire and Devour: Stories of Blood and Sweat;* my intense kidnapping thriller, *Fog: A Novel of Desire and Reprisal;* my violent, homoerotic Civil War fiction, *Purgatory: A Novel of the Civil War,* and *Camp Allegheny,* included in *History's Passion: Stories of Sex Before Stonewall.* There's surely enough candid queer material in *Edge: Travels of an Appalachian Leather Bear* and *Binding the God: Ursine Essays from the Mountain South,* my two essay collections, to put them off. *Loving Mountains, Loving Men* is tamer, fairly free of explicit Eros, if readers can tolerate discussions of the conflicts between my gay and Appalachian identities. But even *Ash: Poems from Norse Mythology* has a few gay love poems, as well as "Valhalla Revised," which details enthusiastic man-on-man fucking in a queered version of the Norse afterlife.

My more recent poems, only a handful of which have appeared in literary magazines, tend toward two topics, neither of which is likely to garner me many mainstream fans: (1) frustrated middle-aged lust for men much younger than myself and (2) the Confederate experience in the Civil War.

"There's no fool like an old fool," my mother used to sigh, referring to my father's wandering eye. I say that to myself sometimes, as I quietly admire assorted young men half my age. Yes, I know: how banal, what a cliché, a middle-aged man yearning after much younger flesh. No one would guess what vigorous fantasies I entertain behind my polite professional façade, my smiling equipoise. Being a university teacher doesn't help: virile scenery everywhere. Neither does living in Pulaski, with its plentiful array of hot country boys/scruffy mountain men: younger versions of myself, exactly the type I'm most attracted to.

Of course I would never approach a student with seduction in mind. The power inequality makes that unethical, and the potential consequences to my professional life might be disastrous. (These concerns, needless to say, have not always deterred other middle-aged men in my position, most of them straight.) At least one of my essays in *Edge, "*Drambuie," deals with this kind of socially forbidden desire—a deep erotic appreciation I felt for a student on Study Abroad nearly twenty years ago. Almost all of my new poems in this vein are about lust and Eros in suspension, frustrated, never acted upon. "The Old Lecher Does Not Seduce an Overnight Guest" is an illustrative title. I have enough of these poems for a meaty volume. I'd like to title the book *Boys I Can't Fuck,* but I suspect I'll go with the milder *Boys I Can't Keep.* If I can't ravish them, I can, by God, write poems about them. That volcanic lust has to have some outlet.

Then there are the few poems about successful encounters with younger men who, thank all the god/desses of concupiscence, appreciate older men, a "Daddybear" in my case. These poems not only fly in the face of those who insist on monogamy—as I do not—but are likely to disgust people who find the concept of sex over thirty repulsive. More verboten and unsavory verse!

Most of the poetry I've produced over the last four years has been based on the same research that spawned the Civil War fiction mentioned above. I'm not African American and I'm not a Yankee, so I do not write about the Black or Northern experience of that war. My paternal grandmother's maternal grandfather was Isaac Green Carden, a Confederate soldier. I myself grew up around Confederate monuments, in both Covington and Hinton. Therefore, I write with clear Southern sympathies, though often from a gay perspective. My work "queers" the war, so to speak.

Though the ladies' club members, most of them Southern-born, might appreciate some of these poems, as would many denizens of Covington, Hinton, and Pulaski, I can assure you that the faculty and students at Virginia Tech do not. (The staff is another matter: most of them are locals.) The majority of people living in Blacksburg and connected with the university are not native Southerners. To them, my fondness for the Stars and Bars and "Dixie," my admiration for Robert E. Lee, Stonewall Jackson, Turner Ashby, and Jeb Stuart are downright incomprehensible. At least one colleague—or so it was furtively reported to me—during my tenure bid expressed "great concern" over my essay about the Confederate flag, "Unreconstructed Queer." Those in my department who might know of my work—and very few do, from what I can tell—probably assume that I'm a redneck, a hillbilly, poor white trash who's managed to infiltrate the ivory tower. If they don't know I have Black in-laws and a biracial nephew, they might also assume that I'm a raving racist. My bushy beard, faded denims, cowboy boots, tattoos, rusty pickup truck, and enthusiasm for country music don't help.

SO THE openly queer and often erotic elements in my work are likely to offend lots of Southerners/Appalachians/conservative country folk, and my sympathy for white Southern citizens and Rebel soldiers in the destructive War between the States is likely to offend city folks/liberals. What audience is left?

Not a lot. I've managed to develop a small literary reputation in both Appalachian literature and LGBT publishing, and I'm thankful for that. Bear Bones Books, an imprint of Lethe Press, has been particularly supportive: they've reprinted two of my books and published four more. But I have a strong suspicion that I'd have a far larger audience if I weren't compulsively drawn to such contentious topics. Once in a while, an enthusiastic reader e-mails me, and that means a great deal. I cherish those messages as evidence that my work does indeed reach the like-minded. Still, I get few invitations to give readings, and my books receive few reviews.

Edge, my first book of prose, received a handful of reviews; in one published in *Journal of Appalachian Studies,* the writer described me as "contrarian." I like that word. He was right. When I was younger, I used to rejoice in my openly expressed difference; it made me feel special, unique, courageous. Lately though, I'm tired of always being in a minority, tired of being the one to talk honestly about forbidden topics most people don't want to hear about. It's demoralizing and isolating. It makes for regular conflict, both internal and external, and after several decades that can be exhausting.

The outright attacks have been the most unpleasant. During my first semester as an untenured professor, an anonymous homophobe e-mailed all the presidents of Virginia Tech's alumni chapters railing about my publications. After *Loving Mountains, Loving Men* appeared, another anonymous e-mail told me to "Get medical help!" One editor, when his literary journal published an essay of mine detailing my semi-tongue-in-cheek lust for country music singer Tim McGraw, spent a full paragraph in his introduction to the issue explaining why he would not have accepted the piece, had he been the nonfiction editor. I was mortified, then furious, then sneeringly amused.

MY FATHER always encouraged me to be a nonconformist, to ignore that suffocating small-town constriction, "What will people *think*?!" My mother was just the opposite: she was very concerned about reputation and others' opinions. That difference made their marriage difficult, and I contain their conflicting voices in my head. When I write about provocative topics, my frank defiance of convention is always mixed with self-doubt and uncertainty; I vacillate between extremes of pride and shame. At the same time that I think my writing should be as honest as it possibly can (my father's influence), I dislike giving offense (my mother's influence). My self seems split, like a fallen oak trunk's axe-cleft heartwood. This painful ambivalence will, I fear, never be resolved.

Today I'm weary and sad. Writing this essay has been clarifying but disheartening. Tomorrow, most likely, my brain chemistry will shift, and I will feel better. One thing's certain: I'll keep writing what I feel driven to write, however unsavory, offensive, and forbidden the topics might be. Not to do so would be cowardice.

We Civil War buffs are always thinking in terms of victory and defeat. Often I feel defeated, especially when I remember the high hopes of literary fame and prestige I once entertained and compare them to my present career. In order to continue, however, I must remind myself that true defeat, complete defeat, is to be silenced, to fall silent. I feel confident, despite my despairs, doubts, and dissatis-factions, that I will not be silenced by anything short of incapacitating illness or death. When I think of truth-tellers of the past—men and women who suffered and died in terrible ways—I contemplate my comfortable existence as a professor, feel thankful to have a home amid the beauty of my native mountains, and remind myself that there are far worse fates than literary obscurity.

JANE SPRINGER

Lo Siento, the Only People Who Know Where Lake Canasauga Is Live There & Aren't Telling

SO WE THREE are family, again, with a real job, and move to N.Y., upstate, journey to the falls, Chittenango, little soldier booth, $5 entry, we can afford to pay for the view & lack of riffraff, our fabulous shoes, no holes, all beasts tased & carted elsewhere, so we can't harm them for plundering our waste-can food—above the picnic area shitter's sink, signs warn: Don't drink the water, E. coli, from farm chemical runoff, we never seen such healthy cornfields, sidling up by state park, saint park, we walk through the so-called woods, to the silvery falls, arrows every 5 yards point the way so we can't get lost, even if we want, plus it's a just a sinewy pig path flanked by an 8 ft. chain-link with more signs posted to that: Don't smoke, litter, or feed the wildlife, & watch them, your children, don't jump, don't dive/ swim, so we can't wholly picture them—the leaves & falls—it's just us & our single-filing-family monk-feet, packing down wrapper-free dirt behind marmot-draped tourists, one with a kid struggling against her leash, she wants to see what's beyond us—at the pinnacle, a sign signifies a boulder, like we don't know one, which it's more a couch, anyway, where to pose for the ideal picture's marked with more arrows—we get the idea, we slip front or back of that spot? Ranger's going to frisk us, which popo-types do downstate, anyway, if they want to, if they got suspicion of a gun, which even though we aren't packing—we do look it, guilty of something, not like the 75+ Amish who barefoot a ball in their hats & hairthings, fieldside of the parking lot where, once you have your money's worth of pristine, you can drive back, changed-good for not touching anything, anything in nature—we better behave.

Ya'll haven't always tried to, behave. Before this journey, the so-called free home-wrecker weekend, no fence between couples, you smoked your chemical runoff, corn whiskey highball hitting wood floor, wood splintering into a wild-pig forest you call Canasauga, in the mythical lore of Georgia, you spiraled up, then down again, looking for the state park, devil park, three times, no signs, wheels flung rocks down twin ravines either side of midnight, headlights struck red eyes of god-knows-what flesh-starved wildcat, & between death journeys, you asked directions in the valley below's 24-hour Circle K, where the clerk said *Lo siento,* it didn't exist, this place, you fed the wildlife: Pizza flavored Combos, pork rinds, Twinkies, Cokes, anything denying health existed, you avid hawk, you bullfrog unbelting in the baby-clothes closet with Fang, trees looking the same, it all reminded you, once you found the mountain sites by accident, by animal instinct, unrangered, unmown—of the down-home white-boy gang bang, Juliana & Lollie with their throats slit in the Appalachian Trail tent, a decade hence, lawless chicory fragrance, Dickey's fabulous sex-slaughters, twang & shotgun blast, wreckage of fern-ripped, ATVs droned in the close-by, muck-stink of morning, bugs buzzed like struck matches, it felt good, at the time, though, unfettered marsh lark, the took permission to touch rare wildflowers in that neglected chain of foothills—the baby alone, asleep, in the next room's manger, Muddy Waters, loud, played, while next year's ghost shat between trees—O ruiner of holy things, orange butterflies flared out from a lightning-struck stump, you the lightning, rift & decay, brushing fire ants off your face.

WEIRDLY, DOWN from Chittenango a ways, we took our boy, Hallows' Eve or All Saints' Day, to a haunted corn maze, cider, organic pumpkin seeds, kids dressed as princesses & killers from various films. The dusk hayride proved convincing, if more terror-struck than expected, the wagon's jerk & reeling over frost-crusted dry humps in the fieldpath, fog-ghosted pond scum, figures hung & swinging in the wind-torched trees, they wore orange jumpsuits, their faces a deep shade of stuffed panty hose—we paid to take the hayride twice, for confirmation we saw the lynching we seen, this far North, this millennium, yesterday, we did!—But kept it from our son, little Zeus, little Arab-Jew, still, it made sense, Chittenango, wanting physical signs to point the way out—so the next trip, we went to Aida, laptops in this version of Egypt, every opera singer belting out Italian was walnut-, persimmon-, birch-, or ash-tongued, we didn't understand a word of it, but connected so viscerally, we wept.

WEIRDLY, THE third night at Canasauga, a white truck circled your tent, so haunted you locked yourself in your car—but with no keys to move it, you tried ducking under the dash, too fat, the muscle-necked, shotgun-toting devil fenced in your jalopy & approached, anyway, through dusky, rain-whelped trees, no husband, no child—you felt alone in the place you thought you couldn't recover from the apocalyptic past or present, yours, or that of others, & beside the brute stalked a spit-slinging pit bull, off-leash—you made the rash decision to open your door & meet death—but the man said he was just Roger, hunting wild boar he donated to the local meat locker, for the poor, which you used to be, when you ate squirrel, one pig could save a family of twelve from starving, Roger said, & all the firewood lay soaked with the afternoon torrents, so Roger sped down dirt & brought you back two dry truckfuls, he refused your beer & left—but built you a big, warm fire, before vanishing.

I GET so turned around sometimes, poor then lame, broken then rich enough to own sneakers nobody but me has ever tried on, or worn—wild then fixed, I don't know where, or who, I am, or was, will be, or between you & me, if there's any difference, woods being so various— what's your sign? Mine's the Starfish-Amputee, located at the crossroads where the Southern Cross/Polaris meet & I'm amazed by you—your brand-new limbs.

JULIA WATTS

Quare Theory: Some Thoughts on LGBT Appalachian Writing

"THAT CRICKET NEEDHAM is funny turned," my nana often said. This comment was in response to the fact that Cricket, the adult son of the most prosperous funeral home director in our tiny Appalachian town, liked to parade down Main Street wearing a white ermine jacket and thigh-high fuchsia boots, his hair bleached Barbie blond, his face aglow with bronzer.

My nana certainly wasn't the only person in town who noted that Cricket was funny turned, but while people may have talked behind his back, they didn't say anything to his face, in large part because he was from the richest family in town, and in small-town life, the caste system trumps all other prejudices. I was a little girl when I observed Cricket turning Main Street into his own personal fashion runway, and while I was unfamiliar with both the word and the concept "gay," I found him fascinating and fabulous.

My second encounter with a hometown homo was less idyllic. When I was in eighth grade, the powers that be in my junior high school determined that since I was "gifted," I should be placed in a special algebra course (never mind that I wasn't actually gifted *in math*). The algebra teacher was Miss Lois Swafford. She always emphasized the "Miss" by saying, "I am a Miss because I have been missed." Miss Swafford looked like a caricature evangelicals might draw to warn impressionable young women away from the dangers of lesbianism. Or its fashion dangers, anyway. She wore a self-inflicted mannish haircut and men's aviator glasses. Her favorite outfit, based on the frequency with which she wore it, was a powder-blue polyester leisure suit, with an accompanying faux-silk polyester shirt, the collars of which spanned the width of her broad shoulders. The ensemble was accessorized with a Western belt with a saucer-sized buckle and roach-stomping cowboy boots.

I had a high tolerance for Miss Swafford's sartorial eccentricities, as I was developing a few of my own, but for some reason I got along with her as badly as I got along with . . . well, algebra. Maybe her systematizing brain was frustrated by my creative, chaotic one. Or maybe it was gaydar—maybe she knew I saw her queerness just as she could see mine, as maybe like does call out to like. Or in this case, dyke calls out to dyke. In a more open, tolerant atmosphere, this kinship might have turned into a mutually fulfilling mentor-mentee relationship, but in small-town Southeastern Kentucky, it turned into animosity. Recognition was dangerous. And I should add that while I recognized her for what she was, at the age of fourteen, I was nowhere near recognizing myself. In fact, like the protagonist of a certain Dusty Springfield song, I was dating the son of a preacher man. A Southern Baptist preacher man, no less.

I *was* beginning to figure out that I was a writer. But just what kind of writer I might be was still as unformed as my identity. I was resentful of the limitations of the culture around me. I didn't want to live in rural Southeastern Kentucky, where the only radio stations were country or gospel. I wanted to be a sophisticated urbanite living in a cramped, book-filled apartment like the people in Woody Allen movies. It didn't matter that Appalachian language and stories lived inside me because I didn't even consider writing about my home region. Didn't all worthwhile stories take place somewhere else? As a result, my adolescent writing sounds like what an unsophisticated girl thinks of as sophisticated. Imagine a teenaged Kentucky shiksa trying to channel the style of an urbanite New York Jew.

Now admittedly, by this time I had read and loved some Southern writers, Flannery O'Connor and Eudora Welty, especially. But their Deep South of the '50s and '60s was different from my Appalachia of the '80s. It wasn't until I got my hands on a copy of Bobbie Ann Mason's *In Country* that the idea of writing about my own region exploded in my mind. Sam, the protagonist of Mason's novel, is a teenaged girl in a small Kentucky town, trying to figure out her identity and her relationship with her family and her country's history. Many of Sam's experiences were mine as well, and thanks to Mason, I saw that a story didn't have to take place in the big Somewhere Else to be good. I quickly discovered that I could write about Kentuckians way better than I could write about New Yorkers.

It took me longer to figure out the gay thing—a couple more years of high school, then a couple of years of college taking women's studies classes while dating a bong- and beer-besotted boyfriend until my life became gay enough for my art to imitate it. At this point, I'd only read one work of lesbian-themed literature set in the South: Rita Mae Brown's *Rubyfruit Jungle*. And while *RFJ*'s importance as a breakthrough lesbian novel cannot be understated, it barely qualifies as a work of gay regionalism. The narrator Molly Bolt bolts from the South as soon as she is able. And in the parts of the novel that are set in the South, readers don't see much of the gay culture of the region because Molly doesn't really seek out a gay community, and she mostly seduces straight girls.

My first attempt at writing Appalachian lesbian (Appalesbian?) fiction came after I'd spent a summer back home between terms at the University of Tennessee. I spent the entire summer feeling shell-shocked, unable to return from being the independent bohemian I was on campus to being the person I was when I lived at home with my parents. It was standard "you can't go home again" stuff, nothing Thomas Wolfe hadn't said before and better. But some things made my story different. The first was the nature of my family's home—a cabin in a holler off a gravel road, the nearest neighbor a clapboard Pentecostal church. When I sat on the porch swing in the evenings, petting the dopey hound dogs that are de rigueur for Appalachian porches, I would breathe in the clean air and let my eyes follow the feminine curves of the mountains. Breaking the silence were sounds from farther down the holler: singing and shouting from a tent revival and the crowing of one of the roosters that a neighbor raised to fight to the death in the ring. These are the sights and sounds of rural Appalachia to me: the light of natural beauty and tranquility with the shadows of dogmatic religion and violence.

That was also the summer my grandparents' health started to fail. Papaw, who had begun working in the coal mines at the age of twelve, was suffering from a respiratory disease that required the constant use of supplemental oxygen. Nana, a coal miner's daughter and then a coal miner's wife, was losing her mind. Imagined conversations with her long-dead Maw and Paw and brother Harold were becoming realer to her than the words of the living. In her muddled thoughts, she was no longer a mother or grandmother, but a little girl again, living in the coal camp. Somehow mixed in with the emotional climate of that summer was me having figured out I was queer (or "quare," as Appalachians pronounce it). I hadn't told anyone yet, and I knew that while my parents would ultimately be fine with it, my grandparents could never know.

I called the short story that resulted from all this turmoil "Far from the Tree," and it was rejected by twenty-two publications before it finally found a home. Half of the publications rejected it because they didn't like the Appalachian angle, the other half because they didn't like the "gay thing." It was a fitting welcome to the world of writing gay regional fiction.

Since becoming a "grown-up writer," I have written nine novels focusing on lesbian and gay characters, all of them set in Appalachia, most of them in Southeastern Kentucky. In my work, I try to show the gay lives that are not often depicted in contemporary literature, to show that not all small-town Southern gays flee to New York or San Francisco or Chicago. Some of them, like me, flee a relatively short distance, to the nearest decent-sized city in their region—Dorothys who don't go off to the Land of Oz but to, say, Kansas City instead. Others stay in their small towns of origin, some of them closeted, some of them, like the admirable Cricket Needhams and Lois Swaffords, flamboyantly obvious. I want to show the complexities of the lives in these places and also to show, as a sign frequently seen at LGBT pride marches says, "We are everywhere."

That being said, I try to be truthful in how I depict the region in my work. Some Appalachian authors feel that all writing about the region should be positive in order to combat negative stereotypes. Though I'm all for combating stereotypes, I am not just a local colorist. I wouldn't be an honest writer if I depicted gay and lesbian life in Appalachia as being perpetually peaceful and perfect. A straight Appalachian writer friend once asked me why H.F., the sixteen-year-old lesbian protagonist of my novel *Finding H.F.,* spends so much time in the novel longing to escape her small-town surroundings. My answer was that escape is the only means through which a girl of her age and situation can imagine acceptance.

Straight writers who have chosen to stay in Appalachia are not the only ones with questions. Recently, while visiting one of my dearest friends, a gay writer who fled the South to settle in New England, I was kvetching about the South's political leanings (backward and to the right). My friend asked, "Why do you stay?" At the time I answered by babbling some inanities about my partners' and my job security, but I thought about his question a lot afterward.

The real answer to why I live in and write about Appalachia is love. While I don't love the beliefs of some of my fellow Appalachians, especially when it comes to politics and social and environmental issues, I still love the region: its language, its mountains, its stories—both written and oral. I am far from the norm in Appalachia. In my own less fashion-conscious way, I am just as "funny turned" as Cricket Needham. But somehow this queer feeling of simultaneously being an outsider and an insider feeds my creativity. Like a tempestuous long-term love affair, my relationship with the region is complicated; there are periods of bliss as well as periods of turmoil in which I wonder if the two of us might not be good for each other at all. But then I see the mountains burst into fiery fall colors or I taste a particularly good hunk of corn bread or hear someone say something in that mountain twang I remember from my childhood. And I realize that even if I did try to relocate, I could never truly be moved from Appalachia. Contrary to how it feels sometimes, my relationship with the region, both as resident and writer, is a marriage, for better or for worse.

MELISSA RANGE
Outsider Appalachian

MY GRANDFATHER WAS a carpenter and a sometime raging drunk, part real and part cliché. Driving the Hillbilly Highway to Cincinnati on union jobs in the 1950s (at least during times that he was not on a tear), it's a wonder he ever came back, but he did. He did not move my grandmother and their four kids to Ohio, even though there was an enclave of Appalachian ex-pats there. He would not leave the place he'd lived all his life, would not risk becoming an outsider to his people, to the mountains. He kept coming back to Upper East Tennessee, the tip of the state, closer to Virginia and North Carolina than to most other parts of Tennessee. It's a wonder he didn't die drunk on the highway, but he didn't, although sometimes, as Aunt Phyllis told me once, he'd get back, throw the car into park, open the car door, and fall right out into the front yard. But it was a by God Upper East Tennessee front yard, even if it was always the front yard of one rental place after another—the carpenter being unable to hang onto the money in his paychecks, to put some by for some land and the boards to nail together a house for his own family.

There is no homeplace I return to on this side of the family—the nervous, angry side—no ancestral mountainside home ringed by scrappy tobacco patches, though that's an image carved into my brain by one Appalachian writer after another, in many books that have formed me and that I love. My high-strung grandfather couldn't hold on to land or to money, though when he was sober, it's told, he was brilliant, generous, handy, compassionate. When he wasn't drinking, he built sound houses for other people, substitute-taught geometry and physics on just his high school education, coached winning baseball teams, and gave away perhaps more of the family's food and clothes than he should have to those who had less than they did. When Grandaddy was on a tear, he'd stay gone for weeks—to hear tell, he spent these drunken days wrecking cars, getting into fights, and writing one bad check after another—sometimes not coming back until someone bailed him out of jail and physically carried him home. It's a wonder he came back at all, a wonder my grandmother kept taking him back, a wonder that they kept managing to have a house for him to come back to. By the time I was born, in the early 1970s, Grandaddy had cleaned up. He drank endless cups of black coffee from his Elizabethton High School Fighting Cyclones mug and chomped celery all day long, I assume to calm his nerves. It's a wonder he made it until the mid-1980s, when he fell over dead from a heart attack on the Astroturf-carpeted front porch of another one of my grandparents' rental houses.

Like my grandfather, I left home, but unlike him, I stayed gone. I left home at eighteen to go to Old Rocky Top, the University of Tennessee in Knoxville, and left East Tennessee altogether after college, at age twenty-two, eighteen years ago. It's a wonder I've never come back to those hills to stay. The mountains that ring my valley town do exert, powerful strong, that famous pull Appalachian novelists and poets are always writing about. Or maybe it's not a wonder at all, for although part of me will always be driving toward that place and its smudged hills with untraceable, presumably Cherokee, names—Unaka, Watauga, Unicoi—I think another part of me will always be driving away. Although I yearn for the mythical Appalachian homeplace I've read about in books, I have had to resign myself to the fact that I have become the outsider who is vilified in both Appalachian art and Appalachian life—and that I became an outsider not only from my own desire and my own doing but because, perhaps, I was an outsider before I even left home.

GROWING UP in Upper East Tennessee, just outside the city limits of the former rayon boomtown of Elizabethton, roaming the woods behind my father's house (the side of the family that hung onto land so stubbornly that siblings fought over it for decades) and getting tangled in blackberry briars, the hills making a ring around every step I took for eighteen years, I felt deeply connected to the land. And I still do: when I get back into those hills after a year or more away, something in my chest opens up, and something in my nerves settles down. But I felt at odds with its people even as a child, and at times, they also felt at odds with me. My mother tells the story of how my kindergarten teacher asked her, after the first week of school, "Where's *she* from?" "She," meaning me. My mother, confused, responded that, since she herself had lived her whole life in Elizabethton, and I was her child, then, of course, I was from *here*. The teacher said, "Well, she doesn't talk like us." Meaning, I think, that I talked rapidly (and still do) and that my accent, though strong enough to be remarked upon by everyone I have met since I left East Tennessee, was not as strong as hers or as the other students' accents. Meaning, I think, that I was using words I had picked up from my reading (I had learned to read before I started school) that were too "big" or highfalutin for me to know, not just as a child but as an *Appalachian* child. The older I grew, the differenter I felt, and much of this feeling came from my reading. The more I read, the more my mind broadened, the more my vocabulary became an oddity, and the more I wanted to see the places I'd read about, meet people who were different from me. Coupled with this desire to "go off" and see more of the world I'd read about were vague stirrings about words: I had written stories and poems nearly as long as I'd been reading, and I began to admit, only to myself at first, that I wanted to create books, since books had been so important to me. As I began to voice these desires as a teenager, the response I got from many of my friends, most of my family, and even some of my teachers, was, "Aw, you won't go off and do anything like that," or "That's a lot of big talkin'," or "You think you're too good for us, Miss Priss?"

IN MANY of the Appalachian novels and poems I have read—and I certainly don't pretend to have read even a fraction of them—there's a certain attitude toward those who "go off" from home and either don't come back or come back too changed. Those of us who leave for any other reason than to find work (in other words, those of us who leave because we want to, rather than because we have to) are often portrayed as uppity and no-count, traitors to the land and to family. In many of these books, those hillbillies who leave home to get an education end up devaluing the old ways, which are typically portrayed as rural ways (no matter that there are cities in Appalachia) and as better ways, more authentic than city ways. Those of us who leave place more value on our book learnin', which is typically regarded with skepticism and amusement, at best, or with derision and hostility, at worst.

For example, in Lee Smith's *Oral History*, a book I love that I first studied when I was an undergraduate at the University of Tennessee with the late fiction writer Wilma Dykeman, the old-time tales of family history are framed by the narrative of Jennifer, the college girl from Abingdon (which is an Appalachian town, and not even a big one), who is portrayed as foolish and disconnected from the old ways, letting her book learning interfere with her good sense. In Denise Giardina's *Storming Heaven*, a book that's so important to me that I teach it, Miles Bishop, who leaves his family in Grapevine, Kentucky, to go to college up at Berea, becomes a coal-company man and something of a traitor, or at least a patsy of absentee coal-company owners. Miles's education causes him to be snooty and disconnected from his people, the land, and the old ways. The character of Rondal Lloyd in the same novel rejects his dream of medical school to go down in the mines because he will cease to be "one of them"—that is, one of the people—if he goes off and goes to school and tries to come back. He'll be an outsider because of his education. And of course Thomas Wolfe said it first: you can't go home again. Once you leave, in this figuration, you're an outsider forever.

Depictions like this suggest that book learnin' corrupts and that going away from home ruins you. I am corrupted and ruint, then, and by my own doing, because I felt the freedom to be myself only when, as a child, I had my nose in a book, and later, when I was older, when I left home. No amount of hillbilly nostalgia (which, like many Appalachians, I have in spades) for some mythic and inaccessible version of the uncorrupted land and its good-hearted people can make me feel that I should have stayed. Raised in a town that was mostly white, straight, evangelically Christian, and politically conservative, I wanted to meet people who didn't fit those descriptions. Raised in a town that expected a few basic and particular things from women— get married, have children, hold the family together at whatever the cost to you—I wanted to find a place where I had different options. Raised in a place that was often suspicious of intellectuals and non-conformists, I wanted more space to test out being both of those things. Raised in a town where no one I knew thought being a writer was a real thing anybody did or ever could do, I wanted to find some-place where what I wanted most didn't seem so impossible.

So I went out, and I've stayed out. And while a fundamental part of me yearns for the mountains, for the twang, for that familiar hard set of the mouth and no-nonsense look in the eyes I associate with people who are from where I'm from, another fundamental part of me loves the bustle of cities, the interesting diversity of people to meet in them, the exciting variety of things to do and options to explore. I've stayed out, on purpose, and that's what makes me an outsider. I didn't do it to find work, like my grandaddy did. I did it because I was born restless, because I had a wandering itch to scratch. Most of all, I did it to find out who I was. And that, I've found, judg-ing not only from my family and hometown friends, but also from many Appalachian writers I have read, makes it less acceptable.

As Denise Giardina's character Carrie Bishop in *Storming Heaven* says: "I have traveled outside the mountains, but never lived apart from them. I always feared mountains could be as jealous, as un-forgiving, as any spurned lover. Leave them and they may never take you back. Besides, I never felt a need to go. There is enough to study in these hills to last a lifetime." Here is one among many literary depictions of the Noble Appalachian, who would expire if too far beyond reach of the mountains, and who wouldn't leave the land unless cheated out of it, which, of course, happened over and over again, and is still happening. But sometimes I wonder if this depiction is entirely true, or if it's at least partly a creation of lit-erature. My family—mom, dad, aunts, uncles, sister, cousins—and many of my childhood friends might insist on the truth of Car-rie Bishop's experience. Yet the most Appalachian woman I have known, my grandmother Ena, who lived in Upper East Tennessee her whole life, once told me, toward the end of her eighty-six years, and in a confidence I am breaking now, "Melissa, I love my children more than anything, and I'm glad I had them, and I wouldn't take anything for them. But if I had my life to do over again, I wouldn't have children at all. I'd travel. I'd get out and go somewhere and see the world some." I wonder how many other insider Appalachians have a little bit of outsider Appalachian in their hearts. Even Car-rie Bishop dreams of the outsider who will come into her close-knit community and astonish her, even as she fears becoming that outsider herself. I didn't fear becoming an outsider because I already was one, even as I was an insider, too.

WHEN I told my high school guidance counselor I wanted to go away to college, she responded, "Why?" I exclaimed, in all of my sixteen-year-old exuberance, "To see the world!" I had no idea how to apply to college and was hoping for scholarship advice, but her response was skepticism and a question about why I didn't just stay at home and go to the commuter college in the bigger town ten minutes away. Yet I didn't feel any conflict between being who I was—a lower-class white kid from East Tennessee who would be the first person in her family to graduate from college—and wanting what I wanted: to go adventuring, to see what I could see out in the big world I'd read about and never seen, only imagined. And now, as a grown woman, I don't feel any awkwardness in moving from discussing ramp festivals and Carter Family songs to discussing something else I find compelling, whether that's interpretations of *Beowulf* or same-sex marriage or prison justice or some new theory about Emily Dickinson's construction of her fascicles. In my work, whether I'm teaching a class full of undergraduates, giving a poetry reading, or presenting a talk, I don't see any reason why I can't braid together both ways I naturally talk, which might, on any given day, include some combination of "might could have," "cultural moment," "fixin' to," "spondee," "genre theory," "y'all," and, copiously, "ain't." I think East Tennessee is beautiful, but I love New York, love Boston, love Atlanta, love Paris, love San Francisco, and I'm glad I've found a way to get to see these places.

I've carried my hillbilly ways with me to the outside, on my back, like I'm some weird variety of mountain turtle. Wherever I roam, I evangelize about the Appalachian trinity of soup beans, corn bread, and chow-chow; I stump against mountaintop removal coal mining; and I stand up and question both the mockery and the aestheticizing of "white trash" and "rednecks" and "hillbillies" in pop culture, in small talk, in the academy. No one who knows me here on the outside would ever be hard-pressed to remember where I'm from and how it makes me who I am. Yet when I go home once a year to visit family and old friends, I am again reminded that I'm an outsider because of my education, my experiences, and my interests. I'm an outsider even though I often pronounce once "oncet," often say "warsh" for "wash." I'm still an ill fit for that place, and it's true that I don't really want to fit in any better than I do.

But the camp of Appalachian insiders—those who never want you to leave, or change, or get above your raisin'—may naysay me here, and tell me that I'm too big for my britches.

SINCE FOR so many writers and readers, poetry is rooted in personal experience, it's likely a wonder to folks that my writing hasn't much come back, either, though it does sometimes. Although I do occasionally write about Upper East Tennessee, and though I also do use our particular flavor of Appalachian dialect in some of my poems, I'm more often to be found researching some interesting historical topic, like illuminated manuscripts or archaic weapons or the abolitionist movement, and writing poems about that. A question I get sometimes at poetry readings is, "Why don't you write about where you're from?" I think this honest question arises from the classification of Appalachian writing as writing that is defined by its subjects. Appalachian writing is, at least popularly, about place. It's about land, and home, and while it may be about a hundred other things, too—environment, gender, race, class, sexuality, family—it is grounded in the land that gives it its name.

Although I claim the moniker "Appalachian writer" for myself, I also realize that I don't quite fit the bill, at least as the bill is typically writ. Am I an Appalachian writer if most of my poetry is born from my book learnin', instead of from my honest by God experiences and memories in Upper East Tennessee? Am I an Appalachian writer if I question the stereotypes and nostalgia I see in the books I've loved, and try to do something other than perpetuate them? What makes my writing Appalachian, to me, is its musical language, its underdog eye, its anger at injustice, its violence, its investment in the natural world, its terrifying God. But I don't know if that's enough for the insiders to claim me as one of their own, or if they should.

WHEN I first catch sight of the mountains on that stretch of I-81 as I drive back home, I feel a lightness and a rightness and a joy that's nearly matched by the oppression and anxiety I feel when I'm back in my hometown for more than a day or two. And when I set back out again, nothing feels near as good as leaving, though nothing feels as painful. When I write, nothing feels as natural as writing in the language of those hills, yet nothing feels as impossible as assenting unreservedly to that culture—to my people, who told me, time and again, that I could not be myself if I wanted to be one of them. I can't pretend that I fit in back home, but I also can't pretend I feel quite at home anywhere else I go, either. Writing from such a rootless place feels very *un*-Appalachian, at least in comparison to the groundedness in place and custom and family that's at the heart of many of the Appalachian books I've read. But I *am* Appalachian, and that is my experience. I wonder if there is a place for my particular brand of insider-turned-outsider in the famously insular ethos of these hills that formed me, choked me, freed me, hound me, and continually pull on me. Or if I am instead what I suspect: an exile at home and away, in the mountains and outside of them, on the page and off, one more wayfaring stranger, like the old-timers love to sing about.

WAYFARING STRANGER

TENNESSEE JONES

Getting Out: The Grief of Transformation

> I'm going to come back to West Virginia when this is over.
> There's something ancient and deeply-rooted in my soul.
> I like to think that I have left my ghost up one of those
> hollows, and I'll never really be able to leave for good until
> I find it. And I don't want to look for it, because I might
> find it and have to leave.
>
> —*Breece D'J Pancake, from a letter to his mother*

WHEN I LEFT the hollers of East Tennessee to move into a disintegrating Victorian abused by a decade's worth of basement punk shows in Richmond, Virginia, I was a morbidly shy eighteen-year-old girl, so terrified of people I could barely order food in a restaurant. I had very little money, no skills, and no financial support system to fall back on. I had a mountain accent so thick it made Richmonders nervous, and though I had no language for it then, a deeply uneasy relationship to my own body, which had never quite curved into the shape of a woman. I had no idea, really, what the fuck was going on. I just had the sense that there was something deeply wrong—whether it was with me or with the rest of the world, I wasn't quite sure.

Though this story begins with getting out—I have lived the life of a writer in New York for the last twelve years—this is not a story of great escape. Rather, it is a story that troubles the getting out myth, a myth that is inextricably tied to the American Dream, an ideal predicated on the assumption that circumstances are equal for all of us, and that success is most accurately and meaningfully measured in economic striving. My story is one that questions the ideal of "strength," and the frameworks on which this myth rests. As such, it is a narrative about power, that essential ghost that haunts all of us, regardless of our upbringing or experience.

I was an intellectually and spiritually curious child, and that curiosity, when it threatened long-held beliefs, was forbidden. Though my mother was proud when my report card showed a straight line of As, my books—gotten at first from the library and later stolen from a chain bookstore—attracted derision, contempt, and outright hatred and fear from my parents. My household was one in which the only book was the Bible, a volume that my mother clung to and my father alternately praised and damned. My father, a sheet metal mechanic and tobacco farmer with the self-loathing and self-inflated importance of a drunk, sometimes threw my books against the wall with the curse that I was never going to amount to shit. My mother, going one better than my father's occasional threats to burn the mess of Devil's work that was ruining his child, actually did burn my writing in the backyard when I was thirteen.

I was raised to embrace the expectation of tragedy, and to take the measure of what I could endure of it as the measure of myself. This is, of course, not the experience of every Appalachian: not everyone in Appalachia lives in the holler, not everyone is poor, not every family grows tobacco or lives within sight distance on the same land for four generations. Not everyone is an addict, not everyone raises his or her children to believe their position in life is unchangeable, and to believe, even more deeply, that this unchangeability is their own fault. However, this core of fatalism is a spiritual hollow in which all of my Appalachian friends have dwelt, and still struggle, in varying degrees, to escape.

My parents were miserable people, and this misery was manifest in the set of their faces, their physical ailments, their long silences and frequent cussing matches. My father's drunkenness and emotional abuse was perhaps the original central aspect of my life, and my mother, who never touched a bottle, was so cowed by our circumstances that she would not accept a promotion at her sewing factory job, though we desperately needed the money, because she was afraid of the responsibility. She sat in the evenings—if he wasn't chewing her out over some little thing—staring blankly into space, sometimes so far gone that one had to say her name over and over again for her to respond. And, yet, my parents took pride in this misery and hardship. They insisted life wasn't that bad even as they insisted it was terrible, and more still, they insisted that there was no choice. Life was hard because it was supposed to be, and the measure of a person's strength was how much was left after the rigors of living had worn them away. My parents abused and punished me for believing I could be anything different from what they had been, for my unwillingness or inability to believe that the fates of human beings are fixed.

It was always my parents' misery—which was my own misery—that was at the core of my need to write. Writing is a pursuit I don't think I would have taken up had I not been so desperate, had it not been so integral to my survival. I wrote down the contents of each day, the bits of story my parents told me, the rotten core of the hateful things they said to each other and to me. In them, I had role models made of the negative space: I did not know what I would do with my life, but what I would not do. I saw in my mother's blank stare that she had no dreams, and perhaps did not remember a time when she did.

As I grew older, I detached more and more from the "real" world, and I embraced the notion, iterated to me by the people I loved, that I was crazy. Indeed, the spiritual, social, and political paradigms presented to me as common sense—the kind of life I was supposed to expect for myself—seemed utterly insane. In retrospect, my path away seems both highly deliberate and full of serendipities I might have very easily missed. My freshman year of high school, I became best friends with a skinny kid named Mike, whose older brother was a skater and a punk. This was in the early nineties, in a town of five thousand, and this friendship eventually connected me to a larger punk underground. When I was fifteen I started compiling my writing into zines and sent these out for review, and made more friends all over the country. It was this zine that eventually led me to that fucked-up house in Richmond. It was in that house, in a very real way, that my life began.

Once I was out, once I was away from the holler, I went through an intense process of forgetting, of distancing. I cut myself off from my family, from the region, as if it were a rotten limb. I hated my parents for the way they had chosen to live their lives, and for what they had done to me, a hatred that was aggravated by my love for them.

The people I loved and who loved me had stabbed me in the heart for as long as I could remember to try to prepare me for the hardness of the world. From this I learned to stab myself, again and again, just to see if I could stand it. I relied for many years on the myth of my own strength. I believed there was something special about me that separated me from those I'd grown up with who didn't leave, or never had the wherewithal to entertain the possibility. I was hard on other people, and even harder on myself. I did not realize, then, that self-hate is perhaps the highest form of selfishness we can re-create. It is the oil that allows the wheels of the big evils to turn.

My writing was forbidden in my household, but it is intellectual curiosity that has made me as much an outcast in the world at large as being a girl who looked and acted like a boy made me an outcast in Appalachia. This is the essential paradox, this is the necessity of delving into what is forbidden, of saying what is unsayable: what made me less than human, when I examined the content of it, allowed me to see the possibility of a different world. I am thankful for the scars I bear from living at the intersections of crossroads of power—in the examination of these wounds I have found the necessity of radical love both for people I've known and will never know who bear wounds of a different shape or color, scored into them by the particular lines of power that have shaped their lives.

There is a vast difference between people who expect life to be incredibly difficult and full of tragedy, and those who do not expect tragedy as a way of life. It is, in part, the expectation of hardship—this deeply ingrained fatalism—that I have spent my entire life trying to understand and recover from. It has made me, as an individual, very slow to change, as Appalachia itself is slow to change. This fatalism—the deep-seated tautology that things are the way they are because that is the way things are—shapes the content of our hope, our horizons of possibility, our ability to act and love. This affects how we treat our children. It affects, ultimately, the shape and content of our souls.

I've always believed another world is possible, because it simply has to be.

FAST FORWARD now, to three years after that initial dingy house in Virginia, to Brooklyn, to another falling-apart Victorian populated by punks and activists when I moved there in 2001, six months before 9/11. These were people I had met during a two-week jail stint following an arrest at the 2000 Republican National Convention in Philadelphia. I had put my body on the line at the time because at the age of twenty I couldn't think of anything else to do; I was absolutely burning up with the knowledge that there are people all over the world treated as less than human, and unwilling to be complicit with that evil for a moment longer.

I had no money in New York, had no idea how I would survive, much less succeed, only that I knew I had to—and that part of this success entailed eventually making money. The mountains were still thick on me, and I had no idea how to enact my own value and usefulness. I wrote, in the midst of panic attacks and sleepless nights over money, I watched my couple hundred of dollars disappear, I took a couple of shitty jobs, I eventually got lucky and talked my way into a job with a small press run out of a studio apartment on Suffolk Street. I was making eight bucks an hour, but I was doing something I believed in—and that was all I really cared about. My attempts to work regular wage jobs had always ended badly—I couldn't get that feeling of dread out of me when I woke up in the morning to punch a clock, couldn't get the stench of my parents' misery out of my nose. I'd always been fired or quit or walked off jobs when working made me feeling like I was drowning.

In New York, I wanted to fit in, even though I was resistant to the idea I would ever have a home. And I was willing to do whatever erasure of culture necessary to remove roadblocks to economic success, and I talked shit about the place I'd come from, when I talked about it at all. I knew they were a joke, my people, and I laughed at them to separate myself from them. My background was too horrible and grotesque, too stereotypical, to be real. I thought the jokes I told at parties were dealing with my past, owning it even as I held it at arm's length, insisting that though I came from Appalachia, I was better than it because I'd had the sense to leave. I thought the acerbic jokes made me whiter—and by that I mean more middle-class—than I was. My hatred of the place covered my shame, and the pain of separation was one that I did not want to touch. My parents did not understand what I was doing and begged me to come back home, despite the countless times they'd told me I made them sick to their stomachs for my queerness, my insanity, my stupidity, my sickness. For years, I rarely returned their calls.

The more time I spent in New York, the angrier I got. I was surrounded by people who in their youth were dedicated to class suicide and voluntary poverty, but I also knew that, for the most part, these were people who did not have the experience of poverty without choice. I understand and agreed with the political thought behind the rejection of economic comfort, but was resentful of the privilege this choice entailed. For me poverty was not a choice. It seemed like both a life and a death sentence. I had never encountered such levels of privilege, such great existential economic ease among people before. I'm talking about my friends, most of them radicals who believed in impossible things, who were eaten up by the same fire of believing the world must change, who had been ostracized in some way from their respective growing-up situations because of this belief. One of my primary political focuses became race, and I slowly began to realize I was not the same color white as my middle-class friends. They had bank accounts, had gone to good colleges, they thought that more for them was possible. They thought I had had the same experience. I realized that being white, along with the cultural capital I'd acquired, rendered my class reality invisible.

This visceral anger helped me understand how my upbringing had affected not just my mind or financial situation or material comfort, but what I'd been able to imagine was possible for me. This led me to begin to remember, to write about my family and Appalachia. As I wrote against my own erasure, I recognized that the whitewashing of white ethnicity is also a part of white supremacy, that the imagined homogeneity of white experience is a necessary component of the construction of whiteness and its continuing dominance, I began to place Appalachia and the people I'd dearly loved and had to leave within the larger framework of capital and power that I was uncovering through living my life. I started trying to talk to those ghosts, and they started talking to me; they helped me remember what I'd tried to forget.

As I began to take ownership of my heritage, to reclaim and remember it, the deep anger I felt was, at times, unbearably heavy. I sought out other working-class people because I felt driven near mad by the unconscious ignorance of privilege enacted by middle- and upper-middle-class people. I thought of myself and my people as not quite white, but gray ghosts, and through the articulation of our experience, hoped to bring color, fullness, to our existence. At the same time, I could not quite accept the truth of my own story or experience, because whiteness gave me a kind of power that would not wash off. The self-flagellating nature of this youth activist culture was remarkably similar in its way to the self-hating ways of where I'd come from.

I eventually left political circles to focus on writing. My social maladjustment and dogged feelings of inefficacy—I had not yet learned the word "trauma"—caused so much anxiety that I decided to focus on the work I'd always been called to do, and that I felt I was actually good at. I remembered working in the tobacco fields with the sun growing long toward dusk, being so tired in my muscles that it made me sick and angry, and also looking at that brown dirt, and knowing, still more, *feeling,* that it was a part of me, and I of it. I couldn't reconcile my fear and hate, my deep tiredness, with that love. I began work on a novel about the region, born out of this anger and the thwarted and stubborn love I felt for my family, and out of my own grief and anger and restlessness. There was, at the center of me, always some restless haunting, some hole. I could not recognize it, then, as a missing part of my soul.

I went to school, grudgingly, to get a BA. I was resistant to entering an institution that would colonize my thoughts more than they had already been colonized, but I felt, by that time in my midtwenties, that I had to go to school if I was ever going to get out of the poverty trap. I designed my own program, an amalgamation of religion, politics, and creative writing that sought to answer the question, *What happened to my people, and why?* Part of my course work was continued work on the novel I'd started, but I knew I wasn't only asking the question of who gets to be human and who does not about myself or Appalachians. I was asking it about all of us.

While in school, I published my first book, a collection of short stories, and went on a cross-country tour, explicitly out as a transsexual— I'd transitioned three years before—and talked about the reality of this experience and the construction of gender. This was uncomfortable and it was inspiring. People's ignorance and disgust deadened me; the people who needed to see me talk gave me the courage to go on. I came home from this book tour burnt, and sick of my own goddamn identity. After I finished my BA, I entered into a competitive and respected MFA program, with a fair amount of skepticism that anyone could learn writing in a classroom. There, I stopped, for the first time, writing about queer people, in part because the messages I received from my professors, editors, and agents, and many of my colleagues, was that there is no market, no interest, in these stories. I thought I was making a wise career decision by going into the closet as a trans person. It would take many years, a nervous breakdown, and a very dark stint with addiction to come out the other side of this and realize I was once again falling on my own sword.

I applied for writing fellowships and made a choice to employ the myth of my own exceptionalism, my "getting out" story, as the centerpiece of the applications. I omitted my queerness. I received a large fellowship that allowed me to live at a middle-class level for the first time in my life. Having money for the first time had a strange side effect for me: my capacity for empathy for the ones around me decreased. Where I had once felt kinship with people who were poor, I began to feel separation, contempt. Though I've been vehemently anticapitalist from the time I was fifteen or so, I could not let go of the idea that one must attain a certain level of economic stability in order to consider one's life a success. This was part of what it meant, for me, to "get out." I strove to understand and dismantle systems of power within my head and heart, and later, in my soul, while unknowingly re-creating different versions of these systems within myself. It was the abject fear of poverty—and the failure I felt poverty naturally entailed—that kept me in thrall to the myth of strength and exceptionalism. This is the deepest possible abdication of responsibility, to oneself and to others, a fatalism and selfishness that is referred to as "personal responsibility" within the ideological framework of dominator culture.

For all of my success and comfort—at the time I was living with a woman I loved very much, we had a middle-class income, and were looking to buy a brownstone in Brooklyn—I sensed there was something deeply wrong, just cosmically off, about the novel I was working on. Set in Appalachia and about my family, it was flat in a way that other stories I'd written were not. I couldn't trace the source of this flatness, couldn't put my fingers around the edges of it in order to unearth it. It kept me up at night. I knew there was something there, but I couldn't see it, touch it. In this way, I felt profoundly haunted, profoundly ill at ease. I wrote. It was all I did: tens of thousands of words, hundreds of pages that I would later write over or discard because the wound they tried to examine was a bloodless one. The people on the page were cardboard cutouts, and I could not figure out why.

REVELATION OFTEN comes to us when we least expect it. By this point in my life, my late twenties, I'd started going back to the mountains often, about twice a year. My father was dead, and my mother had remarried, and had for the first time in her life any kind of semblance of safety and happiness. She had accepted me as a man, in part because my presentation of masculinity is very traditional, and in part because of the transformative power of unconditional love. My presence as a man, I think, also put the trajectory of my childhood into a new perspective for her, and many of the ways in which I'd seemed nonsensical at the time made perfect sense after I transitioned.

The primary reason I began going home was to do research on the novel. It had, by this time, moved from being primarily about class and Appalachian experience to the exploration of how racism had affected the white people living in the small mountain town in which the story takes place. This was based on my own experience. I grew up in the sundown town of Erwin, Tennessee—a town in which all the people of color had been forcefully expelled, and then kept out through formal and informal enforcement—an experience which has led me to have a near-pathological obsession with white/black race dynamics. I knew, growing up, that something terrible had happened in my town—everyone knew this—and the fact of the place being all-white was something talked about, denied, and revered. It was a source of strange, complicated, and circumspect pride. To be adamantly racist was the cultural norm, in my family and school, and the expression of this was hateful, it was violent, it was fucking evil. It was a mercurial poison that seeped into the air and water, no matter what one's natural resistance to it might have been.

When I decided to focus on the historical violence of the town, and how this affected the white generations that came after, I visited the Appalachian archive at the university the next town over from where I grew up to dig up what I'd known my entire life but didn't actually *know*. On these trips, searching for historical documents that for the most part didn't exist, I could not escape the feeling the lynching and expulsion that had occurred in 1916 had been partially excised from the historical record (there was far more on record about the elephant that had been hanged in the town the same year). I spent more and more time with my family, still feeling the gnawing certainty the characters I was writing were not breathing real breath.

I was sitting in my grandmother's living room, talking to her, listening to her tell stories from decades before, when I noticed the almost grotesquely long and thick thumbnail that had grown that way after she'd smashed it into a car door. I remembered watching her dig out the pits of cherries she picked by the gallon on some hillside, the way that thumbnail had torn into the deep red flesh to separate seed from fruit, the lines of cherry juice running down the side of a five-gallon bucket, dark as blood.

It hit me like a bolt out of the blue, looking at my maw, far past eighty years old, that I'd ceased to see my actual family as full human beings. My own getting-out story had superseded the experiences of those who had loved and reared me. I was writing about them from the perspective of a "winner," of what I perceived to be the "right" side of power, and this power had blinded me to the fact of their unimpeachable existence as human beings. It was this that had kept me up at night: I did not believe in the central humanness of my own characters because I did not believe in the *humanness* of my people. I was better than them. I was special. I had gotten "out."

So what to do with this simple, horrible truth? I had swallowed the dominant culture's narrative about Appalachian people so thoroughly that this hatred and dehumanization had become entirely transparent to me. This is the greatest disappearing trick of power— that we begin to believe perpetrator ideology so completely and thoroughly that the damage and hating we begin to do is to the ones we love and to ourselves. I realized the depths of my own hubris and self-hatred—that I could reiterate the dominant culture's narrative about Appalachians even as I consciously worked toward resisting and undermining this narrative in my life and in my work—and it was terrifying. The implications of this reached across the breadth and scope of my entire life.

JAMES BALDWIN writes that what one does not remember is the serpent in the garden of one's dreams. The temptation to forget is a great one. The temptation of our own survival at the cost of the livelihood and subjugation of others is a great one. The myth of strength and exceptionalism—the American Dream—makes this commonplace. I wrote myself out of Appalachia, my particular nexus of what had to be escaped and denied in order to survive, and I wrote myself back there again. By learning how to love my family—these people who had damaged and raised and loved me—I was able to enter more deeply into the examination of the modes of power I was writing about. This love allowed me to see where the intersections of power had left their scar tissue on me, had left great and previously unknowable holes. I was able to see there is no separation between success and failure, that the distinction between the two is a false one. I admitted to myself the depths of my own racism, and it was through this admission that the novel began to take on yet another complexity: I began to write the history of the lynching in my town as if it had not been a foregone conclusion, if they had not believed their own survival had to come at the cost of the subjugation of others. I looked at my neighbors on the street in Bushwick, Brooklyn, and I realized the source of my obsession with race was not the fact that my skin is white and theirs is brown, but that I had believed whiteness actually exists.

Part of this journey was confronting everything I'd ever been scared of, and in so doing, confronting what I had not yet known I feared. I remembered more of what I'd forgotten: the texture of that place, the million shades of green, so many that it would take a lifetime, perhaps generations of lifetimes, to see them all. I remembered my family, at the end of a day of hard labor, looking at those hills, the willows and pines and poplars, and breathing deep. I allowed my body to feel its natural pull toward that place, and I began going home more and more often, spending time with my family when I could. The writing began to take on these shades of green, this texture, and the characters began to blush with blood and to move around with agency in the light of this love, this fullness. The people in my book began to act in ways that I did not expect and had previously been unable to imagine. They said things that surprised and delighted and were full of insight that I often did not understand as I wrote their dialogue. And through this work, I began to understand more of the shape, the magnitude, of the parts of my soul that were hung up in the trees, still, the parts that were straight-up missing from my life.

I remembered also that it had not been my mother who had burned my writing in the backyard, as I'd written in my college and fellowship applications. It had been me, a thirteen-year-old girl, who had taken her journals and stories and set fire to them as if they were a pile of brush. It was too personal, too unsayable, to admit this when I was younger. To make my mother responsible for fear and intolerance was one thing; to admit my own self-hatred, my own willingness to destroy part of myself because to do so would have perhaps made my life superficially easier—because I wanted to forget—was quite another.

At the same time these breakthroughs in my creative work and spiritual life began to happen in my early thirties, my sanity began to fall apart. I fell off the tightrope and into the abyss that I'd always feared was waiting for me. I became an addict like my father, and the density of self-hatred—for I had always been smarter than this, hadn't I?—had the gravitational force of a black hole. It crushed the dreams right out of me. For three years, I tried to drink myself to death as I worked on my novel. I remembered what I had for my entire life tried not to remember even as I thought I was remembering it, and the traumas of the converging lines of power, both systemic and highly personal, severed me from the "real" world in a way over which I had no control. I was driven crazy by so many things—the attempt to actually *feel* what life had been like for my parents, the desire to see the true implications of the racial legacy of my hometown, the content of my hatred of self because I am trans—and it was simply too much. I sat with the horror of how power has been enacted across history, and I totally fucking lost it.

There is always great grief in transformation. There is no foregone conclusion that we might survive it. What is forbidden, what is unsayable, these things are forbidden, too, as a measure of safety. To truly drop into them, to go to the other side of the looking glass, requires that one lose what is referred to as "sanity." We are, I think, meant to make this journey, and it is our evolution, our continuing existence, that depends upon this. We do not face what is unsayable to save the world. We do it to save ourselves. What I had to give up in order to understand this was the myth of my own strength. I had to understand that my worth as a human being would still be intact, that it was unimpeachable, even if I failed.

So this is not a story of great escape, of getting out. I didn't leave because there's a damn thing special about me that's not special about every human being on the planet. Great escape always implies that the process ends. That there is a getting-out, and then the struggle is over. Struggle is never over, transformation never over. The escape is not of one place, one abuse, or one time. It is not one region, one family, one way of thinking, one particular trauma. I know that my mother and father did not mean to impress the dents in their shoulders onto my own. I know they did not want to hurt me, or stunt my life. I know they did nothing more than impress me with what they considered common sense. Had I been a different kind of person, with a different vocation, I might never have known parts of my soul were missing, might not have found the path through the green hills and blue smoke, to find them, let them be, and grow them back.

Two old friends, one of them from the region, have been maintaining a land project for over a decade in the mountains, one mile from the county line, as the crow flies, from where I grew up. In 2012 I spent two summer months there, writing and doing work on the land. For the first time in my life, I felt full integration, being in those mountains, unafraid of who and what I am. I felt a need, almost a moral decree, after being on that land, to talk to my mother about the effect my childhood has had on my adult life. To talk to her about the effect her childhood had had on her life, about generational trauma, about the vision of a new world. We sat on the porch looking out over her husband's land in the August sun. I was at the time newly emerging from a nervous breakdown, and about six months sober. She asked me, flat-out, "Tennessee, what's wrong with you?"

And what is wrong with me indeed? And so I told her. I told her the content of my life's work. I told her everything I had been unwilling to tell her before. My mother cried, we both cried, we talked about her own childhood with an abusive, alcoholic father and a mother so cowed she would not even work. She told me she had watched her father pick up her mother, a tiny woman, by the throat and hold her up against the wall. "I still didn't know any better, when you were growing up," she said. "Didn't know things could be different." She told me she was sorry. She told me she'd never had a chance, which was one of the things my father had said to me when I was still a teenager, about his choice—but he framed it as though there never really had been a choice—to drink. "I could've been something different, 'cept nobody did anything different," he said, this man who was so taciturn he rarely spoke, and when he did, his speech was so thick with accent and missing teeth it was barely intelligible.

My mother told me she was sorry for what she had tried to do to me—break my spirit—to protect me from the world. We cried together over the things that had been handed down to us. She told me she was proud of me for getting out. Before that moment, how could my mother have known? And how could I have known when I was younger what had happened to her? How could I have known my hatred and contempt, my bitter jokes and the grotesque, tragic stories I made funny at parties after I moved to New York, were hatred for myself, my own inability to dream, my failure to imagine?

It is the faith in a changeable world that gave me back my mother. And for what we had no way of knowing, we must forgive others. This begins by forgiving ourselves. And forgiveness requires giving up what one believes one can't live without. And this is in part why things that are unsayable are unsayable. To say them requires us to look at the world as it is. And if we see the world as it is, the hatred and atrocity that is transparent and forgotten becomes visible, and we are moved to change it. This is a huge responsibility. It is the ultimate responsibility. I am not talking about the urge to change the world; I am talking about the work required to change the self. Perhaps at the end of the day *this* is the knowledge that is forbidden, because the responsibility for enacting it is too great: that we are all equally and inexorably human.

CRYSTAL WILKINSON
Strange Fruit Your Imagination Bears

IF YOU SAID you remembered her packed suitcase or her salty kiss on your forehead before she left you, you'd be lying. If you said you remembered her whispers or the muffled cries, if you said you heard the dog's bark followed by the engine of your grandfather's car, then the crunch of the gravel as they headed out of the holler carrying her away from you, you'd be lying. But somehow all of this is true. You've carried versions of your mother, versions of her leaving, with you your entire life. Inventing and then reinventing your mother's story. Turning your mother over and holding her up to the light like a stone.

YOU WERE six weeks old when she brought you to Indian Creek, Kentucky, to live with her parents, and you were a year old when she left the creek for Lexington to go off and have another nervous breakdown at Eastern State Hospital. This was her second one. The first one had happened two years before you were born.

You imagine birds chirping, then stopping to take a look at your mother being settled into the backseat of your grandfather's Ford Mercury. Or in one story they'll tell you it was the sheriff's car that carried her away. In any case, you write of how the birds paused in the branches that morning to look at your wild-eyed mother before they rustled the leaves of the hickory tree and flew away. Then you delete that passage. You imagine it, like a black-and-white film, the car kicking up dust along the gravel road until it disappeared beyond the horizon, the car fading where the dirt road met the sky. And the baby, oh, as a mother you can't help but try to see the baby—you—nestled in the curve of your grandmother's arm. Maybe you were asleep. Maybe you sat up, cocked your head, and cried a little sad cry until your grandmother offered you a sup of milk. Your mind's eye follows the car from the womb of the hills all the way to the county line and eventually to the city, where your country-girl mother looks up at the red brick buildings and then looks back at your grandfather, standing stoic in his bib overalls. She is dressed in a flowered dress, strands of her long hair hanging loose from a ponytail. The orderlies escort her away and a steel door shuts, lacerating something between your mother and your grandfather that will never heal. Or maybe she was frightened in the presence of the law. Maybe she was dragged along a sidewalk by deputies, screaming, "Let me alone. I want to see my baby!" You can't help but to believe that you were her obsession even at the peak of her madness. She's always told you this.

YOU IMAGINE yourself and your grandmother back home on the hill—the sounds of beans being snapped for supper, your grand-mother's soft cries into the dishpan, your chubby legs chasing a spi-der across the linoleum, you saying, "Mommy? Mommy? Where's Mommy?" But this is all a lie.

Your first real memories are filled with how shiny and black your patent leather shoes were against your white lacy socks because your head was always down, your eyes on the floor. You remember the whis-pers passed through the cupped hands of the women you love (aunties, your grandmother, your great-aunt). When they speak of your moth-er's illness, a mostly forbidden subject, it always sounds as if she had just taken a vacation, that she was simply off somewhere doing some-thing restorative. You catch them shaking their heads in pity in your di-rection. This is how they'll look at you (at funerals and family reunions and church dinners and at Christmas) until they die. You will always be the crazy woman's daughter, no matter what fruit your imagination bears. There will always be a woman in your family with her hands on her hips, stretching her long neck to see what has become of you.

NESTLED IN the western rural corridor of Casey County, Indian Creek is cradled by knobs. You remember in your fifth-grade Ken-tucky history class learning that your county was the only county com-pletely in the Knobs Region. Long after your mother is taken from you that first time, it becomes your habit to go to the backyard and climb up to the top of the knobs and imagine that if you tried hard enough you could dream her there, four counties away, in the city, looking out the window of Ward 6 at the mental institution, thinking of you. She comes to you a 1960s-era vision of mother, in a sleek, blue dress and red lipstick, puffing elegantly on a cigarette, a melancholy look on her face, her legs crossed, the buildings rising up around her, her heart aching for you and the land she knows back down home.

You will be nearly grown, a mother too, before you realize that your mother's journey through mental illness was not just a case of the blues, not just her going off someplace to convalesce, to get herself together. You will be horrified to know that during those early years, while you toddled behind your grandmother, captivated by the magic of earthworms and butterflies and penniwinkles in the creek, your mother was enduring a battery of treatments for her paranoid schizophrenia. That she didn't have anything familiar to look at. No hills. No creeks. No garden full of backyard bounty. No trees. No gravel road. No baby. That most days she was confined behind brick walls like a prisoner. The view out her window: buildings, sidewalk, buildings. You will cry when you learn that your mother, who can't stand to be cold and wears a sweater even in summer, was subjected to ice baths when she was rowdy, to calm her nerves. You will learn that she underwent electroshock therapy, which left huge gouges in her long-term memory. She still can't remember important milestones in her early years. This worries you. You wonder sometimes if she even remembers you. Sometimes you feel guilty for testing her. "What time of day was I born?" you ask her. You feel even guiltier when she sadly says she doesn't know. Beyond those testing moments, silence is the easiest form of communication between the two of you. You spend lots of moments in silence, an occasional glance at each other, a smile, but at those times, even with a lifetime of words to say, you are both mutes. Black women don't speak their pain. Black women don't speak of madness. The Wilkinson women don't talk about it. Wilkinson women don't talk about anything but the children and meals that need to be prepared, the cleaning, the shirts to be starched and ironed. You were bold once and asked her what was it like being there at Eastern State. She looked past you into the air, as though she was searching for an answer, and finally said, "I don't know. Not anything good, for sure."

Now, more than fifty years of psychotropic drugs have left her body ravaged with kidney failure and hypertension and she walks with the help of a walker. Her waist-long hair is gray and she twists it up with her arthritic hands to make a bun. Her shoulders are stooped. She runs her thumb over the fingers of her right hand constantly as if she's strumming something invisible. All your mother's ailments are exacerbated by the drugs that have kept her sane.

WHAT KIND of mother would she have been, had she been able to really mother you? You wonder this even as you slide into your fifties and should be rid of those romantic notions of what a mother is. You still compare yourself to her and wonder if your children are the crazy woman's children, too.

Though you have always felt abandoned by her as a child, you still remember your mother as a regal vision in her black high heels, form-fitting dresses, her hair pulled elegantly back from her face and her lips dark red when she would return to the creek to visit you for holidays, dressed to the nines. She was fancy and no longer belonged next to your grandmother. Even the house with its woodstove, the tin white pot to pee in that sat in the bedroom corner, and the buckets of well water near the doorway in the kitchen seemed to not welcome her any more. The dog barked in the yard as though she were a stranger and you wondered if the birds, the squirrels, the branch, the oak, and the hickory had forgotten her, too. She kissed you on the lips and hugged you so tightly that sometimes you feared her. She always looked as if she was about to cry when she saw you. You, somehow, always knew she loved you, though, and you knew it was a mighty love.

Your grandmother watched your mother as though she was afraid that something awful might happen. And back then you didn't know the dangers of her disease. That she once pulled a butcher knife on your grandfather. That one time she threw an iron at your grandmother's head for saying, "You smoke too much." They say she whipped you harder than she should have when she was off her medication. But you still don't believe that. She loves you so much that even as a grown woman you can't bring your mouth to say the word *abuse*. There is not a word that comes to your mind for it, but it was not abuse: this you know for sure.

To you she was somebody out of *Jet* magazine or straight off the television set. To you she was a strange, beautiful black woman who was your beautiful, strange black mother. And by then you could see yourself beginning to show in the shape of her nose, her smile, the discoloration under her eyes, like little half-moons. You were steadily becoming her beautiful, strange black daughter.

Sometimes you felt as though your real mother was dead or lost, that she had been replaced with this woman who was whispered about, a woman whom you barely knew. But even as she was the woman who sometimes saw things that no one else could see, sometimes said things that made others uncomfortable, your mother played piano by ear and produced beautiful art with pencil and paint. Later you would boast that all of your imaginative leanings came straight from her. You heard things and saw things, too. You became a writer.

In your other life, the one you imagined for the two of you back then, she held your hand everywhere you went, took you to the city for swim lessons, taught you to play the piano like her, and told you of the days after she was released from the hospital and moved to Louisville to become a beautician. She told you stories. You wrote stories. You imagine yourself at her feet, your head in her lap, the awe of her washing over you.

In reality, you spent most of your youth thinking of your mother as a sister of sorts. Your grandmother was the one who held you when you were sick and dressed you for school. Your grandmother was steady, sturdy as barbed wire and could solve any problem, had a balm ready for the bee sting, the bicycle wreck, skinned knees and elbows, the fishbone that got stuck in your hand. Your mother was lovely and fragile and was not to be counted on. There was always that story about the time she almost let you drown in the creek. Your mother bought you tea sets and clothes that were too small. She straightened your hair with her beautician tools and put bows around your plaits. Your mother laughed sometimes at people and things that no one could see but her. There was always that look in her eye that you couldn't quite identify. Something wild always beneath the surface of her corneas threatening to show itself. She told you she loved you constantly, sometimes dozens of times within fifteen or twenty minutes. You came to think that she loved you too much. At one point you decided that perhaps it was her love for you that had driven her crazy. Can anyone stand to be loved this much? You are both fascinated by this kind of love and fearful that such excess exists.

WHEN YOU were in your late teens and had left the creek for college, you drove thirty minutes from Richmond to Lexington to visit your mother's little apartment on the Northside. The apartment was on the second floor, and the bright orange door stood out from the lime green doors of the other apartments. You thought that even this was a sign of her strangeness. Inside, the apartment was clean, but always reeked of cigarettes and the smell of fried meat. Your mother wore an Afro sometimes back then, and worked in a hotel. She always invited you to look through her costume jewelry for a trinket to take back to college with you. Sometimes she had boyfriends who would either leave when you arrived or slip up and down the hall like ghosts until you left. You would learn later that they were Army vets, hotel barkeeps, dock loaders, insurance salesmen, and occasionally roustabouts. You always felt as though your mother was still trying to coax some greater love from you than you were capable of giving. She would pull out the picture albums and you would both reminisce of the old days on the creek. You would run your finger across the plastic images of you and your grandparents, the gray tar-papered house that you and your mother grew up in, the rusted glider in the backyard, the smokehouse, Pine Lick Baptist Church. You would take something small from the yellow velvet jewelry box to make her happy. A smiley face pin, a mood ring, earrings, a bangle—things you kept but rarely wore. You taught yourself to always thank her.

These visits were awkward, and often the two of you sat in her living room or at her kitchen table just staring at each other, then at the walls or the floor. Sometimes she would fix you something to eat, but she didn't know any of your favorites the way you thought a real mother should. At these times you'd think of your visits back to the creek, where your grandmother welcomed you with a plate of meatloaf, mashed potatoes, and a spoonful of homemade relish on the side because she knew what you liked. Once, your mother made salmon croquettes. She was embarrassed when you said, "Oh Mommy, I'm allergic to fish." By this time, her illness was controlled with the medication, but still you felt as though the both of you were learning the ways of strangers. But during those college years your mother and you grew fond of one another. You began to forge some hybrid relationship—sister/friend/mother/daughter. Your mother was the first person you called when you became pregnant as a second-semester freshman, instead of your grandmother. You told her your secret as though she was a girlfriend. You were frightened to tell your grandmother. You didn't want her to be disappointed in you.

YOUR MOTHER saw your son shortly after he was born, days before your grandmother saw him. Your mother came to stay with you in your apartment in Richmond for a few days. You recall an image of your mother holding him, her shaking hand under his little head. She held your son as if she had never held a baby before, but you remember wishing you had a camera to freeze the moment. If there had been a photograph it would have looked like any grandmother holding any grandchild anywhere in the world. That would have been a nice heirloom to pass on to your son. You remember taking him back into your arms, whispering in his tiny ear, promising to be a better mother to him than she had been to you. When you looked up from him, she was there standing in your tiny kitchen, stirring canned soup and staring at you holding your son. You were not sure if she'd heard you, so you smiled and rose with the baby nestled in the crook of your arm and hugged her. She cried (with joy you think now). You cried and felt guilty and lonely and wished your grandmother was there to smooth that moment away like a wrinkle in a sheet. You called your grandmother later and she barely said anything. "You needed a baby like a hole in the head," she said to you, then asked about your new son and his father before she asked if you were eating enough, and hurried you off the phone.

You drove those thirty minutes to visit your mother often, and when you graduated from college you moved to Lexington to be close to her. In the years that followed, she and you and your children traveled back to the creek to see your grandparents as a fully realized family. You think now that by then both you and your mother had become city women, and you wonder now what your grandmother thought about the two of you there together after all those years apart. Those were good times, for the most part, and you felt greedy then for always wanting more, feeling as if those good days with your mother weren't enough. It's true you wanted more from her back then than your mother was capable of giving. Sometimes you still do. You imagine and reimagine a new mother for yourself. You summon your dream mother, your dream mother with outstretched arms and plates of cookies and sound advice.

Your real, flesh-and-blood mother leans on you for her own salvation, depending on you as much as your children do. You were her caretaker before you reached your thirties. You continue to remind yourself that she is your mother, your mother, *your* mother. You felt horrible when each of your grandparents died because you didn't want to have loved them more than you loved your mother, but you did.

SHE LOVES YOU.

She loves you.

You remind yourself of this constantly. Sometimes when she talks of your childhood as if she was the greatest part of it, she tries to reassure you. "Your grandmother wouldn't let me have you," she says, "because . . ." And she can never get beyond saying, "because I was sick." And that is when she wants to hug you tightly, as if you might disappear again, and she kisses you so hard that you fear your cheek will bruise. You want to push her away but you don't, because she is your mother.

She's your mother.

She's your mother.

And you hold your own self up to the light and turn yourself around like a stone. You are a mother, too. You know what *mother* is from the inside out. So you let her kiss you so hard that you feel the scrape of her chapped lips and the outlines of her teeth through her mouth bear into your cheekbone. And you feel that smothering mother-love that she has for you. You see it rising up in her, even before she kisses you, a powerful kind of love that is cloaked in fear and pain. You flinch as if you are about to be slapped. There is nothing you want to do more than push her aside and run away, but you, you hold steady as she showers you with all the love that a mother can muster for a child. It is in these moments that you try not to overreact, try not to cry, try not to re-create yourself a girlhood with her as some other mother. She is your mother and you allow her to love you with as thick a love as you both can stand. It's her job to love you and it's your job to not replace her with anyone else. She is your mother, the only mother you will ever have, and it's your job to brace yourself for her overwhelming love and to just keep on finding ways to love her back.

DAVID HUDDLE

Above My Raising: A Narrative of Betrayal

THE CHIP ON my shoulder has a name —Ivanhoe, Virginia. Some-times it's there because I'm out to prove I may be a hillbilly but I'm just as world-savvy as my friends and colleagues who grew up in cities. Other times it means I'm deeply, deeply ashamed of where I grew up, and I'm trying my hardest not to let it be visible in my speech or behavior. Days of attitude, days of mortification—even hour to hour I don't always know which it's going to be.

Didn't listen to country and bluegrass until I was long gone from Ivanhoe—even though that music was born in the same place I was. Never liked cornbread or buttermilk or collard greens. Embarrass-ment about my accent started when I was twelve and began riding the bus to high school. The Wytheville kids made fun of how we Ivanhoe kids talked. I still mostly don't like to hear the accent of the southern Appalachians. I never aspired to write anything "Appala-chian" and still don't. I have more affection for the Upper West Side of Manhattan, where I lived for the two years I attended Columbia, than I do for Ivanhoe, where three generations of Huddles lived and where my parents and grandparents are buried.

I grew up in a family that valued education, art, cultural aware-ness, conversational substance, and good manners. Never mind that we were still getting used to having indoor plumbing. Huddles were among the half dozen or so "nice families" of Ivanhoe—my father and grandfather had good jobs, which meant they had money to spend on books and records, hobbies like oil painting, watch repairing, and fly-fishing. Understandably, the other-than-nice families (which is to say, the poor families) resented Huddles. We were people who felt an obligation to "make something of ourselves." Thus, my parents sent my brothers and me to the University of Virginia, where we spent our father's hard-earned money on drinking and carousing with young men from Richmond, Norfolk, and Falls Church.

Because my fellow students at U.Va. mocked me for my accent, I continued the project I'd begun in Wytheville, trying to sound more like the people around me. I also bought tweed sports jackets, oxford cloth button-down shirts, repp ties, and Weejuns in Charlottesville so as to dress like my peers, most of whom could afford to shop for those clothes at Eljo's and Ed Michtom's. Preppy rich boy from Richmond or Tidewater was the look I sought.

I do acknowledge the downside of such snobbery—it's what delayed my appreciation of the extraordinary music that came up out of the southern mountains. Nowadays I can't get enough of Bill Monroe and Earl Scruggs, the Carter family, June Carter Cash, and the guitar virtuoso Doc Watson; I feel like I have to make up for what I was too snooty to pay any attention to when I was a young man. I still use the word *trashy* to describe certain general categories of behavior, food, music, fashion, language, unsophisticated art. E.g., velvet paintings of Elvis or Jesus. E.g., an after-school snack in Ivanhoe would have been to go to Price's Store, buy a little package of Planter's Peanuts and a bottle of Dr Pepper, then pour the peanuts directly into the soda for simultaneous eating and drinking pleasure. Because I consider it trashy, I've never even tasted that snack. And because I have these notions of the unacceptable, I deny myself any claim to authenticity. *Yeah, I'm from Ivanhoe, but you won't catch me dipping snuff or chewing tobacco or even sitting on a porch stoop like I don't have anything better to do.*

The other (nonsnobbish) half of my Appalachian antipathy is more legitimate. My great-grandfather was shot and killed in daylight in front of his store in Ivanhoe. The big boys picked on me in elementary school and later on the school bus riding to high school. Leon Jones pulled a knife on me and would have sliced open my belly if I hadn't been lucky and just agile enough. A hired man entered our home one night when we were all at the drive-in and rubbed poison ivy all over the inside of my mother's swimming suit so that she spent all of July and August in a state of agony. That particular assault on my family was horrendous enough to go through as a boy; as an adult

I'm trying to come to terms with such a perverse act directed toward my *mother*. When my wife described this occurrence to a friend of hers and the friend expressed how appalled she was, my wife said, "That's Appalachia for you."

A classmate from grade school, after he'd quit sixth grade at about age seventeen, quarreled with a neighbor, then went into his house to fetch a butcher knife, chased the neighbor, jumped on the neighbor's back, cut his throat, then watched him die right there in the dirt alleyway. Around 1990, when my parents were taking their fat old dog, Daisy, for a walk out on the dirt and gravel road from their house, two teenage boys with rifles coming the other way shot and killed Daisy, then ran away laughing. And finally, in an act that I can't help seeing in personally symbolic terms, an Ivanhoe pyromaniac set fire to my grandparents' home while it was empty and under repair and burnt it to the ground.

These are the specific instances from my experience of a general atmosphere of meanness, violence, and belligerent ignorance practiced by my schoolmates toward each other and toward any vulnerable outsider. It goes without saying that this atmosphere was passed down to my peers by family members and adults of the community. Ivanhoe was this way in large part because it was unincorporated— which meant that there was no government in the town, and the deputy sheriff responsible for the area lived several miles away from the center of Ivanhoe. There was almost nothing to stop people from doing whatever they wanted to. Black people lived elsewhere and stayed away. Girls learned to defend themselves as best they could from constant harassment. Tales of wife-beating were ordinary and usually provoked laughter as a kind of joke about domestic life. If you gave any evidence of difference, you paid a price. For example, during the six months or so that I took piano lessons from Mrs. MacGavock, who drove over from Draper one a day a week to teach piano in Mrs. Sisk's parlor to a few girls (and me during those few months), my peers called me names and threw rocks at me when I walked to and from my lessons. Teachers, ministers, and a few decent and/or educated people made some effort to improve life in Ivanhoe, but everyone understood these do-gooders were powerless to change the basic community ethic: In this place you are at liberty to do as you wish.

By the time I was twelve I knew I didn't want to live in the place where I was growing up. If I had to make a list of the places in the world I'd least like to live, Ivanhoe, Virginia, would be first on the list.

And yet, and yet—How did I make my way to the writing life I have? What was the topic of *Paper Boy,* my first book of poems? And the topic of *Only the Little Bone,* my second book of short stories? "Ivanhoe, sweet Ivanhoe," as my father once said when he was hospitalized and desperately wanted to go home—that place was my topic, and I rarely had a kind word to write about it. In the poem where I quote my father's vision of Ivanhoe, I go on to say, "that sorry / town where we'd all grown up, that cruel joke / / of a town so poor, so mean, and so ugly / that all you had to do was say the name / in Wytheville and somebody would swear he / almost got killed there one night."

Okay, there was an upside—my family life, the natural world all around my childhood home, some of the illiterate, dirt-poor, and deeply humble men who worked for my grandfather and helped raise me. Among my fondest memories are waking up to the view outside my bedroom window of a misty summertime sunrise over the mountain on the far side of New River. I also have to say that Monkey Dunford, with whom I spent many of my boyhood hours milking cows, feeding chickens, and slopping hogs, was the poorest man and the most deeply Christian person I've ever known. It's a fact that stares me down whenever I start ranting like this: Ivanhoe gave me my writing life. It is because I both love (as one can't help loving an abusive parent) and despise Ivanhoe that I have been able (or compelled) to write about it with urgency.

I lived there with my family from my birth in 1942 until I entered the University of Virginia in 1960. Afterward, though I spent the occasional week or month there, I really never lived in Ivanhoe again. In the fifty-one years since then, I've lived in Charlottesville, Virginia; Fort Jackson, South Carolina; Baltimore, Maryland; Stuttgart and Mainz, Germany; Cu Chi and Binh Chanh, Vietnam; Roanoke, Virginia; New York City; Colchester, Essex Center, and Burlington, Vermont. Eighteen years in Ivanhoe; twenty-two years in one place and another; then thirty-one years in Vermont.

If you ask me where I'm from, I'll probably say Vermont because for the past ten years I've coached myself to do so. Even now,

I'll probably tediously explain to you that I'm actually from Ivanhoe, Virginia, but geographically, culturally, spiritually, and politically I'm a Vermonter.

Which leads me to the intemperate and reckless (and forbidden!) part of what I have to say—how the Tea Party and Appalachia have lined up beside each other in my brain. I know the Tea Party did not come from Appalachia—in my view it was invented and foisted off on the American people by Karl Rove, Dick Armey, Fox News, the Koch brothers, and Rush Limbaugh. The Tea Party began organizing protests and supporting candidates around 2009. According to *The New York Times,* "The Tea Party agenda is not well defined, though it is anti-government, anti-spending, anti-immigration and anti-compromise politics." What *The New York Times* doesn't say about the Tea Party is that it is racist, ignorant, backward-thinking, and belligerent.

Because I don't live there anymore but because I've made considerable use of it in my writing, whereas in my life I've made a concerted effort to put Ivanhoe behind me, the national utterances of the Tea Party have struck this very exposed nerve in me and have kept on hammering away at it. The place in me that hurts gets a daily exacerbation from the news. What Fox News has to say about immigration and the Affordable Health Care Act and President Obama himself could have been composed by the men sitting on the steps of the Ivanhoe post office. When the Tea Party started getting vocal, it was as if my upbringing was calling to me—*Oh, David, Mr. High and Mighty Educated Liberal, listen to us preach the politics of your upbringing—Obama's a socialist and a Muslim, Obama's going to set up death panels and take our guns away from us, Obama is selling America out to the United Nations, Obama's going to send in the black helicopters.*

If I didn't know better I'd swear that Jim DeMint, Rick Perry, and Michele Bachmann have recruited Grandmama Huddle to channel her old batshit craziness into my ears from all the way down in her corner of hell. I know, I know—there are at least as many kind and decent and smart people as there are mean-spirited, sexist, racist, small-souled, conniving, gun-nut wack-jobs in Wythe County, Virginia. It's just that these Tea Party zealots have captured the media microphone, the financial backing of cynical billionaires, and some powerful places in our government. The most shameful aspect of my background is receiving attention, funding, and traction. Forgive me for being paranoid, but it's as if the Ivanhoe that I have spent my life escaping has transmogrified itself into the national monster that is American right-wing extremist politics. On a day that I write a poem and work on my novel, a guy in Charlottesville carries a rifle into a Kroger's to demonstrate his constitutional rights. And another guy in Alabama—a Vietnam vet with PTSD—holds a five-year-old boy hostage in a bunker so that he can sound off through a ventilation pipe about his contempt for government.

I would like to be able to say that these Tea Party types are not my people, and in fact they are not. Legally, genetically, and geographically they are not. I have every reason to say it loudly and clearly— THESE ARE NOT MY PEOPLE!

It's just that I can never convince myself. In my mind I will forever recognize them. Politically, psychologically, and spiritually, I can't ever deny them. They are my townspeople and my kin.

Am I trying to rise above my upbringing? You're damn right I am. But it's been a futile project and getting more so every day. At the time of this writing, my wife and I have still not resolved the issue of where we'll be buried. Actually, we've pretty well resolved it for her— she's going to be buried with her family in the mountains of Virginia. I guess when I hear the clods of dirt banging down on my coffin lid I'll know at last whether I succeeded in my quest to rise above where I came from. Vermont's mud-season muck will mean I made my escape into civilization, art, and enlightenment. Virginia's hard-packed red clay will tell me I never made it out of that hellhole.

CHARLES DODD WHITE
What We Gain in the Hurt

MY COUNTRY HAD just taken me back, and I sensed, not for the first time, what it was to feel stranded between extremities. When I came across from Canada I had a passport in my pocket that showed I'd been away longer than was strictly legal, so I was grateful to be given passage, even if I was bound to suffer the suspicion of the men watching the American side of the border. There seemed to be a lot of bluff going on, something that had gotten more pronounced and paranoid since September 11th. Even six years later, they were probably sorting out the best way to perform their genial menace. Stepping across official boundaries has always unnerved me. Even tollbooths make me antsy. I'm not sure why this is the case, but the reaction is physically palpable. In that moment the gulf between here and there seems impossibly distant. But the pressure of coming back into your home country is of another cut altogether. You're going back into all the familiar turbulences you left behind, and while there is a kind of adventure in coming home, there's also this feeling that you've forgotten some of the hard math that reminds you who you are and what you should have become.

I got back to the mountains of Asheville, North Carolina, in the middle of the night after fifteen hours on the road straight from Toronto, and I had little more on me than a single suitcase and an idea for a book. That was part of the risk. The other part was in trying to repair what damage I'd done by going away to chase down a relationship with a girlfriend that had been a long time in its dying. A year in Texas and another in Canada. I had a ten-year-old boy that

I'd seen fewer than half a dozen times over the past couple of years. Better intentions had been to make the trip back to Carolina once a month, but those plans were eclipsed by several small and predictable failures. Regardless, I was now back for good, and I meant to see what that might mean for everyone and everything involved.

I let myself into my mother's trailer; she had left the door unlocked when I'd called ahead to let her know I was coming in. It was late enough that I knew she'd already be in bed, so I moved quietly to the front bedroom and put my few personal effects away and crawled between the sheets with a bottle of Absolut Citron. I'd developed the nasty habit of drinking through my bouts of self-pity in the past few months, and vodka had become my drink of choice in that period of time.

The trailer was an excellent setting for depression. The mattress was prickly with feather quills, the walls composed of pressboard. Additionally, I was without a job or a real plan. From where I lay with my simple cocktail, I could see the neighbor flew a trim Confederate battle flag beneath a sodium light. When I closed my eyes I could smell the faint whiff of dog shit in the carpet. I drank the bottle down but couldn't sleep.

I ROSE early the next morning and sat over coffee and thawed supermarket biscuits with my mother while she watched television. We hadn't been able to really talk to each other since I'd first started dating my ex-wife, twelve years earlier, and being gone for two years had done no kindness to the break between us. There has always been shame and pettiness in any house we shared, and we were at our best when we pretended a different history. She often had told others that she had raised me alone. It was true that my father, when he was still alive, was never around. But I remember being with my grandmother or uncle more than I remember time spent with my mother, though that may be a fault of my partial memory. I can confidently say that she has always struggled to adjust herself to the routine demands of survival. Something in her has never fully developed, caught in a version of the past that only she can recognize, and I have never been able to meet her where she is. I still wonder who has been more injured by this.

She had moved up to the mountains with me the summer I turned eighteen, attaching to my desire to leave home and somehow managing to come along despite my best countermanding efforts. She had spent all of her life in Atlanta, and the mountains and small-town living of Asheville promised something vaguely pastoral and nostalgic. I had begun reading Thomas Wolfe when I was sixteen and was desperate to make a material connection between the hidden power of words and the living, breathing world evoked in Wolfe's fictional version of Asheville in his first novel, *Look Homeward, Angel*. I wanted to be able to write like that, to see like that. I had convinced myself there would be room enough there for both my mother's and my escapes.

In the years since, I've always found myself drawn back to the mountains. I've drifted across the country for much of the past two decades, but it's always been this place, this meeting of sky and ground, that writes something permanent in my heart. I wandered the Georgia woods as a boy because there's a sadly beautiful isolation when you give yourself over to the natural world, and that sense is made larger by the age and reach of the southern Appalachian high country. The mountains here are granite, not limestone, so there's no coal to drag out, no mineral wealth to decimate. Instead, you have the feeling that this is a profoundly old world, rounded off by the soft rays of a distant sun. Menial use seems beneath it, somehow. Men have imported all kinds of architectural ugliness to the ridgelines, but that blight is temporary. With all the plaster and presswood they've warped into place, you get the feeling that time and weather will have little trouble dispensing with the thin timbers, the sliding foundations. This belief that the mountains had abided and would still abide was the elastic that kept pulling me back to my adopted home.

And too, there was this idea for the book. After years of trying to find what it was that I should write, I had finally heard the voice of a true character, a man from the mountains, from the hollows and pocket ridges. My imagination had traveled home before I had. Walking the icy sidewalks of Toronto a few months before, sitting over beers in a narrow pub off Bloor Street, I already knew this man who would propel the story, knew his regrets and strength. I started writing and the words were, for the first time, it seemed, my own. I had to get back to see what this meant, to see how my story about a father and son a century ago would coincide with the story of what had happened to me as a failed father, and how I might be able to salvage some important part of the future.

THERE WERE no jobs back in Asheville, no offers to teach. I'd run out of a perfectly good PhD program when I'd gone up to Canada and now I had little to offer other than a few pale efforts at freelance writing, a hope which is tenuous even in the best of markets. But the national economy had just plunged, and those lucky enough to have steady work weren't sharing any connections with part-time teaching gigs they might snag for themselves. I couldn't blame them. Most Americans believe college teachers are firmly ensconced in middle-class insularity. They still see cartoons of camel hair and elbow patches, as if the modern professoriate has stepped from the pages of a 1950s *American Scholar* magazine cover. The reality for many college teachers under forty is something radically different. Patchwork employment is available if you drive between two or three colleges, teaching introductory classes on contract, often missing pay periods for long stretches at a time, particularly over the holidays. One doesn't need much of an imagination to understand how quickly this can convert someone into a Marxist, and it explains why so many teachers are frankly befuddled that much of Middle America sees the concept of redistributing the wealth as an inherently nefarious concept.

So I fell back on something I knew well: security. When I'd served in the peacetime Marine Corps several years earlier, I'd been part of a short-term program that cross-trained enlisted personnel in a secondary MOS, an acronym for what is commonly known in the civilian world as a job. While I'd spent most of my time as a M1A1 Tank crewman, I did have the dubious advantage of some law enforcement training as an MP, and I remembered being told that would somehow benefit me down the line.

I had resisted walking a security beat at first, figuring I might find something through a temporary service. The only place that appeared to be hiring at the time was a hard labor company that administered a test before putting you in the availability pool, a test that asked things like if you'd ever been in a fistfight or rough horseplay on the job site and if so, had anyone been sent to the hospital as a result. I decided to answer honestly, which was yes on the first count. It's hard to imagine having gone a week on the tank ramp without some kind of light scuffle with one rival or another. Frankly, it's considered good for *esprit*. My honesty, as it turned out, was well exercised. I passed the test and was told to show up the next morning at four a.m. That was when the trucks would come around if they needed mule labor to jump in and roll. I decided maybe my ethics about security work weren't as fastidious as I'd earlier led myself to believe.

I was hired in to the security firm pretty much on the spot because of my service record and probably because I was the closest thing to professional the desk manager had seen in the past six months. He was himself an old vet as well as ex-cop. He could tell I needed money as soon as I could get it, so he put me on the only open shift he had, watching a couple of fire trucks that had to be parked outside overnight while renovations were made to the firehouse bay. They were twelve-hour shifts, five days a week, from eight at night until eight the next morning, paying a little over eight bucks an hour. All those eights lining up seemed to be telling me something worth paying attention to, so I signed on right away and collected my new uniform from the office's wardrobe closet.

I managed to get my old Bronco II running and drove out to the firehouse the next evening. The truck had been sitting idle for most of the past couple of years and it had a tendency to overheat if I ran it for too long. Fortunately, I didn't have to drive too far. The job itself was simple. Sit in the truck and be ready to place a phone call with my cell in case anyone started snooping around. It was cool at night and the place was fairly rural, so there was little chance of trouble I couldn't handle. The one consistent enemy in security work is sleepiness and tedium. To stave this off, I started writing, wrestling my laptop around in the slim cab to simulate as comfortable a study as I could. The empty night was perfect. I felt like I'd slipped outside an easy idea of time and imported all of my characters with me.

As soon as I claimed a couple of paychecks I was able to find a place in town to rent with a roommate. I contacted him through Craigslist and went over to tour the apartment and introduce myself. Parker was an affable man in his early fifties with two wild-assed dogs, a black boxer named Canaan and an antique and irascible chocolate lab named Cleo. He showed me a small room in the finished basement of the eighty-year-old bungalow. It was tiny but newly refurbished with laminate flooring and had a small private bath attached. Though we would have to share the upstairs kitchen, I had my own private entrance around back. At the end of the tour Parker somewhat nervously told me that he wanted to make sure I understood that he was gay and that I didn't have a problem with that before committing to a rental agreement. I was surprised he felt the need to say as much, but I answered that was no problem with me as long as he understood I really liked to drink beer and whiskey. We shook hands and I began moving my few things in that afternoon.

After the firehouse job was finished, the security shifts I got were sporadic and tended to be short-term. I tried not to worry about making enough money to keep up with bills while I wrote during the day in the basement room. I had a nice view of the large backyard, a yard that was jungle-thick, shading us through the worst of the summer heat. There was a large cicada hatch that year, and each afternoon was surrounded with their collective thunder. It was distracting, but only in that way that beautiful and weird things can distract you. Ultimately, it made for good company.

I BEGAN seeing my son, Ethan, and had him stay with me whenever he could. Because the room was so small, I bought a folding cot at Walmart and tried to pad it up the best I could with extra bedclothes. We would switch off nights on who had the benefit of the big bed. Ethan has always been remarkably adaptable and stoic. He accepted this arrangement as well as he had all the others, without complaint or disfavor. Even then, I saw the man in him, the complete person that can never escape the dumb pride I feel at being his father. Both of us are quiet people, and we have that odd tension that stoppers words between men who want to share more of themselves with one another than they readily can. But you can feel the effort, the underlying ease, and that sometimes can be a great and true comfort for all the complicated errancy that invades a normal life.

He told me little of what had happened in his life while I was away. He had close friends through his church, a foreign concept to me. I had all I could stand of organized religion when I was a boy, and then later when my ex-wife had insisted on attending Sunday services. Then, as well as now, I've felt the fundamental absurdity of believing in a God above your own sense of right and wrong. Archaic dictates seem to have little to do with my idea of good and bad. Still, I knew it wasn't my place to comment on what value he derived from the community he found within the demands of his God. I believe discussing this part of himself made him uncomfortable, perhaps thinking I repudiated this part of him that existed outside of my first-hand knowledge. But even in this reticence, I sensed the force of his personality. I recognized how much was familiar and how much distinct and strong.

It was difficult when I would take him back to his mother's. During that time, they lived in a small upstairs apartment of an old building along a wooded road in West Asheville. There was a Japanese maple in the front yard that burned dramatically with fall colors, leaves softly rattling in the breeze like a chain of paper fans. I walked him up the big wooden halls and watched him go in, saying goodbye but rarely exchanging a hug. When I would go back down and back out to the truck, I felt like the displaced stranger I'd let myself become.

BY THE end of the summer a new security position had come in to work the graveyard shift at the city high school. There had been a recent news report of the building being haunted, so the company had gone through a couple of guards to find one who wasn't superstitious. It promised to be steady employment and offered a private office. My only responsibilities would be to tour the campus every hour and make sure no doors were left unsecured. There would be vast fields of time, a lack of definition I could fill however I chose. There could be no better place to help a book discover what it is supposed to be.

Many events in a writer's life form the elusive quality of voice. But perhaps the elements which seem the slightest may in fact prove the most evenly articulate. The space we inhabit with words is somewhere hard to discuss in plain terms. Overlay and revision are the ways we come to know what matters in our quietest moments. Those long nights were when those moments came to take on meaning for me. The cold halls and the vagrant winds popping at the jambs of unsecured double doors brought truer ghosts than those more easily reckoned. Those Gothic voices became mine. They demanded entry.

Searching for something wise exacts a debt. You can see this in the books of people who live toward their stories. In writing, the hurt we take on is part of the larger hurt about the good struggles of strong people. If this is not what we should strive to tell, then what? We are all crossing back and forth, between countries, between shame and dignity, all of us. In this radical life we must find the salvation of what is real, never shying from the severe and strange. That is what writers do if they are honest, what they inflict and grant.

The book was written across those endless nights at the high school. My character, Hiram Tobit, was the best truth I could find, and the book, *Lambs of Men,* was all I have to say about what fathers and sons are to each other. The completeness of that experience is not meant to be flexible, nor is it able to change the small troubles of my own life. That is the uncompromising totality of art, the privilege of having created a hypothetical world. I believe the violence poets accomplish is preeminent and necessary, but it cannot be confused with the price that we all pay in an effort to understand the hard beauty between who we are and what we say. My writing is often sad, but I am not a sad person. This emptiness between words and writers is where the world makes what it will, and any warning otherwise is so often ignored.

I am home now, still in the mountains. Like you, I still find plenty of ways to hurt, but I cannot be prized from where my feet fall. This is the permanent return, the family ground. Only a fool believes he is without a home country.

JACINDA TOWNSEND
Casablanca

I.

I'm standing in the international flight lounge of the Casablanca airport, waiting for a flight to the Islamic Republic of Mauritania. It isn't miles away. It is 4,000 miles from where I grew up, but it may as well be another planet. Despite the heat, no one wears shorts or T-shirts: in this airport, women wear *hijab* and greet one another with a kiss on each cheek. There's no respecting the queue: men routinely jump the security and ticket lines in front of women. There is no thick, lush bluegrass here. There are no mountains, either, to speak of—travel several hours south from Casablanca, and you're in the Sahara desert.

Across the lounge, people stand in line at a station for *emballage*, a process by which their suitcases are sheathed in industrial-strength Saran wrap before heading to less-developed countries, where they'll otherwise be opened by baggage handlers looking to ransack electronics and other valuables. Like the curious, gawping American I still am, even after all these years and countries of African travel, I snap a photo with my disposable camera. I will develop it as proof—proof of one of Africa's more outrageous yet perfectly necessary travel practices. Proof, also, that I've gotten out of my tight American skin and seen—touched—the world. I've used my freedom to meet new frontiers. To escape old restrictions.

I'm happily thinking all this, how I'll show this photo to my American friends while offering explanation, when a man walks up to me and starts yelling, angrily, in Dharija and then in French. "Supprimez-ça," he says, meaning *Delete that photo*. He presses his thumb down against his bent forefinger to pantomime his instruction.

"This isn't a cell phone," I tell him, in my own nervous French. "There's no way to delete. I just want a photo of this. We don't do this in the United States."

We argue. He indicts all Americans, all tourists. "C'est interdit ici," he says, again and again—it's prohibited here. We both know that's a lie. I can take photos if I please. It might be rude, and it might not be a custom, but it's not prohibited.

And in the end I win, simply because I'm carrying a disposable camera in the year 2013, I can't *supprimer* anything, and he doesn't know what to make of that.

But then I lose, because even after we walk our separate ways, him to some far-off recess of the airport and me to a café table where I can sit and read while waiting for my flight, I'm shaking. I'm having to sit down in this café because basically, after this encounter where I straightened up on my feet and defended myself, my knees won't let me stand.

II.

Why am I shaking? In part because I fear the Casablanca airport. I don't trust it, not its faux marble walls or its clean tile floors or its PA system or its neat little *gare* with trains connecting to the city of Casablanca and points north and east. I don't trust the Royal Air Maroc ticket agents in their maroon uniforms—they are rude, especially to sub-Saharan Africans and other travelers, like me, whose skin is darker than theirs. On this, my fourth trip to Morocco, I have taken pains to avoid the Casablanca airport by flying into Marrakech.

But now, because I'm traveling to the neighboring country of Mauritania, where I will meet up with that country's leading anti-slavery activists and continue some essential research, I must use the Casablanca airport and its network of international flights.

I wasn't, however, always a person with this fear of an inanimate building.

One summer before, in 2012, I brought my kids to Morocco with me. I was prepared for the in-flight rudeness, and even the nasty way the ticket agent would speak to me at the counter, but I wasn't prepared for what made me lose my breath with fear—the ticket agent, that summer on my way back to the United States, told me that my children's tickets from Casablanca to Madrid had both been canceled.

After an airline manager in Casablanca confirmed this, I bought new tickets, to the tune of $600, and my children and I made the flight just minutes before it left. When I got to Madrid, I discovered that the tickets had never been canceled—I'd been a victim of one of Royal Air Maroc's many customer service nightmares. Months later, after much hassle, Iberia gave me a partial refund. But the damage to my psyche had been done. As a traveler, I felt newly fragile. The unexpected had happened on the turn of a dime and I had been unable to scare it away with my bravado: I couldn't do something as simple as getting my children on a flight.

III.

I grew up in Bowling Green, Kentucky, the daughter of a mother who never traveled. On her honeymoon, she'd been to Niagara Falls—that would be her only time ever setting foot outside the country. She didn't see the point of traveling, at all, ever—after they divorced, it was my father who took us to Disneyland, to Phoenix, to Montreal. My mother almost never left town.

Even when she went to Nashville, or even to a neighboring county, she often felt that she had to take a man with her, particularly if we were traveling at night. I had a 4-H speech competition one evening in Morgantown, Kentucky, only half an hour away; she recruited her uncle to drive us. When it was time for my senior prom, she insisted that I not go without my then-boyfriend, whom I'd just unceremoniously dumped. "You can't go by yourself," she said. "And you're not driving." So my boyfriend who was no longer even my boyfriend drove my car, that I'd gotten for my sixteenth birthday, because my mother thought it would be crazy if people saw me driving myself to the prom.

It was important, always, in the Kentucky of my youth, that a woman always be chaperoned or accompanied. Particularly when traveling.

IV.

I have left the Casablanca airport and I'm on my way to Mauritania's capital city, Nouakchott. On the flight, I read background materials on Mauritanian society and the persistent, pernicious problem of modern-day slavery. Twenty percent of Mauritania's citizens are enslaved, often brutally, by its ruling caste. Escaping slavery, in this vast and mostly Saharan country, is almost impossible because of its punishing desert climate; because "slave" is a caste of Mauritanian society, successfully effecting a postslavery life, in which one might find gainful employment, is almost unheard of. Mauritania has only recently even made enslavement a crime punishable by law, and in the six years between then and now, only one slave owner has been successfully prosecuted, despite the evidence of slavery that is everywhere.

Reading, digesting, writing—despite the shocking subject matter of my research, these are still moments of normalcy. Moments I usually have on planes. But I'm reminded, during this moment on this flight from the Casablanca airport, that I'm doing something most American women don't usually do. Not in groups, not in pairs, and certainly not alone. And I'm reminded, during this moment on this flight from the Casablanca airport, with my disposable camera and its shot of *emballage* in my bag, that not even twelve months prior, I failed miserably at this traveling thing. I wonder, as I often do: As long as you still carry the memory of living something, will you really ever get past having lived it?

V.

I often think that if I made a list of all the things that Kentucky-grown girls were told not to do growing up because "good girls don't," that list would eventually have to roll itself into a huge, heavy scroll, one that, if it were unrolled to exposure, would unfurl itself down a long corridor and around a building. In south-central Kentucky—Bowling Green, to be exact—we were offered many rules of engagement.

No dresses above the knee, I was told as a kindergartener, and then again as a first-grader at a fundamentalist Christian school. If you have pierced ears, I was told in junior high school, you have to wear earrings when you go out in public. No empty holes. They're trashy. There were rules of engagement even for specific venues, such as church—women can't cross the pulpit—and later, there were rules of engagement with the very planet itself. One of these rules was that girls—and even grown women—were not to travel solo.

My mother and numerous others drummed this into me, that the world was a forbidding place, not open for female exploration. And so, when I was admitted to Harvard at age sixteen, my parents—and everyone else—tried to dissuade me. It was literally a thousand miles away from Kentucky, and, as a woman at the neighborhood convenience store told me, "you don't need to go all the way up there to go to college." But it was Harvard, after all, and so my parents relented. But there were rules. No riding the subway (I broke this rule before Freshman Week was finished); no going to a hair appointment downtown unless your father is in Boston to take you.

I broke these rules. I broke others. I went to law school in North Carolina. Got an MFA in Iowa. Worked as a journalist and then a lawyer in New York City. Traveled solo to Albuquerque, San Francisco, Greece. And in 2001, I was awarded a Fulbright for a year's study in the West African country of Côte d'Ivoire. The old dissuaders came out full force. My mother begged me not to go. My mother's best friend faxed me an article about a young American woman who had disappeared in South Africa. But it was a Fulbright, and I was going.

At the end of my Fulbright year I scheduled a layover in Morocco and fell in love with that country. I have returned again and again—I've been back alone and I've been back with first one and then both of my children, but I've never taken a man. And for the most part, that's been fine. I learned how to cook with a propane tank and I learned how to speak enough Dharija to get by, and above all, I always stayed safe and healthy and showed my children a good time.

Until that moment, in 2012, in the Casablanca airport, with a lying ticket agent and two terrified children.

VI.

What did that moment—that previous summer when I was with my children—what did it do? It undid almost every moment that came before it. It left me six hundred dollars poorer, for one thing. It humiliated me, this moment, made me wonder if maybe my French was better or my Arabic was better or if I'd just been standing straighter at the ticket counter or if I'd just seemed like someone with more moxie, I might have prevailed.

It reminded me of what many Moroccans thought about my dark skin—that it signified my being a fool, undeserving of proper customer service, accepting of any kind of treatment. That moment, that series of moments when I was running back and forth between the first- and second-floor ticket counters with two children under the age of seven and three suitcases—that moment unnerved me so, I'd left the bag with my laptop in the ticket line and hadn't realized until I was already upstairs in the airline's customer service lounge with both my children and the rest of our baggage.

That moment made me crumble, in front of my own daughters. It made me wonder if maybe I shouldn't have attempted this with no man. It made me go back to Indiana and think I might never return to Morocco.

VII.

It is 2013 and I'm back, of course I am, because I've read a CNN news story about slavery in Mauritania and tracked down the abolitionists mentioned in the article, who are overjoyed to learn of my interest. Because I'm writing a novel set partially in Morocco and partially in Mauritania, this shouldn't be that big of a deal, I think—it's just the kind of thing I always do when researching. But Americans almost never travel to Mauritania, and in the process of acquiring a visa to this Islamic republic, I begin to understand why. It takes months to get the visa, and I have to lie about my reasons for visiting the country, and my sister, who lives in Washington, D.C., has to go to the Mauritanian embassy with her French-speaking boyfriend in order to inquire after its delay.

Dissuaders come out again. This time they are cosmopolitan, urbane, well-traveled dissuaders, even. Al Qaeda is in the north of the country now, says a friend, who has someone from the embassy in Mali send me a semiclassified report. There are landmines there, says a former Peace Corps volunteer who left Mauritania a few years prior. You can't go overland. You shouldn't go at all. Why do you need to do this, exactly? they ask me.

I schedule a June trip to the country, using Morocco as a home base of sorts, and promising myself to take a flight to Mauritania rather than going overland—2012's moment in the Casablanca airport has taken that much nerve away from me, that I don't want to spend my whole three weeks in an unfamiliar place.

Also, I've not brought my children.

It's a fruitful trip, if a difficult one. It's Ramadan, this summer of 2013, and there's almost no food or drink to be had in the 116-degree weather, but my first full day in the country, one of my hosts, Brahim Bilal Ramdhane, allows me to nap for hours in his living room and invites me to a lovely *iftar* in his home when it is time to break the fast.

My second day in Mauritania, I meet with the grandpapa of all Mauritanian abolitionists, Bouboucar Messaoud. The son of slaves, who became a lawyer and then an abolitionist, this man has a presence like none I've ever witnessed. In the afternoon, he takes me to visit a family of escaped slaves who are living in a tent on the edge of Nouakchott. The mother of the family—much to everyone's seeming horror, there is no father—has eight children, all of whom have been conceived with different men, because her master "leased" her as a prostitute. As she tells me her story, with the help of a local student who translates her Hasaniya into a sort of "franglais" that I can understand, I look at her children, who alternately smile and hide their faces under veils. I hold her four-month-old, the only child who has been born outside of slavery. I brush the flies off her feet and unwrap her face from the stifling blanket, noting her little ears pierced with gold studs. I kiss her gently on the cheek, taking care to leave her sleeping. I bring her close to my own bosom, the way I always held my own children when they were infants. I breathe in her smell. I feel what people have felt through the centuries, when they've escaped a bad thing to make a better way for their children. God is good, I think. *Allahu akbar.*

VIII.

I return to Casablanca from Nouakchott with gastrointestinal issues of the highest order, but I have, too, something unnameable, something previously unspeakable—I have my power. It's not even that I have it back. No—I have a power now, and a peace, that I didn't previously have. I've faced my fears, even the ones I didn't realize I had. I've lied to a corrupt government to get a visa and entered a country that doesn't want the world to know what happens within its borders. I've met up with men I barely know, allowed them to drive me around a strange city, eaten and slept in their homes. I've seen and touched something that will affect me forever—the slavery experience—and simply let that experience overwhelm me with its attendant emotion. I've traveled in an Islamic republic where I was forced by custom to wear *hijab*, in a country that is an Al-Qaeda target, a place where I'll stand out as an American and won't even begin to know all the subtle reasons why.

I've gone to the moneychangers on the corner of the Nouakchott street and converted an obscene—nay, deadly—amount of currency and then, when I ran out of that currency, gone in the night to one of the three ATMs in the country, only to find that my bank card won't work. I've gone, the following day, to find a bank open late during Ramadan, where I've had to persuade the teller to let me go behind her counter and log into her computer to get the password for my wire transfer. And I've done all this in my French, which has never been that stellar.

Most importantly, what I've realized is that I've not ignored fear on this trip to Nouakchott—I just haven't had it. All the travel that has come before has come with a little voice in the back of my head, that voice asking the insistent question *Why are you doing this with no man?* In the Islamic Republic of Mauritania, which is culturally further from Western Kentucky than I've ever been, I've heard no such voice. The only voice I've heard is the one telling me that this is an important thing I need to witness, that this is an important group of people to whom I need to give voice. What I've felt, on this trip, isn't so much *You should be doing this in some safer way.* What I've felt is more *You should be doing this.*

IX.

I am scheduling another trip to Morocco with my children for fall of 2014. While I am avoiding the Casablanca airport, I'm doing so not out of fear, but desire—if we fly into Marrakech, we get to spend more time there, and there's not really a reason for me to spend time in Casablanca.

My children are still young—nine and four. They will not remember that moment, two summers earlier, that I crumbled in front of them. But it's important for me to take them back. Before, I was just pretending to be free, pretending to be outside my uptight American skin, outside the skin of that uptight little Kentucky-raised girl who was told not to walk on the street after dark. Kentucky is a state settled by those who emigrated from the same sort of hills and mountains in Wales and Scotland and kept their clans tight in those nooks and crannies—one of the biggest lessons one learns, growing up in

Kentucky, is that one is never supposed to leave it. Not to pursue an educational opportunity, not to give voice to the voiceless, not to grow or learn or change. And if you were a girl, growing up in Kentucky at a certain time, it is a lesson that others drummed into you—traveling isn't something to be done without a male presence.

Now, those thoughts fail me completely. In that small moment of entering a taxi—of negotiating, in the hard-won French that always comes back to me instantly, with the driver who wants to charge me three times what he'd charge a Moroccan for the same ride—I can demonstrate, for my daughters, how to get out of Dodge. I am not the mother who shook before a ticket agent. I am the mother who can keep them safe and show them the world. I am a woman who is solid in her skin on this planet because I seek to understand it more than I fear not understanding it.

JOYCE DYER

A Tiger in Your Backyard

YOU GREW UP in a company town, though it wasn't strictly in Appalachia. No mountains stood anywhere—even in the distance. Sandstone hills reared up sometimes, but mountains were not part of your topography.

An "outmigrant"—that's what people call you still. You know something about the Appalachian experience, but only secondhand. Firestone Park, the community Harvey S. Firestone built in the early 1900s for his workers in Akron, Ohio—your city, a city called the Rubber Capital of the World when you were a girl—was a colony of migrants, and you lived among them. Your paternal grandfather, as well as your father when he was a boy, worked in the anthracite coal mines of Pennsylvania before coming to Rubber Town, and your maternal uncles traveled to Akron from West Virginia to make rubber belts for engines and to marry your aunts. Akron rubber companies recruited workers from up and down the Appalachian strain, and men came for better pay.

Coal and rubber are the same to you, though you know they shouldn't be. Your daddy didn't wear a miner's helmet when he went off to work at Xylos, Firestone's reclaim plant, but he still came home with thick seams of black down his cheeks, his arms, even the white shirts he wore during the years he was plant manager. It was called "lampblack," that substance that marked him, and it eventually found its way into his lungs and sealed them up, just like tar.

Until all the trouble started for Tom Coyne (and the trouble began long before the tumor formed), you thought Firestone Park was the best place in the whole world—even better than Hollywood Beach, Florida, where your family vacationed one week each July in a pink motel, when the rates were low.

The world made sense to you from the day you drew your first breath of factory air in the leeward wind. You knew what it was made of even before your brain was fully formed: A park at the center of town where you could play and a street called Crescent that bent around the hill that framed it—the way a high moon sometimes arches earth. An annual visit by the Ringling Brothers and Barnum & Bailey Circus and an annual Christmas party in the Firestone Clubhouse, with performing dogs and a visit from Santa—events sponsored by the Firestone Tire & Rubber Company for families of employees. And that meant you.

Once a tiger escaped from the circus and strolled through your backyard. You didn't see the animal, or hear its growl, but your neighbors said they did. You saw the tiger later, when it wasn't there. What you did see then in that backyard of yours, just a short walk down a pathway and through some high grass, was a statue of Harvey S. Firestone on the corner of South Main Street and Firestone Boulevard—at the entrance to your community.

He sat on a hillock, a bronze man in a bronze throne. Harvey was sculpted to look like Lincoln on the National Mall, and surrounded by a stone exedra carved with naked classical figures. How could you resist a thing like that? It was your playground, and you would climb into your founder's lap (with a boost) and stare as fixedly as he did at the line of Firestone factories just below the little rise you both were on.

Harvey S. Firestone was in all the rhythms of your daily life. He *was* the rhythm. Your family banked at the Firestone Bank, bought food and household items at the Firestone Employees Store down by the plants, purchased tickets to spaghetti dinners held in the basement of the Firestone Park Methodist Church or Firestone Park Presbyterian Church (even though you weren't members), paid for medicine at the Firestone Park Pharmacy, filed claims with the Firestone Park Insurance Agency when your daddy wrecked the car. You attended Firestone Park Elementary School, designed by Harvey in the shape of a castle—with turrets and crenels—and you learned many years later that Harvey himself drove the tractor that leveled the ground behind the building, readying it for a parking lot. Each day when you entered your school, you noticed a six-foot painting on the right of George Washington and a six-foot painting on the left of Harvey S. Firestone. You felt the importance of your town in American history from the time you were five years old. Washington, D.C., and Akron, Ohio, were indistinguishable to you.

You loved Harvey S. Firestone, but your father loved him more. He had met him once, he told you, but Harvey died in 1938, so you never did. But no one was more alive in your imagination than Harvey was—more trustworthy or good. Until the day when your father stopped wearing his white shirts, stopped going to the Clubhouse with other men for lunch, stopped laughing hard with that toothy grin of his. Until the day your father started burping and taking Maalox tablets, growing more and more silent, wearing to work the clothes he wore only to mow the grass, carrying a brown bag with an American cheese sandwich in it and a sloppy dill pickle in wax paper, and, later on, disappearing into the night with groups of other quiet men.

In the 1960s, your father was stripped of his job as manager of Xylos, and then subjected to further demotions, until he was fired a year before his pension was scheduled to kick in. He was told in a letter that he wasn't needed anymore because he had no college degree. Like the tires that arrived at his dock on the train each morning, ready to be ground for reclaim, your daddy was all used up.

But a tiny loophole gave Tom Coyne one more chance. He had begun his career at Firestone as a union man, and once a man joined the union, he stayed a member all his life. No one could take that from him, and so your father was able to remain at Firestone even though the company didn't like it much. Didn't like it at all when they found out. He could punch a time card, the way he had decades before—and wait to turn into an old man so he could retire and keep some of his pension check.

On the heels of that decision, the company quickly demoted him one last time—to janitor. *Take it or leave it,* they said, and in spite of his poor health, he took it. A few weeks after that, in the dark of night, he became a union activist, though you wouldn't know this until long after he was dead.

You wrote the story of your father several decades after you left home. As hard as you tried, you couldn't separate it from the story of the company town he had loved for so long—or from the Firestone Tire & Rubber Company that built it. You talked to people still alive who had worked with him, read company minutes, developed and studied glass plate negatives Bridgestone/Firestone representatives gave to you of interiors of your father's plant. You learned about United Rubber Workers, Local 7, clock card #9786—the person your father had been in the 1930s, and then became again. You read about environmental hazards in the rubber plants and interviewed chemists and asked doctors what had really happened to your dad's poor lungs and liver. You tried to understand how the industry was changing in the 1960s, and why it would forget a man as loyal as your father was.

And when the writing about your father was over, you thought about how sad it had made you to realize that your daddy had no escape once he sold that soul of his to the company town. He had absorbed Firestone into his system so completely that he had been fooled into thinking that Firestone Park was a place of perpetual moonlight, and that nothing could happen to him because he had a great benefactor—the bronze man—who kept an eye on things, and because he lived on a street named Evergreen, on the edge of a crescent moon. All of you—Annabelle, Tom, and Joyce Ann—lived in a little Tudor house, "a one-of-a-kind, a house built for executives, honey!" your father used to say to you, because that's what the company had said to him. But that house was not one-of-a-kind, you later found out, but a part of the mail-order Sears Modern Homes program the company had bought into. It was a house that arrived on a train in a package and was untied and then assembled on Evergreen Avenue, and then you lived in it for a while.

You didn't tell everything, though. You didn't write about the fear the book provoked. Yes, you told about the sadness, but not the fear. Firestone had been absorbed into Bridgestone by the time you wrote your book, but something of the company remained—and almost all of it lingered in your memory. Did you have the right to take away so much from your father? To nullify decades of his life? And couldn't there be consequences for your unruly behavior on the page, even now, and where was your gratitude for all the good that happened during those years Tom Coyne had been so happy?

The worry you felt when you wrote that book was not inside its pages. This is the first time you've recorded it. You made it seem as if you strode without a care into those corporate offices to conduct your little interviews. Made it sound as if you weren't worried all the time about whether you were stepping cautiously enough, getting things right, covering your tracks, staying out of too much trouble. As if you felt confident that you had the right to attack and criticize the company that had supported you and your family for so many years and even awarded you a Firestone Scholarship (for children of hourly employees) shortly after your father was fired, allowing you to attend college, something that would not have been possible otherwise. Was it your right to relinquish gratitude, and what kind of loyalty was that, young lady?

Oh, your father's worry was on the page, but not yours. You kept that out.

You ended your book with your father's death, and assumed that would be your last word about the company town.

You thought the town was gone from your life once you buried your dad. By then the idea of the company town had ended—for Akron, Ohio, gone bust, and, most certainly, for your family. But you have come to understand that you were wrong. You had been exposed. The town had gotten into your blood, wound its way around your nerves and flesh even more than it did your daddy's. It didn't vanish just because you left Firestone Park, and it didn't die because your father did.

It lived right on in you.

You were as susceptible to the lie as he was.

You may have suspected this even while you were writing your father's story. But the story of the second "company town"—the one you chose—was going to be even harder to tell, so you put it off. It's difficult to write about another's disease, but it's almost impossible to write about your own.

Heir to the idea of the company town, you held its familiar script in your hands and walked right onto a new set. The second play had two acts, just as the first play did. Act I—The Seduction. You can talk about this act because it's not difficult for you to poke fun at yourself—to recognize your foolishness. In the new play, foolishness and fear appear in separate acts, so the first act is easier to tell. You shake your head when you think of your Seduction, but you don't quiver much when you read your lines.

When you were thirty, you did it again, but this time entirely on your own. You walked right into a new town and signed the papers. You took a job at a boarding school in Ohio, and for many years didn't notice—probably refused to notice—the resemblances it bore to the company town you had left not long before. No factories here, no smoke spewing into the air, so you failed to make the connection. But you should have looked for signs, because they were present all along. A Headmaster (just the word . . .)? An Assistant Headmaster? And they were always men, and always had the final say. Few decisions were reached by committee, and no important committees had faculty on them. You of course noticed how low the salaries were, and regretted the school's decision not to pay into your pension plan because you didn't coach a sport, but you were so enticed by the benefits and the beauty of the place and the history of the school that you came anyway. Why, the school had thought about the faculty and provided them with privileges—a gym and swimming pool for you and your family to use anytime you wanted, free housing on campus, three square meals a day in the dining hall, an on-campus Christmas party for the children of faculty (with a movie and gifts) sponsored by the Headmaster's wife. One day your son would receive full tuition to attend this school, your contract promised, because "faculty brats" went free. Without teaching here, how could you have afforded an education like that for your child?

So things went smoothly, and well, and you were happy and people liked you, and your son was happy and people liked him, until something happened at the school twelve years after you arrived that caused you to resign. You weren't fired, the way Tom Coyne had been, but someone else was, and after that it would be impossible for you to stay.

That brings you to the second act—you'll call it Protest—the same part of the story you had trouble talking about when it was your father's story, but are having even more trouble with now, when it is your own.

Two kinds of Protest are evoked by egregious episodes in the life of a company town, and both are difficult. The Protest you display when life is actually happening, and, later, the Protest on the page, as you look back.

For a second time, discrimination by those more powerful unsettled a life. For Tom Coyne, the issue was education. At the boarding school where you taught, the issue was race. Of course you can't prove it was race that led to the firing of a black musician who was the heart of the school—had been here twenty-five years. After it happened, the lawyers quickly stepped in, and both administrators and Mr. William T. Appling were placed under gag rule. No one spoke a word. To anyone. The lawyers were the only ones who spoke, and only to each other. The silence continued and no public explanation was offered by either side. But you were older now, and the man was dear to you. You knew what you had seen, and what he had said to you, and the world suddenly turned Kafkaesque.

Mr. Appling had become the school itself for you. Its passion and its beauty. When you first met him, you didn't know that he had played piano with the Cleveland Orchestra, and directed its chorus. That early in his career, young William won first prize in piano from the National Association of Negro Musicians. Or that people in the music world loved and admired him and knew that as a black man he had been born just a little too soon to be appointed to the choral positions his talent deserved, and so he was here at your school instead, embellishing it whenever he held his baton or sat at the piano bench. But even in those first weeks and months after you met him, you knew this: Bill was a little like a psychic, or the man at a carnival who guesses your weight within a pound, or a doctor who knows what's wrong with you before the blood tests come back. You and your husband knew this was a person you wanted in your life—a great man—and you wanted him in your son's life, too. Your son was in first grade when you arrived, but you were sure he would find Bill and Bill would find him, and in eight years you would be right. Your son would love growing up in this safe place, on the "lawn's wide sweep" that the school's Alma Mater promised, with ponds and other boys and hills to sled down, and you hoped that Bill would soon be his teacher (his counselor) and lead him to music (which he did), but you had not imagined that your son, in the terrible innocence of his youth, would try to save this man one day.

The story you need to write is about what you did (not nearly enough), about race in America, about how William T. Appling unintentionally radicalized your son and changed the course of his life. It's not all your story—it's your son's—but you have to tell about the part that affected you. It's a story from twenty-five years ago that people kept private then and that has been kept private for all this time, a story that led people besides you to leave the school, a story about social justice and art and armbands and black turtlenecks, a story that is connected to John Brown because his father, Owen, helped found the school 150 years before and also left it in sorrow and anger because of race, a story that made national news—a story that magnified the contest between anger and docility, courage and cowardice in your soul. Your company soul.

I would never do anything to hurt you, said the Company Town. And you believed it. *Yes I would,* the Town said. And you believed that too.

Your father found courage, and organized for the union *because he had to.* You and your father are company people at heart, and don't come by courage easily or naturally. You both want to believe that ideal communities exist somewhere, and that they look out for the people who live in them—and make fair rules by which all its members can play. You wonder if maybe Appalachians have been too much this way, at least the ones who came north or west from the mountains when the company called. Your people, in other words.

But you're like your father in that other way, too, and that's what you found out when you lived in a company town the second time—in a place you chose. You remained too docile in the years and days before the lawyers came—listening, trying to understand, doing your best, wanting to heal things, watching your son grow—but when there was *nothing left to do,* just that horrible silence, no recourse at all, you became active, and disappeared into the night to do what you could, the way your father had.

You did a few things then, but your son was stronger and more eloquent than you were, and he was seventeen.

But now, twenty-five years later, the silence that persists has become unbearable and you know it's time to write. You will soon disappear again into the night, where secrets strike the page, *because you have to.* You have no desire to go, only dread, but you will proceed. In your family, people join the union or they write, and both are done in darkness, under duress.

So at this moment—sitting at your computer in an upstairs room—you know you are going to reconstruct the way things ended for Mr. Appling, for you, and for your son at the school the three of you loved and shared. You still love the school, but you will find the courage to tell, because this silence cannot continue. After twenty-five years of it, you will get the story down as best you can, with all its history just a few blocks away in the old buildings of campus up the hill from your house, with the spirit of John and Owen Brown right beside you, with Appalachian coal miners somewhere in the distance clinking their pails, with the memory of your father sneaking out of the house late at night to tell his own secrets in the union hall, with that tiger creeping closer to your door. And so you begin.

Mr. Appling and the woman were both concert pianists, you will write, *and they lived together with two beautiful daughters and two grand pianos in a brown house at the edge of town. Genius lived in that house,* you will say, *and late at night the man and the woman would play duets. They'd play all the composers who had written music for two pianists, not one—Mozart and Schubert and Brahms and Debussy and Stravinsky. Some compositions were written for four hands at a single instrument and others for two pianos,* you will continue, *but Mr. Appling and the woman would play both, each night finding themselves either seated side by side or staring across the room into the other's eyes.* You will tell more about Stravinsky, but at first you won't know why. *It was revolutionary music that the couple chose,* you will write, and then you will name Stravinsky duets and let the notes you hear in your head admonish you for your long silence . . .

CONNIE MAY FOWLER
Rose

1. JEWELRY

I wear memories of my Appalachian roots as if they're pearls strung on a frayed silk string. Even as I sift through what is known and suspected, recollections born from coal dust and poverty slip through my fingers, the metaphoric necklace perpetually breaking.

A pearl here, a pearl there. The faded and torn photograph trapped in the frame of a broken mirror, the exhalation of a half-uttered and therefore meaningless sentence, that long gaze peering into the distance as it seeks some semblance of home: this pastiche of impulse and desire is what I call my heritage.

2. THIEF

Let us be exact. Mine are stolen memories, gathered in a haze of cigarette smoke and the slosh of bourbon poured too freely, memories proffered through tears that filmed my mother's eyes but did not fall.

Though she is long dead, at the most unexpected times—while wiping clean the curved underside of a tomato's bright leaf, the moment before I softly gasp when my husband caresses my hip, the ritualistic reach over a hot stove as I search for just the right slotted spoon—I see my Appalachian-born mother with unnatural clarity.

I love those moments.

3. VASE

There she sits at a kitchen table by the sea (a distant and lovely exile), cigarette aglow, a dirty dinner plate at her elbow, her gaze pinned to a past that stalks her, sustains her, buoys her, destroys her. In this swirl of time and tobacco and booze and my youth and her regret, the words flow. They crowd that hot, breathless room like wings.

Her refrain reminds me of death and hope, as though she is little more than a speck of dirt that will one day catch a ride on a bright red bird. Black lung. Poverty. Sorrow. Song. The lonely maw of a green holler cloaked in the mist of her dreams. Dawn's ecstatic light trembling like a lip on the golden edge of a high mountain cloud. Bone-breaking wind filling the bowl of her empty belly. A snake handler whom she loves. Pretty, pretty wildflowers growing beside a cold, clear stream.

She remembers life not in its totality, but in its infinite parts, as if time were nothing more than a series of doors slamming shut at her approach.

In my memory, she shares this image: She—a teenager of unadorned beauty—stands at that cold, clear stream and floats her hands over the tremblers of Queen Anne's Lace but thinks twice about plucking them, can barely consider the act of stuffing them—a celebration of sorts—into a clear, chipped drinking glass. She refuses to admit how pretty they would look in the window of the dirt-floored shack she calls home because the truth of it is, flowers remind her of death.

4. BODIES

Death is always with her. There isn't a vase of flowers in all of Appalachia that can obliterate these memories: Her daddy's big hands beating down on his wife and child as if feminine flesh required reshaping. Her mama—*isn't Rose the most beautiful name?*—dying in childbirth in that mountain shack and buried in a star-patterned quilt of her own making, her mama whose final gift to this world was a stillborn baby boy.

My mother swore her daddy wailed deep into the first night he spent without the woman he had beaten, "Rose. No flowers. Just thorns. Rose."

5. RHYTHM

One morning, as I sit at a different kitchen table by the same sea, I wonder if Mother remembered all these moments and maybe others as she gathered her long black hair over her thin shoulder, slipped on her shoes, and left Grundy with, as she liked to say, only the clothes on her back, thus turning the children she would have into exiles: people who live in the subtropics but who, every time they hear the high lonesome whine of a mandolin or fiddle, rise to their feet and dance, keeping the beat, swinging their arms, swaying their heads, moving in lockstep to rumors that bear the weight of truth.

6. LEAP

When I could bear the weight and rumor no longer, I went to the mountain, a prodigal daughter returning to a home she never knew.

7. NIGHT

I didn't ascend the mountain. I got a room in one of those places that prefer cash to credit, where the sheets are threadbare but clean and towels bear the warning, scrawled in indelible ink, Property of the Lonesome Pine Motor Lodge.

I got under the covers and pretended that in just over eight hours, I would be wanted, remembered, loved.

This was, of course, a conceited and laughable pretense. I was officially unknown at this elevation. And because so many years had passed, how could a memory of my mother persist? It couldn't, I told myself. You're a fool, just like Mother always said.

So I slept.

8. COMPASS

When I awoke, the quilt lay twisted by my side, looking not unlike a slumbering lover, a napping child, a dog dead or asleep. Who could know?

I tried not to pray for fear of what that might conjure.

Instead, I listened to the early morning dew, wet with birdsong.

There will be disbelievers, but I know what I heard:

Do not brush your hair. Do not. Last night's dreams linger in your tangled curls. You will need their narratives—their cut-up pieces of life—membrane and cell, bone and rumor—when you stand inside a cabin that frightens you, a cabin stinking of coal and tears, blood and memory, a cabin that carries the scent of someone you once loved. Do not.

In the scattering darkness, I understood. I knew what the birds knew.

Time to fly.

9. HOME

The mountain was a pine-pierced nautilus forever turning in on itself, rising from a vanquished ocean, the violent geology of change buckling Appalachia's wide backbone.

Finally, the sea made sense to me.

10. HUMILITY

I am a flatlander, but my people—those strangers I'm kin to, those strangers known only to me in the lilt and acid of my mother's departed voice—are all sons and daughters of this high, ancient spiral born of stardust and sea fossil.

That's what I told myself as I entered the only restaurant in town that was open—a Pizza Hut. I fought to retain a smidge of dignity—to not sound deranged—as I explained to the plump, fresh-faced, eighteen-year-old waitress the circumstances that had brought me to Grundy.

"I don't know your mama. That was way before my time. But given your last name, you've got to be related to everybody in town. There's the pay phone right over there. I'd just start calling folks."

11. QUARTERS

No invitations to Sunday dinner. No suggestions for Monday breakfast. No definite recall of any of my people.

And then I dialed someone named Marie Looney because Precious Looney (I cold-called her because I liked her name) recommended it. "Marie Looney knows everybody's business," Precious said, a confident clip to her mountain drawl.

Marie Looney was old. But her memory was sharp. She sounded like a hillbilly reciting an Appalachian version of Genesis.

Now John Looney was probably your great-great-great-granddaddy. He was a Cherokee, pretty high up, and he sired three daughters, not a son in sight. I think the girls' names were Mary, Inez, and Kathryn. Inez married George, who was also a Looney, but not the same family, so it was okay— you see there are white Looneys and Indian Looneys—and they had a whole passel of children. I think that's where Rose, your grandmother, comes from. Yes, two lines of Looneys. Irish and Indian. Plus the Boyds and the Smiths and the Yeats. I could go on and on. But that was a long time ago and I can't be sure of any of it. Old Mrs. Smith, now, she would know more, but she up and died last month. Maybe you ought to go out to Looney holler. There's an old abandoned cabin there.

12. BLOOD

The cabin leaned squat in the black dirt, spare as a collarbone, hidden in a holler among many hollers, a dry brown silent carcass, testament to my mother's stubborn insistence to abandon the dirt floor of her birth.

13. LINGER

I stood where my mother once crawled and spied through the lens of a broken windowpane red birds on the wing.

From the floor, I gathered my mother's dirt. A good fistful. Impulses stained with hazy memories rushed through me. I longed to press my face against my grandmother's cheek—a woman known to me only in stories told in the incandescent glow of a naked bulb—and feel in the chambers of my seashell ear breath born of these words: "You really do have people, honey. You really are a granddaughter. You are *my* granddaughter."

I sifted the dirt through my fingers, pearls for the dead, and then looked around the room for a jar or a pop bottle—anything to gather the dirt so I could take a piece of this place home with me. As I turned a full circle, I felt a ghost brush my hand. For a moment, we were knuckle-to-knuckle, ageless and dead. And then it moved on.

Licking the dirt from my palm, I recalled a favored fact. Sharks taste with their skin. I ingested the mineral compost of time and loss and wondered if my familial past—its broken bones and untended rosaries and dreams abandoned as we stared at our visages in mirrors cracked and not—had just consumed me.

I walked back to the broken-paned window. No chipped drinking glass. No picked wildflowers. But a line of them—ragged and bright—trailed across the yard and into a meadow. Perhaps that would have been okay for my mother. Perhaps as long as the flowers remained unpicked and outdoors, death wasn't in the cards.

"How do I know for sure this is where you lived? How do I know this is *it?*" I asked, my voice wavering and loud in the empty cabin.

I gazed at the rough-hewn log walls and the rolling green of the holler. I stepped into the lone doorway, the path in and out being one. I smelled the earth and discerned the promise of rain.

It was pretty here. And quiet except for the wind and birdsong.

Surrounded, I decided to stay a spell, knowing that when I left, I would remain sad and lonely, stubborn and jubilant, because even in exile we carry our places with us.

HALFALACHIAN

LISA LEWIS

Where There Are Mountains, There Must Be Valleys

THE MOUNTAINS I fled cast a shade over everything I must shine a light into. As a young woman, I rode horses up mountain trails, leading neophyte riders who had rented a horse for the afternoon through the beauty of the Blue Ridge I took for granted then. Once I even helped cut a trail through the North Carolina mountains. The wonder of that topography and that version of forest is that there are always openings in the darkness, slits of sun probing the leaf clutter like someone looking for a lost thing. I do that now when I write. I step into a small patch of light and it shines across the toe of my shoe and, if I'm lucky, into what I say, to myself and on the page.

It was in pursuit of writing, though, and a place for writers—Iowa City—that I left the mountains to begin with. I had already been away from the mountains for years when I found myself, a PhD student in Houston, waiting on the lightweight side of the desk in a small windowless faculty office for the famous visiting poet to comment on my work. I admired his poetry greatly though I hadn't read much of it yet, and I was anxious, happy, and expectant. The poet shuffled through the pages of the selection I'd submitted for our meeting and asked me something trivial, trying to make conversation. I replied. I was taciturn. Shy. He said, "Are your parents rural people?"

How often we must say innocent things, or things that seem innocent to us, anyway, which practically blowtorch those we speak to out of their chairs. It wasn't just the words but the poet's patrician tone that torched me in this case, coupled I guess to my knowledge of where he lived, which was always announced as part of his bio. Those who give their national addresses in their bio notes are making a point about something rubbing off, usually something expensive. I don't resent it that much. I react as I'm supposed to, faintly envious, faintly ashamed. But come on, who says "rural people"? Who asks that question in that voice? My address didn't have to be in my bio note. Apparently it was in my voice just as something else was in his. Rural! People! Parents! If only he had known—and if only I had—we might've had one heck of an interesting conversation instead of that pained moment in which I felt unmasked when I hadn't even known the mask was there, and who knows what he felt—boredom, probably. "No," I said. I meant to sound aggrieved, or something, and I was more or less convinced I was telling the truth, but on some level I had to know even then I wasn't.

Yes, my parents were "rural people." I mean, sort of. But I was closer to a multigenerational urban background than I knew, so if my later writing has manifested an obsession with that version of the past, what I wrote then treated only the first symptoms of a chronic unease. My father, whom I have never met, and who is by now old enough I expect him to be dead every time I check his Facebook page where I regularly stalk him, is not "rural." He was born in Washington, D.C., and raised there, and his own bio note, of which he also appears to be quite proud, describes his journeys to New York City and his lengthy career as a journalist rubbing elbows with the most important politicians in the United States. On his website there's a scanned-in note from Nixon praising him for his insights. My mother, the victim of what she described to me thirty-five years after my birth as "date rape"—a term that had only recently been coined—was, like her daughter after her, born in Roanoke, Virginia—which I imagined urban enough to disqualify me from the term "rural"; but unlike me—I was spared some horrors—she grew up mostly in Mullens, West Virginia.

And—I mean—oh, the photos! Nothing in the way she talked about those years would give away the shape of the houses in the background or of her knobby knees showing under those little shifts she wore. In many of the photos she is posing with a white German shepherd. She was a lifelong lover of dogs, as is, predictably enough, perhaps, my rapist nonrural father—and me too, of course. Is that genetic? Do the urban and the rural combine in the lover of dogs, equalized by the ones who make no such distinctions?

Somewhere out there on the Internet there's a funny video, "50 State Stereotypes in 2 Minutes." Virginia's is "From center of civilization to Hicksville in twenty minutes flat." My father was a student at the University of Virginia—itself cradled gorgeously in the ever-loving mist of the Blue Ridge—when my mother, twice his age, played piano there at a dance. For those who don't grasp the complexities of life thinking and writing—for those who use reductive language like "confessional" to describe what is ultimately as much or more a readerly attitude as a writerly one—I should point out here that I always feel like I'm making this up because she spoke so little about her time playing in that stupid "dance band." But her failure to foresee my future destiny as a writer aside, who wouldn't want to bury all that, even developing an aversion, as she did, to the piano in the living room which had been her sixteenth birthday present, since it must've seemed to her the worst mistake she ever made, getting her raped by that rich boy and changing her life?

Such is the punishment for women who step out of line: pregnancy will bring them back and keep them there. And then there's this hybrid who's Appalachian by birth and by voice but who somehow, strangely, seems not to realize that or accept it or understand it. Who is deeply surprised to hear the obvious spoken aloud to her face—that her voice gives away that she's "rural" in the ears of the cultured she aspires to be. And who now wonders about collapsing a hard-earned and presumably less rural writerly voice back into its Appalachian birthplace.

The famous poet that day, blandly throwing my inflections back into my face, probably had little reason to distinguish between the generic "rural" and the far more specific "Appalachian." But when I was growing up, miserably, in Roanoke, one of the most snobbish places I have yet to see, the effort to lift the idea of Roanoke away from the oft-invoked-with-utter-disdain "redneck" or "grit" was more or less endless. We who are in the face of something, there in the very shadow with it, tucked under the armpit of Mill Mountain and the whole weary rest of the monumental ancient ridge, go to some lengths to divide ourselves up in ways that allow us to retain the dignity we think we deserve. Virginia is Virginia! So what if it's about to fall over into the unlovely "southwest" of itself? All the more crucial to draw that line and belittle the wrong side of it. That showed among my friends and family; outside my group, of course, I was a marked girl, unbeknownst to myself. What I must've stood for there I probably still don't want to know. Yet prying into those questions has become the bone and flesh of my life's work, the shrinking-away-something to be pushed back into like a tunnel.

So this is my fundamental birth experience of my home place and my pedigree, such as it is, and what I think now about what it made me, or started to make me: a writer obsessed with dragging secrets out of shadow. You could draw it onto some graph of social class and privilege, throw in the contamination of confusion, so like the dark hollows and sharp curves on those mountain roads, and you'll have something I sometimes miss. But today that impulse to flee the time and place of early nightfall seems to me not quite possible and not quite worthwhile; it is not what I have done, only what I thought I was doing; it is not what has somehow saved me but what came along with me all this long time away when in fact, as I have come to understand, I resisted for reasons I have always wanted to resist: I was obedient to a design of shame. Under that expansive ridge that always looked to me like a giant's blanket carelessly thrown down, I looked out, not up, fearing what I would see.

There are always correspondences and none of them are good. Sometimes now late at night I turn on the TV and there's a program called *Moonshiners*. One night I watched, an old man told what he thought was a funny story about a moonshiner with a still in the trunk of his car driving 40 to Charlotte and daring a state trooper who pulled him over to look inside because he claimed he had a couple of expensive hunting dogs in there who would run away and then the trooper would owe him money. The old man cackled at the punch line—predictably, that the trooper did open the trunk and of course there was a still in there—and then we, the national audience safe and sound anywhere but there, were watching some much younger people, a whole family, wholesome in their wholeness, tending a still on a mountainside that must've been somewhere around Lenoir, North Carolina, site of my later and more troubled adolescence.

Talk about shadowy. Talk about moonshine!

I remember the night some friends and I parked on a logging road—we were always parked on a logging road, though the trees were intact—and though we usually had some drugs to do, at least some pot to smoke, that night we didn't but had driven there out of boredom and habit anyway; and we saw what I still think must've been UFOs—flitting red dashes of light above the mountaintops, moving at speeds nothing else could move. We dared them to come to us as if we were that moonshiner in the story I wouldn't hear for forty years and they were state troopers, who for once we had no reason to fear because we were empty-handed of anything but our ignorant young selves—or at least we thought we were, though if an actual state trooper had found us there, he would have found reason to punish us somehow. It was a country of punishment after all. UFOs darting like water drops on a hot griddle seemed friendly by comparison.

The darkness I found in Caldwell County, North Carolina, would be the darkest of my life, at least until my marriage—another story, though sometimes also tainted by my association with the Blue Ridge, since my husband folded it into his general contempt for me. I tried to show contempt back, but can you be convincingly contemptuous of anything or anywhere if you've grown up in shadow and drunk more moonshine than you've seen, even been arrested for an act of derring-do performed in a field where, for once, trees had in fact been cut down to their stumps, a kind of midnight obstacle course for a girl who an hour before had been chasing white lightning from a gallon jug with grape Kool-Aid stirred for the sleeping children of a friend? Probably not, which is why folk from the Appalachians are forever depicted as telling inane tales and laughing too hard, as funny to others as their scorn would be effectively shaming. No, we are shame ourselves; we are the living punch lines; somewhere someone sucks on a corncob pipe and guffaws.

There are always correspondences and none of them are good—unless they can be stitched together in the haphazard guilty quilt of narrative. A story circulating on Facebook some weeks ago featured a photo of someone described as a Brazilian chieftain of the Kayapo tribe. One must doubt these things, but from what I've been able to discern, the only inaccuracy about the photo is that I saw it as if it were breaking news a year after it originally appeared—and an accompanying warning about the president of Brazil having just signed a law allowing the construction of a dam, the Belo Monte, that would flood the villages of that chieftain and many others, allegedly displacing forty thousand indigenous people. The chieftain is weeping; another man is bending as if to comfort him. Once my grandfather wept like that—maybe more than once, but I saw it once.

We were taking a drive on a Sunday afternoon to see Smith Mountain Lake, which, according to some materials I've looked at, reached "full pond" level in 1966, when I was ten. So though I don't recall the conversation preceding our outing, it seems likely that we were going to survey the finished product, its original construction having begun in 1960—the damming of the Roanoke and Blackwater Rivers to create a lake that became very popular for recreation, as lakes do, and the electricity that probably kept the lights on at my house and all the others in the surrounding area. On the map one can see that Smith Mountain Dam occurs at a spot roughly between Bedford, Franklin, and Pittsylvania Counties in Appalachian Virginia. My grandfather grew up on a farm in Bedford County, and, not unlike the old storyteller on *Moonshiners*, devoted much narrative energy to charming and usually amusing tales of run-ins with various rural troublemakers. But a mule who kicked him over a stump featured more prominently in the versions I heard than any kind of government representative.

Anyway, Smith Mountain Lake covers thirty-two square miles, and, as the relevant Wikipedia entry puts it, "Before the lake's creation, farming and logging were the primary industries." Farming and logging—from what I heard about that farm in Bedford County, the one the government took and my grandfather wept for that Sunday he saw the wide, wide water that buried it and everything he remembered, "industry" seemed a word from a language irrelevant to his. But what other word is there for a straight-faced historical account of what gets swept aside? The people must've seemed hardly there at all, and there was no Internet on which to circulate a photograph of a man weeping. And the people there in the Appalachians—the ones in the places where enough of them gathered to become visible—needed electricity too, needed it more than they needed a swath of valley with a mule or two and the stumps leftover from logging, or at least that became the opinion that mattered.

I read now on a real estate website that the early development around the lake was mostly trailer parks, but during the 1980s started to become more upscale. No surprises there. And I do remember those trailer parks, at least the ones I saw on one later drive with my mother to Smith Mountain Lake, my grandfather not along that time—he never went anywhere near it again. I especially remember my mother's bitter satisfaction that the area surrounding the lake looked so trashy. But how could anyone be satisfied that what had made my grandfather cry like a Brazilian Indian was only trailer parks and electricity, that invisible thing, invisible as he was—as we were—but much more powerful? We had lights before. I know that's what the people who didn't want the dam thought, and if anyone had been able to invent solar energy then, or wind energy, maybe that valley would've stayed dry. Of course it's invented now, but the mountains in West Virginia suffer as the valleys in Virginia did then. Some of them resemble moonscapes, laid bare to the sun in a way no one who lived there would've believed possible before the tops were taken away for the sake of power—the power of money, the power of jobs, the power of keeping the lights on. I partake of my family's bitterness when I see those photos. And I think I hate those "upscale" people with fine houses at Smith Mountain Lake. How nice for them, to be latecomers to a scene they never had to know was quiet carnage. Of course—of course—I could say that of us all.

Yet one difference is—of course—that the weeping Brazilian chieftain reduced to a "meme" on Facebook is an example of what happens to "indigenous people," and my grandfather is not exactly indigenous—though the outcome seems more or less the same, at least in terms of how the two of them must've seen and felt the loss of those lands. The bones of one's ancestors either underwater or disrupted, moved to higher ground—and it occurs to me now that I don't even know where my grandfather was buried.

I know he and my grandmother bought burial plots somewhere in Roanoke, and that quite a fuss was made about those plots; they were expensive and they represented something about social standing that my grandparents wanted, but I think they were both buried in Lenoir instead, since they both died there, having been forced there by my mother's marriage to a man who made his home there after growing up, as she had, in Mullens, West Virginia, and their own infirmity and need to be cared for as they aged. What those four shared was the general plan not to stay where they began, though my grandparents surely wanted to stay in Roanoke; the Brazilian chieftain most likely wants nothing more than to stay where he began, though already he may have changed his mind. Humans are adaptable like that.

I think of how I loved to skip school those years in Lenoir and drive up Blowing Rock Mountain with my equally naughty friends, smoking pot, the sunshine lighting up the valley we didn't dare look into long. We didn't dare stop at the overlooks either, lest the ubiquitous state troopers find us there, and we didn't have the money to pay to go into the park at the top of the mountain, but we knew the myth because the logo on the signs told it—a woman standing on the rock and a man (though at the time I thought it was a child) being blown up to her from below. It's said to be an Indian myth. There haven't been many Indians around Blowing Rock in a long, long time. But maybe I could blow back up the rock like that—though what I've also heard is that in practice you can't hope to see the wind return anything to you once you drop it off the rock, except maybe a scarf. Someone said, I'm sure, that if you so much as tie a knot in the scarf it's gone.

In my childhood home the very pronunciation of the word "Appa-lachian" was such a matter of contention that it often seemed better not to speak it at all. Was it Appa-latch-un? Was it Appa-lay-chun? Only a fool would say the latter, I learned; only someone who didn't know; but there was a feeling of resistance to being named at all. We were either citizens of the world—a phrase no one in that house would've used, and maybe it hadn't even been invented yet—or we didn't exist, and who would want to exist if all they could see, stepping away from themselves, was this history of being displaced or used?

The dam comes and you must go.

The railroad comes and you must serve it; you go where it goes because you go where the coal goes, and you consider yourself lucky that you only see it roll by in a car, not hew it out of the rock with your own hands. Its dust blackens the curtains. The sun sets early outside and begins late; all your days begin in blackness. I got out—after going to college in my own backyard, not Roanoke or Lenoir but unlovely Bristol, where the coal cars also ran, and not even knowing it then, my world was so small.

But the trouble with being not just of "rural people" but of raped, displaced Appalachian people is that you are bound to be found out at every turn as the right kind of person for using up or pushing out but not for writing about it. So I didn't—but so I do.

I have driven back there to the once-unspeakable places a time or two. And what I saw was so much poisonous beauty—poisonous because it was always there and I never even knew. I stood at the top of the hill on Broadway Avenue, in Roanoke, on the sidewalk in front of my childhood home, studying the yard my grandparents planted with dogwood and azalea that was now a small apartment building, the flat one-storey kind with tiny efficiencies and a miniature parking lot in front—and the Blue Ridge arched its back in my face, a mountain landscape the color of shadow and sadness all sunlit and gorgeous, and suddenly I was like those tourists we used to laugh at, license plates from New York or some other place Virginians liked to think was no match for our piece of heaven on earth, those idiots who drove to Roanoke every fall and clogged our streets with their stupid traffic, just to see leaves! What a joke they were.

What a joke *I* was not to have seen what was there—only to have seen that I was somehow set apart, even from the people who lived around me, the children I went to school with. And in some way it was true—most of those children seemed to live lives of apparent peace and safety. If any of them were illegitimate children of wealthy rapists, it certainly didn't show. If any of them were daughters of women who somehow managed to believe that they could be traveling dance band musicians in the 1950s without being made to suffer for it—well, they weren't. Their fathers mowed the lawns and later ran for governor of Virginia. Their fathers were right there. Their fathers were doctors or businessmen. They paid the bills. We imitated them as best we could. My grandfather was a railroad man who worked the second shift and came home smelling of metal and coal and slept all day and once I saw him cry at a shimmering valley of water.

And Lenoir—where my only pleasures came in plastic bags and couldn't be had without a needle and as little blood as you could find the skill in your shaking hands not to spill—it honestly will take your breath away if you come to it fresh, on your own wheels and your own dime, your own piece of freedom you work for, the need to see again, to speak, no longer in a silent rage at the hands of parental force itself gone terribly wrong. Looking at it again on my trip back, driving the streets that seemed to me then only to lead to the stained brick caverns I worked in sometimes, the furniture factories where the unfortunate lopped off fingers and thumbs and inhaled enough dark glaze to drown in cancer, I could see I almost knew even then about the other views—the vista off 321 up Blowing Rock Mountain, just for starters, and that secret place we called Crystal Pool, miles and miles into the mountains on dirt roads where we sometimes went and sometimes someone, not me because I couldn't swim, stripped naked under the influence of a drug called MDA and dived into water that might've been bursting in golden flowers, though more than that I remember finding the bodies of frogs along the banks, their legs chopped off, and realizing that our secret place wasn't as secret as I thought. I don't think I could find that body of water now. I'm probably glad, because I know what America has let happen to all her beauties: they've gone upscale, for the sake of power.

And now I mostly travel on the wireless wings that bring me to photographs I never would've seen otherwise and bland sentences kicking dirt onto the graves of people I never knew, but I am their offspring nonetheless. I disapprove, but it doesn't change anything.

I often think that I have been able to make myself more or less at home for the eighteen years I've taught in Oklahoma because at least here you can see what's coming at you, tornado or trouble of some human kind. But that's not the truth, exactly, about why it's somehow a relief to me not to have mountains in my eyes. I lived in valleys, mostly, because that's the way there—either you hang off the side of something or you stand below it and gaze up or across. Despite all the changes driven by American beliefs about prosperity and economy that have made every lovely landscape the likely prey of anybody with a blueprint for a vacation mansion, it will take more than mountaintop removal mining to change those fundamental matters of perspective.

A month ago I submitted a proposal for money for a trip back to Lenoir just to look at it, and then to write. Because it's an academic proposal, and "looking at" places to make the past return in words is not what academics generally understand as what should be done in the name and on the dime of research, I fully anticipate that my wish will not be granted. I will go, if I go, the way my grandfather moved from Bedford County to Roanoke to Mullens and back, and my grandmother left tiny Elliston, where her father molested a little girl who lived down the road and all the daughters used real rags for their menstrual blood, and my mother fled Charlottesville pregnant with me. I will pay, and I will keep on paying, and writing about it, or from it, or away from it, or in flight directly down its rhododendron-spotted throat because I will be what I have avoided all my life and what I have never been able to avoid—a kind of crossbreed, a fusion or blend in all-mixed-up love and hate with the backcountry in me.

AARON SMITH
For Better or Worse, This Was My Country

I HAVE THE kind of relationship with West Virginia that most people have with their mothers: I can talk shit about her, but *you'd* better watch your mouth. My family moved to West Virginia when I was less than a year old, and I lived there until I was twenty-one. We lived close to the Ohio River and were roughly an hour's drive from the three major "cities": Charleston, Huntington, and Parkersburg. Needless to say, my parents rarely wanted to drive an hour to go shopping or to see a movie, so I spent a lot of days wandering the woods or swimming in our aboveground pool.

What I really wanted, though I couldn't name it then, was the freedom that I associated with cities. I guess it makes sense that as a grown-up I came to think of myself as a gay writer who writes mostly about urban landscapes—Pittsburgh, Boston, and New York City. I think of Frank O'Hara's lines from "Meditations in an Emergency": "I can't even enjoy a blade of grass unless I know there's a subway handy, or a / record store or some other sign that people do not totally regret life." When I started to think about being an Appalachian writer, my first thought was: That's not really who I am. Like many, I bought into the notion that for writing to be considered Appalachian it must be concerned with trees or certain narrow stereotypes such as salt-of-the-earth mountain "folks." But as I started looking through the books I've written, I realized that *my* West Virginia is very much between the pages.

When I left West Virginia in 1996, my intention was to never go back. I visited my born-again parents a few times a year, but mostly I felt like I had escaped (and was happy about it). After each visit, I looked forward to that moment of getting back onto Interstate 77. If I were driving home, say, to Pittsburgh, I looked forward to watching the poisonous smokestack of the aluminum plant where my father worked (the plant I believe gave my grandfather and so many other men in our neighborhood cancer) get smaller with each mile I drove north. For the years I lived in New York City or Boston, I flew out of Charleston and loved how the gold dome of the Capitol building sank beneath the clouds like a lost coin. So you can imagine my surprise when I found myself moving into an apartment in Buckhannon, West Virginia, in the summer of 2008.

I was dying at a desk job in New York City and the dean of my alma mater, West Virginia Wesleyan College, offered me a position as a visiting assistant professor of English. My first thought was: *No, I'm fine, thanks. I'd rather stay where I can have sex and Thai food.* I feared having only a Walmart and fourteen fast-food restaurants in the town where I would live. I knew I'd have to drive Interstate 79 forty minutes to get to the Target in Clarksburg, or travel more than an hour to shop at the only worthwhile bookstore in Morgantown. I had friends in Pittsburgh I could visit if I was willing to make the two-and-a-half-hour trip. (I tried not to even think about the challenge of meeting other gay men.) But like many writers, I was intrigued by the possibility of teaching and thought this was a good opportunity. I reminded myself that I'd spent four years in that town as an undergraduate. How bad could it be?

After seven years, I left the place that I loved most, the place I'd always wanted to live, a place where buildings replace sky and twilight is more brilliantly lit than any rural evening, and moved back to what I refer to as the "scene of the crime." I've always said that I wanted so badly to leave West Virginia that I never bothered to learn the name of anything. (I can't tell the difference between an oak tree and a maple.) I also never felt like I could be happily queer in West Virginia. I believe it's because the scenery there was the backdrop for some of my greatest sadness.

I thought I'd stay for one year, and I ended up staying for five. Yes, the job market in teaching is terrible, but I can't say that's the only reason I stayed. I think I stayed so long because I needed to figure something out. I needed to settle into my head, which I found extremely difficult to do when I lived in New York (part of the reason I stayed there so long). I think ultimately I needed to understand what the place where I grew up meant to me. I needed to understand (make peace with?) its lasting effect on my life both as a writer and as a gay person.

What I learned is that West Virginia, for me, is about resistance. It's what I struggled to break free from, but it's also, I think, what pushed me to try harder, to ask for more. The stubborn independence that people in West Virginia pride themselves on is, oddly, what I believe allowed me to hate the state as much as I appreciate it. It made it okay for me to refuse to pretend that life there was as beautiful for me as the landscape across Route 50. For me to claim West Virginia in my writing means to use the parts I like (such as the direct, honest language of the people I grew up around) and to reject the parts that rejected me (like fundamentalist Christianity), the parts that compelled me to leave. Paul Monette says in *Becoming a Man*, his memoir about growing up gay in a small town in Massachusetts: "I knew I had to leave or I'd be torn apart by wolves." I relate to this statement and wonder who I would have become had I not left.

What I consider to be both gay and Appalachian in my work may be claimed by others—who did not grow up gay or in Appalachia—as part of their childhood and writing life as well. People in Montana hunt, too. Gay kids in Chicago are harassed in gym class. Paul Monette had to get out of Andover just as I felt I had to flee Cottageville. But just as I'm unable to unlink my sexuality from West Virginia, I'm also unable to unlink my obsessions from West Virginia. I guess what I'm getting at is that for me, being a West Virginia writer is more than landscape; it's more than writing a poem set in Buckhannon or Beckley, or writing a poem in awe of mountains (though I've read some great ones). Was it my sexuality alone that compelled me to leave West Virginia? Would I have wanted to leave so badly had I not been gay? Probably. My sister is heterosexual and fled the state with the same ferocity as I did. But it's impossible for me to unlink my sexuality from the landscape, fundamentalist Christianity, and objects of a West Virginia childhood, and since I'm a poet who mines the personal for material, my relationship with West Virginia, and what I consider to be Appalachian—whether I'm living there or not—is ongoing.

To me, West Virginia is men with dirty hands who will pull your car out of a ditch. West Virginia is a lust for those same men that is as thrilling as it is shameful. It's a lifetime of unlearning that shame.

West Virginia is a home with a radio or television constantly on. It's an obsession with shirtless men on TV. It's tabloids. It's the Bible. It's gospel music with close harmonies. It's a judgmental god and a hell as real as the trees outside. It's learning to believe in nothing and being lonelier because of it. It's romanticizing cities. It's renting *Moonstruck* at Carolyn's Video and Tanning three times one summer (and my mom still not wanting to believe I was gay). It's pickup trucks and my mother's arms scarred from burns from cooking at the elementary school. It's colloquial language. It's low-class, but dignified. It's honest. It's direct. It's talking about the things I'm not supposed to talk about because: fuck you. It's wanting to get out. It's getting out. It's going back. To claim Appalachia in my work is to say that West Virginia is where I learned and unlearned values; it's where I found my obsessions. In their totality they form an aesthetic that feels West Virginian.

THE WEST Virginia writer Mary Lee Settle writes in her novel *Charley Bland*:

> For better or for worse, this was my country, and I could not let it go until it blessed me. What form that blessing would take I did not know yet. I only knew that when it came I would recognize it through its disguises. It is this that keeps poets in their countries through namelessness, doors closing, hungers, and there are many kinds, until they are forced to abandon home, which can, in itself, become a blessing.

In the summer of 2013 I left West Virginia again. I took a job at Lesley University in Cambridge, Massachusetts. (Maybe the going out, the coming back, and the going back out is also Appalachian?) But what I took with me this time was different than what I took last time. The first time I ran, annihilating everything—family, friends, religion—that tried to stop me. I carried my shame and anger like a weapon I used mostly against myself. This last time, though, I left happy, with my *blessing*, if you will, with the understanding I had desired of knowing what West Virginia means to me, both creatively and personally. It's a history, a past (and, until recently, a present) that I'll always grapple with. It is both art and the opposite of art. It is being loved and unloved, or being strangely loved. It's a state of exile when I'm not living there, but it's a state of not quite fitting in when I am.

MARY CROCKETT HILL
Confessions of a Halfalachian

THE MEMBERS OF my family are all in our standard movie-watching positions: husband in a recliner, remote control in hand; dog licking her tenders at his feet; twins in a heap on the carpet; daughter on the couch, socked feet propped on a huge stuffed turtle; me on the daybed, notebook open but ignored on my lap, the baby conked out by my side.

We're watching *John Carter* and it's getting serious. John's beloved princess is about to be forced into marriage with a power-mad warmonger. In an elaborate procession, the princess is being carted through the streets of a Martian city, convinced that John has returned to Earth and there's nothing for her to do but wed her enemy. Meanwhile, an evil monk-looking dude is holding John captive on an overpass of the very same city. John makes a desperate attempt to attract the princess's attention as she passes through the street below. He needs her to know that he hasn't left Mars, but alas, he cannot speak.

At the exact same instant, my husband and I shout the obvious solution at the TV: "SPIT ON HER!"

I crack up. "What do you suppose it means," I ask him, "that both you and I think spitting is the best way to get someone's attention?"

"I don't know." He cocks an eyebrow. "We must be from Appalachia."

He was being facetious, of course, but it got me thinking.

We genuinely *are* from Appalachia, but I didn't always identify myself as "Appalachian" exactly. I was reared in a small city in southwestern Virginia. While my hometown might have had a good dose of hick to it, there were more keep-your-bullet-in-your-pocket Barney Fifes than banjo-plucking, jug-puffing, rifle-toting Darlings.

True, my mother did store moonshine in a mason jar tucked behind her silver goblets in the dining room cupboard, but I always suspected that to be an affectation on her part. She had an odd sense of humor and that was her sort of joke, as if she were playing hillbilly and speakeasy ne'er-do-well, all rolled into one. Plus, moonshine has "medicinal value" according to Mama. (Yes, we did call her "Mama," and yes, she occasionally did swig a bit for "medicine.")

As a girl during the Depression, she collected dandelions for wine and helped butcher groundhogs on her uncle's back porch. Yet during my own girlhood she cooked ratatouille, baba ghanoush, and homemade pizza topped with weird stuff like eggplant and green beans. She was not the bonnet-topped mother who stirred a cast-iron pot over the open fire, but she did wrap her hair in scarves (and on more than one occasion, boys' underwear) when she baked bread in our old woodstove, which she dubbed, for some inexplicable reason, "Miss Maloney."

Meanwhile, my father—whose family hailed from a cove way in the backwoods of Wythe County, Virginia—wore ascots, white suits that would make Truman Capote blush, and for at least one embarrassing summer, a horrendous black wig. He, who by rights should have been as hick as they come, wrote papers on Gerard Manley Hopkins and published a prize-winning poem in the *Atlantic Monthly*.

We were rednecks who went to the opera. White trash who ate pâté.

So, what do you do with that kind of paradoxical culture—half French poodle, half groundhog?

I suppose these are the answers I've come up with:

As a girl, you let it confuse you.

As a young woman, you put it behind you.

As a mother, you accept it back into yourself.

As a poet, you take the lines it offers.

The girl and young woman parts of the above equations are pretty self-explanatory. (Whose childhood doesn't confuse her? Whose young adulthood doesn't at least metaphorically skip the light fandango out of town?) So let me speak instead for a moment on the last two variables: motherhood and poetry. And since as both mother and poet I don't feel constrained by the expected placement of things, I will do so in reverse order.

POETRY IS an art of contradiction. In its best moments, it pulls language taut. And nothing creates tension like meaning being stretched in two directions at once. What is the line break, after all, but the opportunity to suspend and redirect understanding? Perhaps this is not the way poetry is meant to be read, but this is the way I read poetry: one line as a poem entire; revised by the next, which is itself also a poem entire; and the two lines together as another little poem; and so on. When all those little poems within a single poem have radically contradictory meanings . . . ah, *wild nights!* I never love a line better than when it is saying two opposite and equally true things in the same breath.

Perhaps my conflicted Appalachian upbringing prepared me for this poetic landscape, where one plus one plus one equals anything but three. In both I have learned to savor the rightness of ideas that don't exactly fit—lines that rub against expectations with bald elbows and knees. I have learned, when knocked on my head, not to right myself immediately, but to take a minute and appreciate the view.

But then there's motherhood, which also has a tendency to knock me on my head. How does motherhood clarify my writing life?

Well for one, no other act has brought me so close to my own birth as that of birthing other little creatures into this world. I cannot be some spit-shined version of myself. There is no pretending here. In motherhood, I am inescapably the one I always was—the words of my mother everywhere in my mouth. Though I've learned when necessary to cloak my southern twang in the flatline intonations of a midwestern weatherman, the language itself has a way of jagging out. It is a weatherman speaking of "rain abrewing."

The words of course were there, but it is motherhood that has caused me to notice them. As my children find their own voices, I hear my crazy mix-and-morph language echo back in their blurry first words. When they speak some random mountainism—"dadburn" or "yep" or "alrighty"—I ask myself where they picked that up. But truth told, I already know. Their words are my words, the words of my mother, the words of our culture. The words we have.

AND THAT, friends, is both the blessing and the curse of being Appalachian. (Or perhaps in my case I should use some hybrid moniker to reflect my hokey-pokeyish one-toe-in/one-toe-out upbringing? App*aurban*? *Half*alachian?) The words of the mountains might label me as hick, but they are mine. They speak of origins and growth—connecting me to both a past and a future that stretches well beyond my own concerns.

When my mother died earlier this year, I was left with too much grief and too little of her physical self. She had been the defining presence in my life, but I had only a grab bag of random images: the flash of a gesture, her face rising into a smile, her eyes peering impishly over her glasses, her long thin hair. But what remains most solid to me is something that ironically was never solid in the first place, her words.

It was her words my brothers and sisters remembered together during the days following her death and burial. My sister Luella said she wanted to think of my mother, who was a great reader, whenever she opened a book, so we made a list of some of Mama's sayings—both mountainisms and those peculiar to herself—and printed them on bookmarks. And because a fortune-teller had long ago told us that our mother was the reincarnation of Benjamin Franklin, we called it Poor Nedra's Almanac.

It's the same old six and seven. . . . You gotta spell ABLE first. . . . I'm cleaning the house with flowers. . . . When Heck was a pup. . . . See, the whole thing of it was. . . . It's brain-food. . . . I'm journey proud. . . . If you hurt my daughter, I'll crick your neck. . . . We're going 'round the pumpkin vine. . . . Eat a banana. . . . Amen, brother Ben!

I once had a teacher suggest that I edit "Dagnabit!" out of a poem in which a drunk man chases hikers off a mountain because, of course, nobody really talks like that. The same teacher told me in reference to a different poem that I couldn't possibly know a groundhog has the capacity to lie low, pointedly pretending to ignore human presence in hopes it won't become a threat. I love and respect this teacher, but I also have heard people say "Dagnabit!" all my life, and on multiple occasions observed a groundhog lying low. I suppose I could have responded with the punch line from a neighborhood joke: "You ain't from around here." (This to be said while cleaning dirt from beneath one's fingernails with the tip of a Bowie knife.) But then again, he genuinely *isn't* from around here, and that would strip all the humor out of what was a pretty lame joke to begin with. While his comments were valid, I like to think that the world of poetry is big enough for an occasional goofy exclamation or supposition about groundhog psychology. They are true to my experience, and so—even if considered by most readers as absurd or out of touch—should I silence them?

I guess my record on that score is 50/50. I cut the exclamation but kept the groundhog, mainly because the respective poems worked fine in my opinion without the one but not the other. I'd be lying, though, if I didn't admit that some small part of me also worried that the "Dagnabit!" line was a bit over-the-top. I'm thankful for my heritage; it has made me the person I am. But it is often socially easier to accentuate my nonhick side when need be. I guess you could call it "passing." After all, what culture in the current age of hypersensitive political correctness is it still acceptable to mock? Hillbillies, of course. The same person who would never think of making a rude remark about someone else's race or religion has no problem telling a West Virginia joke. And even the most soft-bellied tween sitcom will eventually run an episode in which someone dresses up in overalls and says stupid things with a backwoods accent.

This is not to say Appalachian culture isn't funny. We are lovers of the exaggerated, the unexpected, the ironic, the self-deprecating, the wry. There's nothing so healing as laughing at yourself and the folks around you. Of course, that attitude presupposes there's something which needs healing—not a stretch for Appalachia, where a long, sad tale (poverty, drug abuse, isolation, environmental exploitation, inadequate health care, and on and on) tatters like a ribbon in the breeze. The problems are real, but so is the humor. In my experience, we will laugh for the relief of it at those very moments we feel some tragedy tugging at our pants legs. When my sister and I took my mother to the emergency room with heart failure on Christmas morning a few years back, we sat by her bed in the examination room, our chests gripped with worry, our minds numb. But we smiled, and for her sake—for all our sakes—we cut up and kidded one another, as if our silliness might set her heart right. We put to practice the tradition long held in my family of looking loss in the face and calling it a lark. Or to quote my mother, the indomitable Dr. Franklin, "It's better to laugh than cry."

This practice is something, like language, I see myself passing on to my children, whether intentionally or not. And like language, it stretches both before and after my own use for it. My kids don't know how to spin wool or stitch a quilt, but they can talk funny and laugh at themselves, even when some sad thing puddles under their feet. Not much of an inheritance, but it could be worse. At least, should they ever find themselves held hostage on an overpass while their true loves pass below, they'll have sense enough to spit.

ROB AMBERG

Photographing the Forbidden

A COUPLE OF years ago on a July evening, I was walking with my dogs on the road below our house, one of the few remaining dirt roads in the county. The walk has been a regular part of my routine for twenty-five years. I heard a truck coming up behind me and glanced back to see our neighborhood thug, who had just been released from jail after serving a term for breaking and entering and threatening his neighbors. As he inched alongside me, slowing his truck to keep pace with me, he looked over my clothing—shorts, T-shirt, white socks and sneakers—and said, his breath liquored, "Are ye out fer yer little walk tonight, mister?" before driving off in a cloud of dust.

The encounter was a clear reminder that *I ain't from around here*. It was meant to belittle, to threaten, and to proclaim superiority. It left me feeling both vulnerable and sad, with a queasy stomach and shaky hands. Local friends suggested I carry a gun. One, a cop, when told of the incident, remarked, "There's another one that just needs killing."

It wasn't the first time I'd been made to feel like the outsider. For years after moving here, *my* accent, mannerisms, and way of thinking precluded many locals from taking me, or other newcomers, seriously. We were easy enough to stereotype as lazy hippies, rich kids, smart with no common sense, dope and sex fiends. For many locals, we were the forbidden, no less a threat to their culture and livelihoods than my neighbor's thuggish persona was to mine. While that attitude has largely changed over time and through personal contact, there will always be born-in-county residents for whom I will always be an outsider.

BEING AN outsider comes to me easily and readily. As I look back over a lifetime, I see there's always been a distance, looking from the outside in, never quite fully entering the room. I've been involved with friends, family, and community, and those relationships have been long-lasting and committed. But I also recognize my ability to turn inward where I can experience life from the safety and warmth of my own dark places. It's the side of me that is shy, insecure, and self-doubting—an awkward core that steals glimpses and questions motivations, wanting to fit in, but knowing I never will. This fundamental temper of mind, that of the outsider, plays an active role in my life—what I do, where I live, and whom I spend time with.

I grew up a suburban kid, a sheltered Baby Boomer, the first grandson of Italian immigrants, and part of the expanding post–World War II middle class outside of Washington, D.C. It was a comfortable childhood. I received a good education and had a loving and attentive family. We weren't well off, but I don't recall feeling insecure or deprived. We had money to take vacations to Florida beaches and through North Carolina and the Smoky Mountains. What I remember of those trips back in the 1950s and 1960s is a reality I knew little about—small towns, people working in fields, strange accents, and open landscapes. These places and people intrigued me—the attraction of the other, no doubt—and I wanted to know more and somehow *experience* that otherness. But the real joy for me was in the looking, capturing moments of clarity through the blur of a speeding windshield, and imprinting those images on my mind.

Later in college, I did a report for a psychology class that involved a slide/tape presentation that, as I remember it, was a scattered and incoherent affair. The instructor rewarded me with a good grade for the sheer immensity of my effort. But I did love making the photographs and the process of joining the pictures with music. I have a memory of that first experience with a good camera. How it felt in my hands. The weight of it. There was something primal and powerful about the physical object and the control it promised. I loved the camera's ability to render detail, catch light, and stop time. The way it framed its subjects. And its absolute need for an external reality—some *thing* to photograph. For me, that some*thing* would always be people, culture, and the human condition. The camera provided an uneasy access to prohibited places, an opportunity to be with people

I'd had no reason to know. And I could accomplish this from behind a lens, looking in from the outside, only as involved as I wanted to be.

While living in Tucson, Arizona, I took a basic photography course at the local Arts Council. One evening, I brought to class a portfolio of photographs I had made in a local park—photographs of people hanging out, some preaching, some drinking, some being old. The instructor asked me why I was hiding in the bushes with a telephoto lens when I could engage people face to face, in a more honest and open manner. The answer made the question hard—I was scared, and embarrassed. I didn't know how to interact with people different from me and didn't know how to explain my interest in photographing them. I could hardly explain it to myself. That critique, early in my photography career, changed my way of making pictures.

WHAT MY teacher categorized as "hiding in the bushes," students I worked with this past summer called "creeping." And there is something decidedly creepy and voycuristic about the photographic act itself, even without hiding in the bushes. It has to do with a photographer's proficiency, perhaps obsession, at turning living, breathing space and people into a still life, an object of art, or a document holding evidence. Photographers constantly look, even when not carrying a camera, measuring light, watching gestures and expressions, and searching for detail. We are like a banjo player unknowingly picking tunes on the kitchen table with no banjo in sight. It's instinctual, a way to frame the world while providing a buffer to that world—a way to be an insider, but remain the outsider.

I'm thinking here of what I do—social documentary and personal narrative—the type of photography that concerns itself with picturing the real world, as vague, ambivalent, and intimate as that real world might be. Photography has become ubiquitous in our lives; nothing is off limits. With access, photographers are able to make pictures in the most forbidden of places and then, in turn, provide access to those taboos for viewers. They act as bridges between disparate worlds.

But what gives me, or any photographer, the right to make representations of other "real" people? What special dispensation allows me to decide how a person or a scene is remembered? Some indigenous cultures believe a photograph steals a person's soul, a thought that seems primitive and naïve in our modern world. But those peoples are right to be concerned. Photographers don't necessarily want to steal someone's soul and take it away when a photograph is made. But they do want to *capture* that soul, and preserve that essence for themselves and for others who often have no connection at all to the reality pictured. There is arrogance in believing you have the right to perform this unsanctioned act—to steal, or capture, a person's soul and then display it as truth.

I'M A person who doesn't know a stranger and can find common ground with most anyone. This ability to connect—to give the appearance of being an insider and part of the scene—has served me well as a photographer and writer. I've often said if I have a gift, this is it. It has helped my photographs be more about trust and dialogue than confrontation or acquisition. But it also can be a manipulative tool—one that gives me control over situations, allowing me to get the image or the story I want. A friend of mine defined flirtation as a promise of sex, but not a guarantee. Photography can be like that—the promise of connection and common ground, but not a guarantee beyond my getting the image.

Images first brought me to the mountains. Like many boys of my generation, I was fascinated by the lives of Davy Crockett and Daniel Boone. Seeking common ground even then, I had a coonskin cap *and* a rubber tomahawk. I believed the region's people to be as Walt Disney rendered them—heroic, brave, and romantic. So, in 1973, when I moved to Madison County, North Carolina, those stereotypes accompanied me and were what I looked for when I arrived. At that time, those real-world stereotypes—the wrinkled and wizened faces, old women in doorways, and misty mountains—were easy enough to find, and I photographed many of them.

Over time, I began to realize how much of this place I was failing to see, or choosing to ignore. While I was homed in on the romance of the place, the other extreme of the Appalachian stereotype—the clannishness, violence, poverty, and abuse—was also on full display. Many residents, despite their professed fealty to the mountains, blatantly disregarded the land itself, evidenced by straight-piping waste into creeks, trash piles on the sides of roads, and serious erosion from clear-cuts and overuse of chemicals. Ours was one of the ten poorest counties in the state, with a high rate of high school dropouts. The year before my arrival, a young female VISTA worker had been brutally murdered in a remote section of the county, and later, a man was sent to prison for poisoning his young daughter with herbicide.

There were other dynamics in Madison I was missing. Many county natives fit no discernible stereotype. They included teachers, bankers, businessmen, and farmers. They played golf, mowed their lawns, and went to church—more suburban and middle class than my family back in Maryland. By the time of my relocation in the early 1970s, hundreds of new people—retirees, young professionals, artists, Latino immigrants, and back-to-the-landers—had started moving into the county, buying property, raising families, and carving niches. It was not the place I originally imagined it to be.

I've lived in Madison County for forty years now. For most of that time, I've thought of myself as a participant/observer. My desire to live in and fully experience the mountain lifestyle has coexisted with my need to photograph it. Working with firewood, springwater, gardens, animals, and farm maintenance produces tangible results— heat, hydration, food, and stewardship of the land—and offer a counterbalance to the fleeting nature of images on paper or screen.

Helping neighbors with their tobacco, raising children in the county, attending funerals and wakes, and playing a role in community functions all link me to place in an active way that goes far beyond simple observation while providing access for my photography.

The duality can be problematic and can leave me feeling foreign in both worlds. If my role as an observer depends on my being a participant, then certainly the opposite is equally true. My role as a participant includes being the observer. I straddle two identities—that of the community member, chainsaw in hand, ready to dance or help a neighbor, who likes nothing more than to visit—and that of the outlier, the guy who makes 'em pictures, writes 'em books, and holes-up on the mountain.

I DON'T ignore stereotypes, because they exist in real life—at least, they exist in the world I live in. I don't place any particular emphasis on them, but choose to see them as part of the whole. Understanding Madison County, living in it, and documenting it as the traditional, yet evolving community it is—inclusive of a broad diversity of people and ideas, rather than one simply fixed in time—has been an ongoing learning process. And often, people don't want to be reminded of, or want outsiders to see, those parts of themselves deemed to be less than perfect, or unsavory. Thus, Madison County, which has been nicknamed *Bloody Madison* since a brutal massacre of thirteen Union sympathizers during the Civil War, a moniker punctuated over the years by acts of random and family violence, has been reborn as *The Jewel of the Blue Ridge* in an effort to make the county more acceptable. For me, choosing to see and acknowledge forbidden details for the ongoing reality they are becomes a balancing act between community self-image and values on the one hand, and historical honesty and artistic edginess on the other.

The concept of including oneself in the story is a recurring and oft-debated subject in the academic community, one I wrestle with frequently. Am I living the life or documenting the life? Objectivity and truth—elusive and ambivalent at best—become everyday challenges and end points to strive for, areas of gray rather than black and white. An observer's presence on a scene *always* changes that scene's reality—taking it from a scene lived to a scene recorded, to be acted out later in the form of a book or exhibit. Here in Madison County, because I am one of the *actors* as well as the director, my photographs are not only part of my personal past, but also a footnote in the county's history and evolution.

I sometimes find arrowheads and pottery shards when plowing our garden spot next to the creek. I keep those pieces of evidence in a bowl in my kitchen and reference them when confronted with questions of status. At what point do you really become part of a place? When do you stop being an "ain't from around here," and become the neighbor who "lives up the road"? Does it take a certain amount of time? Does it take turning the soil, burying animals and family in it, stewarding it for the time you are on it? Or if you are an observer, does it mean representing that place in a way that conforms to an artificial standard established by others with their own tenuous ties to place?

I don't know the answer. But I do believe the definition of what it means to be "of a place" is changing, even in a relatively isolated and indigenous spot such as Madison County. People have been migrating into and out of this region forever, some staying longer than others, most everyone leaving a footprint on the landscape. How do we judge one footprint to be more native or true than another?

I remember first driving into Marshall, the county seat, looking for the road to my uncle's place. I passed a huge barn with a sign plastered to its side that read, "Get Right With God." It was like an instant message that said, "You don't belong. Don't bring your forbidden ways into our community." After forty years, being an insider comes to me easily here in Madison County. I understand my place and I see ample evidence of my connection to the community. Just last week, we went to a Visitation for the father of a good friend. Van was the patriarch of a native-born family we've known for twenty years. At the entrance to the chapel, there was a memory board with pictures from Van's life—Van with his prize chickens, holding his grandchildren, fishing. In the middle of the collage, the family had placed a large photograph of Van that I had made five years earlier. In it, he is looking away from the camera as he pulls back his shirt to show me his new pacemaker. It was a funny, light, and intimate moment between us, and Van couldn't get over my photographing it, and later exhibiting it at the local Arts Council. "Why would you take a picture of that?" he'd ask whenever I saw him. But I knew the image had relevance beyond a laugh between friends or the embarrassment Van might feel upon seeing it.

Van was a heavy smoker who had been having heart problems for years. But those of us who knew him understood that quitting wasn't likely. Tobacco had played a major role in the county's history and had been a part of Van's life since he was a boy. He loved his smokes. For him, if a machine inserted effortlessly below his collarbone could buy him a few more years with his family and the mountains he loved, that was good enough.

An outsider sees with a more detached eye and a wider perspective. It was the outsider who recognized the importance of medical technology to both Van and Madison County—technology not available in poor mountain counties a generation earlier. And it was the outsider who made the image and chose to exhibit it.

But it could only have happened with an insider's access to forbidden knowledge—the taboos, stories, and embarrassments we are not supposed to share with the outside world. By choosing to share them, the insider runs the risk of being banished to the outside and becoming one of the forbidden himself.

Get Right With God, Marshall Bypass, Madison County, North Carolina, 1974

At the Democratic Party Fish Fry, Marshall, Madison County, North Carolina, 1990

Carnival on the Island, Marshall, Madison County, North Carolina, 1983

At the 4th of July Party, Anderson Branch, Madison County, North Carolina, 1985

At Paul and Sylvia's Wedding, Anderson Branch, Madison County, North Carolina, 1980

Our Pasture and Woods, PawPaw, Madison County, North Carolina, 2013

MICHAEL CROLEY

Homeless

WHEN MY FICTION writing professor found out I was half-Korean and from Appalachia she wondered why I wasn't writing about that. At the time I was writing mostly about middle-aged men based on people I knew in my hometown, and this miffed her. My professor was Mary Ellen Miller, widow of the Appalachian poet Jim Wayne Miller, and she had become my mentor in all matters involving literature. The fiction writing class was my third with her, and in those early stories I produced I was taking my first stabs at writing about Appalachia.

After my second workshop of the semester she asked, "Why all the middle-aged men, Mike?"

"I write about what I'm afraid of," I said. "I don't want to become like the men in my stories." In conference later I asked her if I should be writing about something else.

She didn't explicitly say that I should, only that I had what seemed to her a very original story in my mother's move from Masan, South Korea, to southeastern Kentucky when she was nineteen. Not to mention the material I might have about my own experiences growing up there.

"I don't think I'm ready for that," I said. "I know it sounds morbid, but maybe when she dies."

What I didn't tell her was that a part of me understood why it was interesting to her, but it wasn't all that interesting to me. After all, it had been my life, and I didn't see how my life could necessarily make for a good story, something someone might want to read.

"Well, think about it," she said. "There is probably something there."

I was twenty years old and wanted to be a writer. I loved the way I felt when I wrote, when I felt my consciousness slipping away and I moved into a place deep inside myself, and the words that came out were my truest thoughts and the most clarified and distilled feelings about life. I often described it to my friends at the time, because they were either fraternity brothers or jocks, as being in the zone. On the basketball court it meant my mind had gone somewhere else and my body moved on instinct, in perfect synchronicity. Jump shot after jump shot, I clearly saw the hoop, felt the leather's pebbled grain on the pads of my fingertips, watched as the ball arced high in the air upon release. It was the rarest of feelings, and those movements were like the coalescing of years of practice and attention to detail. In writing, though, I was not practiced in the same way. I had never kept a journal or diary because that had always felt just a bit silly to me and I had sensed I was posturing when I did. But writing in school for an audience, for my teacher or fellow students, was something I loved. Writing in this way, with the inherent knowledge I was writing for someone in order to connect, might have been my innate gift as a beginning writer. The thought that someone else was going to read my words pushed me to be better, but I also wrote then, as I do now, for that feeling of the mind itself at work. The words came to be me unbidden in those moments, and as I searched through my emotional terrain there was a raw, unrefined energy inside me. And so I did sense, through Mary Ellen's suggestion, that if I could push even deeper into the territory I resisted, the territory that seemed walled off to me, I might find myself riding a much different current.

The stories I had turned in to her had been about men waving off the dreams of their youth to do right by their families. My father had been such a man. One, my mother often told my brother and me, who had given up on his dreams because he had a family to take care of. She repeated this more once I reached college, and her tone was one of both caution and longing. Had one thing gone differently for my father, he might have been able to pursue what he really wanted—which was unspecified—and she was also telling us that a family would divert us from our own dreams. Passion would be trumped by practicality.

I left Mary Ellen's office that day and thought about my writing, the subjects I had picked until then. I thought about Gurney Norman's little book of stories, *Kinfolks,* and how reading them at fourteen years old had completely changed my idea of what fiction was. His stories had given me the permission to set my work in Appalachia, to fill them with the kinds of people I grew up around, and realize they and their situations could make for compelling fiction. His book helped me avoid the pitfalls so many young writers make of using settings they have no familiarity with, like New York City and Los Angeles, or other locales they see in movies and television shows, and showed me how a landscape you know best gives your work the texture of authenticity. So even though my stories were set in my hometown and I would write about it for years, in many ways, I still wasn't writing about my Appalachia and my own complex feelings about it.

CORBIN, KENTUCKY, is located right off I-75 in Whitley County. It is the halfway point between Lexington to the north and Knoxville, Tennessee, to the south. It is the home of the first Kentucky Fried Chicken, a fun fact I often tell people on first meeting them that helps them remember me. If most folks saw Corbin I'm not sure they would associate it with Appalachia. This isn't the place of Walker Evans's photographs or LBJ sitting on porches. In many ways, I think of Corbin as resembling suburbia more than most places in Appalachia. We weren't pocked with coal mines like Harlan or Pikeville. We had access to the interstate and could be in a city in an hour and a half, but I always saw cars zooming past us every day as if nothing was worth stopping for. The L&N Railroad built Corbin, and once passenger service stopped the railroad became a freight and service stop for locomotives. So we had a mix of generational residents and newcomers who had been transferred in by what was then CSX when I was a teenager. Corbin was mostly middle class, it seemed to me then, and, in some ways, still is, but we had our share of poverty. We knew to avoid the grocery stores on the first of every month when the checkout lines were long and the lots in our little Trademart Shopping Center were full. Bible thumpers clamored when the school proposed to incorporate sex ed into the curriculum in middle school, and out in the county I saw cars up on blocks and babies running barefoot in diapers. But those weren't everyday images of my hometown, of the people and places that flood my memory when my thoughts turn to home—the word I still use when I refer to Corbin.

I always felt and still feel that Corbin was regarded in Kentucky as a town of great high school sports programs. When I was coming of age in the early '90s, we were a football school with a proud tradition, but we had started coming on in basketball and baseball too. We took pride in being a somewhat scrappy bunch with a mix of both middle-class and lower-income kids in our school of six hundred students. But for me, whatever pride we took in our athletic accomplishments was always ballasted against the other thing we were best known for: our racism. As in football, our reputation seemed to span the state. I was once asked by an African American opponent if we still hung black people in Corbin. Another time, at a high school academic competition, another African American boy asked me where I was from, and when I told him, he took two steps away from me, as if I might attack him. If I could only see those boys now—if I could only be the boy I was then with the sensibilities I have now—I would ask them to look at my face, to see the slant in my eyes, the unruly, black hair that will not bend or ply, the subtle tint of my own complexion. But the boy I was then was still protective of my hometown and its ugly truths and occasional slights.

When my brother, who is six years older, was in high school, a documentary film crew showed up one year and produced a film called *Trouble Behind*. The film's focus was how a singular event in 1919, in which all the African American residents of the town, some 200 men and women, were marched to the train depot at gunpoint, loaded on boxcars, and shipped out of town, had created a legacy of racism in our small southern town. Blacks had never returned to live in Corbin after that, and the documentary sensationalized the subsequent years of racism in Corbin by targeting folks unhappy with Corbin from nearby communities, as well as residents in Corbin oblivious to their own hate-laced rhetoric. There was no real examination of the event in question, which involved a white man being robbed by two black men, which subsequently led to a mob forming. The film glossed over the history and helped perpetuate what the journalist Eliot Jaspin calls "fables" created in towns like mine that tell stories far more benign than what actually occurred. Over the years the story in Corbin had been twisted and distorted into one in which black residents began causing trouble, so they were run off, then allowed to come back to town, but chose not to. We were told growing up that black people chose not to live in Corbin and that we weren't a racist town. The film's evidence to prove the town's legacy was mostly anecdotal hearsay, and so as my brother and I watched it we saw how naked its agenda was. But I also remember I felt put down, as if the film was saying this entire town was filled with nothing but ignorant, bigoted rednecks, and because I was from here, I was no different.

And at the same time, I also knew Corbin never felt like a place open to African Americans, that it had never felt completely open to my brother and me. By virtue of being athletes we had both been "popular" students, but I never felt I belonged to any group. I always felt on the outside. From the second grade on, I had been on guard about my heritage and my memory of growing up in Corbin. And as I've gotten older, told my own anecdotes and reflected on my life as a boy there, I see in ways I couldn't always then that I lived on edge, ready for the moment when someone turned on me. It happened often enough, usually when I made someone angry in school or at a practice, and the easiest, most cutting thing to come at me with was a comment about my race. I was called Ching-Chong, a Japanese motherfucker, a Chinese motherfucker, and a Chink. During an argument with a female classmate, she hatefully said to me, "Why don't you just go back to where you came from?" And I replied, knowing full well how this would spite her, "You mean, up the road?"

Teenage angst forces us all to feel on the outside, but my ethnicity, the Asian features I carried, marked me in a much different way than it did my peers. More often than not, though, when confronted with these slurs, I did nothing. I was a dutiful child, a good student, and probably a bit too conscientious. I was afraid both of losing a fight and of what kind of discipline I might face from the school if I ever met any of these insults with physical force. When I got to high school, though, I had the idea I was becoming a man, and in order to become a man, I needed to start standing up for myself.

My junior year, a teammate on the football team began writing GOOK, in pencil, on my locker. I came up from lunch and there it was, scrawled across the yellow paint, the lead so faint I had to strain at first to read it. Then it was clear and plain to me and I wiped at it, smearing gray smudges onto the locker. I burned the eraser of my pencil down to a nub removing it, and every day for a week I did this. When I was sure of who had written it, I asked my other teammates to confirm, but they refused to out him. After three days of pestering a friend of mine, he finally relented and told me the boy's name, but he didn't want to. He made me promise to not let on he had told me, and the knowledge that he'd have rather protected this boy's identity than help me hurt nearly as much as the act itself.

His name was Duane, and I caught him after lunch one day. We were by the lockers and I hollered to him, lowering my voice a half octave in order to make myself sound tough and mean. I was not small—in fact I'd started on the football team at tight end for two years—but I had never been in a fight and I was nervous. Saying his name was like stepping off a cliff. There was no going back, only the inevitable downward fall. The fear built in my body, my stomach flashed empty, my blood pulsed to my limbs, and I thought about losing the fight and the humiliation that might bring, as well as the physical pain, but I also thought about what he had done and that if I simply took it, then I'd end up taking that kind of shit for the rest of my life. So I did what is often hardest in this world: I stood up for myself.

He denied he'd written anything but I refused to let him off the hook. I wanted to goad him into the fight, to get him to admit what'd he done, and just as I was moving in close to him, ready to push him or throw a punch, an ROTC teacher came hustling down the hall and broke us apart. He asked us what was going on, and as I answered I glared at the boy, never once looking up to the teacher. "This son of a bitch wrote something on my locker I didn't much appreciate." I was aware of the warble in my voice, the syntax and language lifted from cowboy movies, but I wanted to be firm and direct, to let both the boy and the teacher know I was serious and that detention or suspension were not going to be deterrents for me.

The teacher listened to the boy's denials as I explained the situation. He must have seen the anger on my face as I talked because all he did was tell us to go to class. No principal's office or anything else. "I didn't write that shit on your locker, Croley," Duane said as we drifted apart. "Then who did?" I asked. "It wasn't me. I don't know," he said, backing away. Both of us were, it seems now, afraid to turn away from each other. We just inched backward and I told him to stay away from me. To never speak to me again.

MY SENIOR year of college, the writer David Halberstam visited, and I had the honor and pleasure of escorting him to and from campus. On the evening of his talk, I drove him back to his hotel afterward and sheepishly offered to buy him a beer. "Of course," he said. "But stop here first. I'd like something to eat." It seemed surreal to me at the time that he had agreed, and even stranger when we pulled into the Steak 'n Shake drive-thru and the Pulitzer Prize winner leaned across me and ordered a burger, fries, and a shake. Sitting back in his seat, waiting for the food to arrive through our window, he asked what I wanted to do with my life. I confessed my desire to be a writer.

We took the food back to the lobby of his hotel and watched the NCAA Tournament on television. He bought us two Heinekens. By then I had told him I had requested the assignment to be his escort so that I might talk to him about writing. I see now how generous and kind he was with me, because he was very patient and listened to me. He asked what I wrote about and where I was from. I told him I had written some stories about Appalachia and Corbin, that I wanted to be an Appalachian writer and this distinction was important to me. I told him there were a lot of lives there I admired and that I thought were overshadowed and/or stereotyped, and I wanted to write about those people in an honorable way. He mentioned *Harlan County USA* and asked how far my home was from there.

He then spied my features and asked about my parents, if they were from the area. When I told him my mother was from Korea, he raised his eyebrows. "And have you written about this? About your mother or being half-Korean?"

"No," I said, and repeated what I said to Mary Ellen about writing about my parents while they were still alive.

"What will you do when you graduate?"

"I'd like to go to graduate school for creative writing."

He asked which programs I would apply to. He mentioned books he enjoyed from some of the writers at the schools. And then he offered me advice. "Your reason for not writing about your life and your parents is a good one, but if you're going to apply to these graduate schools—and keep in mind, I don't know a lot about these kinds of programs, I'm a journalist—it would seem to me that in very few instances will they be able to spot talent right off the bat. I think that what they may very well be looking for is potential or something that separates you. And that story, this story of being half-Korean and from a small town in Eastern Kentucky, is *your* story. Nobody else is going to have that."

THREE YEARS later I was living in Richmond, Virginia, but I was unemployed and anxious. I still had not written about my life, but one weekend when I was visiting Corbin, my mother told me a remarkable story about her childhood. There was a couple who lived near them, and as a girl she heard them yelling and screaming at all hours of the day and night. Sometimes they would have these great shouting matches and suddenly there would be silence, and she knew it was because the man had struck the wife. She said my grandfather had sometimes struck my grandmother, too. "I think she asked for it," she said. "She wouldn't leave him alone and she would get right up in his face." My mother has a way of getting lost in her own stories, as if a movie reel of images runs in her head as she talks. She didn't say anything more about what happened between her parents or the man and woman in their village, but a flash of images was running in her mind and when it finally stopped, she snapped back, and looked me in the eye. "When I moved to the United States I only promised myself two things. I wouldn't owe anyone any money and I would never let my husband beat me." Something about the line was golden and powerful, and I knew it had to be used.

What spurred my mother's story was my own tale of woe and depression. After college I had taken a job that I quit within a year, in part because I wanted to be a writer. I had been out of work for eight months and was ambling in my attempts to enter the real world. This was right after the dot-com bubble burst and the economy was in a severe downturn, meaning that having any kind of job was a blessing, and I had thrown that away. My parents, in their young lives, had never had the luxury of walking away from a job, and they counseled against it, but supported me nonetheless. My brother offered to let me come live with him in Richmond rent-free and look for work, saying I only needed to work on my writing if that was indeed what I wanted to do, and that I just needed to get any kind of job I could.

And my mother had told me the same thing, saying she and my father would support me financially and cosmically, so long as I was trying to do this thing that I professed to love.

But I felt like a failure then. I had nothing to contribute to my brother's rent, to our grocery bills or well-being. I was as depressed as I had ever been in my young life, and though I looked for jobs relentlessly, nothing came up. My inability to gain work made it hard to feel good about what kind of person I was or might become, and that made it pretty damn hard to sit at the computer and compose a story, which seemed like a fruitless and crazy endeavor. My mother knew the depths of my depression and how I was beating myself up, so the lesson she may have been imparting to me the night she told me her story was this: I didn't have nearly as much on my shoulders as that woman or my grandmother, or as many uncertainties as a nineteen-year-old Korean girl who left everything she knew—language, culture, family, the very food she ate—for the man she had fallen in love with just a year before.

Later on that same weekend visit, I was driving around the country where my father had grown up, where I knew he and my mother had lived for a short time, and I drove down the holler, to his childhood home. I saw the mountains I had grown up around and that had always been comforting and familiar to me, imbued with my mother's words echoing in my head. My imagination leapt backwards to the girl she would have been then, not much younger than I was, and suddenly those mountains were completely new and foreign. At twenty-three I was utterly lost in how to make it in a country where I had spent my entire life, whose culture was woven into me through the power of cable television and popular magazines. I'd been given every advantage to pursue my dreams and education, and if the world seemed that opaque and closed off to me, how could it have felt to her in these hills? In this land that ever since I was eight years old seemed left behind and lost in time compared to Corbin, which, in turn, had also seemed a land left behind from the world at large, how did she manage?

I wrote the first fifteen pages of what I thought would be a short story when I got back to Richmond. The pages came easy, fast and fluid, and when I was done, I realized what I was writing was more than just a short story. I had used her lines as my starting point, and I imagined what it was like to be so young and scared—two emotions

I was pretty familiar with—and to find yourself deep in the heart of Appalachia with a coal mine nearby and poverty even more abject than what you had seen in Korea, a country torn apart by war almost two decades before. I imagined my mother, all those big dreams of her youth—the universal dreams of young age for love and plenty—seeing those old forest-covered mountains, the hills blown away by dynamite, and the ocean she loved nowhere in sight. No short story could tell her tale, get at the difficulty and chances we take for love—the sacrifices we will make. I had a novel and I knew it, but I had no idea how to write a novel.

I had been lucky that some good teachers and published writers thought I had talent, but I was, when I look back on that day, essentially alone. The writing of that book would take eight years—a quarter of my life when I finally finished it—but it was a territory I *had* to explore alone. I didn't confide the novel's subject matter to my family until after two years of writing, and when I did they were wary. They didn't want people in our hometown to misconstrue the fiction as fact, to think the record of the novel was the life my mother had lived.

Once, on the verge of quitting the book for the fear of how it would affect my family, I confided in a writer friend of mine. She told me a story about hearing Pat Conroy give a reading and how he had given himself permission to write his mother's story, saying, "Nobody was going to tell her story unless I did." I thought about that a lot over the next couple of months as I waded deeper into the novel, into blurring imagination with facts, creating circumstances both similar and dissimilar to my mother's as well as my own. And I decided one day that nobody would know how strong and beautiful she was unless I put that to the page. She had raised us two boys in Corbin never seeing a face like her own. Clerks had followed her up and down the aisles at stores. I had watched as people openly stared at her while we were in K-Mart or Kroger. Waitresses had seated and served other customers before her. Women at the insulation factory where she worked picked on her. Once she was badgered by a group of boys on a school bus and she pulled up beside the bus and waved it to a stop. She walked right up the steps and to the very back row, and said to the boys, "You wanted my attention: now you've got it. What do you want to say?" A friend of mine was on that bus and he said it was awesome to see the surprise and fear on their faces.

I THINK about my early attempts in writing a lot now that I'm a professor myself. I teach a lot of students who, like me, want to be writers but are afraid to give themselves permission to tell their stories. I have daily access to the worst of my fears as a college student. I see the hesitant marks in their prose, the way they come into the office, coyly wanting my approval. I ask each of them what their story is, just as my teacher asked me, and, like me, they do not know. They don't know what the one thing they have is that nobody else has. I try to give them the books and the advice that will lead them to it, but I can't make them turn inward. They must do it and see it themselves, and it's hard to just be a guide and not a director. They are afraid of failing, which is a fear I tell them will never go away. They are afraid the words won't be there, which I tell them will also never go away. They care greatly about being original, which I tell them they will probably never be, for there are no new stories. I tell them we are colleagues in this endeavor, this hard, impossible task at bottling beauty and the ineffable. But while I talk, I think about where they are sitting, what words I could not hear at their age.

It's hard to tell a student, or anyone you care about really, to step into the mystery of this complicated human universe. So much can happen, good or bad. But nothing can happen without that step. My mother remains the strongest woman I know and she moved seven thousand miles away from her birthplace to be with my father. To this country she came, to that little patch of Appalachia I will forever carry in the cadence and rhythm of my speech, though I know now, I will never go back. Like her, I am adrift from what I once knew and loved best. There was and there is, in some ways, no other story for me to tell.

SARAH EINSTEIN

Mountain Jews

We're Mountain Jews, halfway between Reformed
and Baptist.

—*My brother Robert*

THIS IS A DISTINCTLY AMERICAN STORY,
BUT NOT A VERY APPALACHIAN ONE

A. I. came to America from Linkuva, Lithuania, where his family
lived on the estate of a Baron Hastings. His father, Joseph, studied
Talmud, though family legend doesn't account for whether Joseph
was a devout scholar or just a bum. Either is possible. His mother,
Sheva Baila, ran the baron's dairy. We have a single black-and-white
photo and so know that she was a stout woman with large hands and
a broad face. Peasant stock, but shrewd. In 1886, she sent the fifteen-
year-old A. I. to Baltimore so that he could make his fortune and send
a little money home.

A. I. bought a hundred-dollar peddler's pack from the Baltimore
Bargain House and moved to Greenbrier County in southeastern
West Virginia. A horse-and-wagon peddler, he traveled through the
small towns and hollows, selling sewing needles, suspenders, bits of
lace, hairpins, and calico to the local folk. In Lithuania, he and the
oldest of his siblings had joined the baron's children in their lessons
with two British tutors, so although he no doubt spoke with a heavy
accent, his English was good enough to haggle. The railroad was just
beginning to reach this part of Appalachia and people needed the
things he carried with him.

He did all right for a year or so, until his wagon got stuck in the ford of the Greenbrier River at Lowell. Unable to afford a new wagon, he opened a general store in the tiny town of Talcott, near the Big Ben Tunnel where twenty years before John Henry had driven down sixteen feet while the steam drill only made nine. A. I. did much better than all right once the railroad started bringing in men to work the mines. In 1891 the rest of the family, including my great-grandfather Lake, emigrated to the US and settled throughout West Virginia. Most, like A. I., became shopkeepers, but buffered by his older brothers' successes, Lake was able to graduate from high school and later went on to Johns Hopkins Medical School. He set up practice in Huntington, West Virginia, which was then a little bustling. A little fashionable. His sons went on to be doctors and businessmen, opening factories to build optics and manufacturing the heavy machinery needed to mine coal. My father joined the family business, as sons-in-law were expected to do, when I was born.

Ours is not a story of eking out a meager living in the mountains. These were not hard times.

NOT DISTINCTLY APPALACHIAN ENOUGH: CORRESPONDENCE WITH AN EDITOR

"As it's an anthology, previous work is good, and nothing need be too overtly Appalachian."

And then, "My coeditor . . . loves your essay, but wonders if it's distinctly Appalachian enough, which is exactly what I told you wasn't absolutely necessary. (My apologies.) I dunno. Maybe he's right. Have you anything else to send along?"

And so I sent along two more essays, both nonfictional accounts of my life in Appalachia and elsewhere. I never heard back from the editors.

The rejection pricks me in a way it wouldn't have if the editors had just said, "Thank you for sending us your work, but it isn't quite right for this book." I'm angered by the idea that my work—essays written from a life spent mostly in Appalachia, informed by being someone born and raised in West Virginia—isn't distinctly Appalachian. That someone with a more expected version of the Appalachian story—one that speaks out of poverty, or a closeness to the land, or a certain sort of Protestantism—feels entitled to make that distinction.

I wonder, *Can I be from here without being of here?*

THERE ARE OTHER STORIES

I will tell you, "We first came to America in Lake's generation," but of course I had four great-grandfathers. One, a broken-down laborer from Peterstown, West Virginia, remembered only as being so soft-spoken that nobody can recall him speaking at all. One, a minister in the South who brought such dissension to his congregations that he had to denomination-hop. One, according to family legend, who came to the US from Ireland as an indentured servant and reinvented himself as a robber-baron. That I can find a birth certificate showing that he was born in the US to parents who were also born in the US doesn't change the way we tell this story; now, we just also say, "Well, he was rich enough to afford to create a pedigree for himself."

And, of course, I had four great-grandmothers. One, a woman named Gracie who was mean as spit and hid beer beneath her apron at night. One, a small-boned lady whose flowered china I inherited and through whom I am entitled to join the DAR (but, of course, I haven't). One—the one married to the minister—about whom I know nothing at all, not even her name. One, Lake's wife, a stout woman with a broad face, named Bertha, whom I come to resemble more and more with each passing year.

I tell you this so that you will understand everything that follows is made up of family legend. We are probably wrong about much of it, but it is what I know of who I am. When I say that we came to this country in my great-grandfather's generation, I am choosing one origin story over others. Still, it's true.

IS THIS AN APPALACHIAN CHRISTMAS?

Through the evening-lit windows, I could see the glow of the televisions, the Christmas tree lights, the crèches on the mantels. The fathers, lean and angular, wore khakis and cardigan sweaters instead of dark suits and starched white dress shirts. The mothers' pot-holdered hands held pies and steaming platters of ham, not brisket and latkes for the Hanukkah feast.

I didn't know these people. The 300 block of Eleventh Avenue in Huntington, West Virginia, was unexplored country. I lived a world away, in the 400 block. There was no real difference; the same brick houses sat back from large yards along the tree-lined boulevard. But I was only two weeks old enough to cross the street, to stay out until the streetlights came on, and this was the first time I'd walked this sidewalk alone, the first time I'd seen into the houses of strangers this way.

Through the glass of their windows, they looked like television families, I remembered thinking, the way families were supposed to look. I wasn't yet old enough to understand that families always, and only, look that way when we peer at them through lighted windows from a cold sidewalk. That from inside the house, all families are messy and complex.

There was a tree at my house, too, and presents. We are the kind of Jews who sing *Frosty the Snowman* and *Rudolph the Red-Nosed Reindeer*, drink eggnog, wait for Santa. But ours was a borrowed holiday and it never quite felt like we got it right. Always, buried in it, was the secret we weren't supposed to tell our friends: Jesus wasn't really the son of God, except perhaps in the way that we are all children of God.

There is a picture from that Christmas morning of me in a fairy costume, a child-sized ermine stole draped around my shoulders, a tiara perched precariously on my tangled brown hair. It was one of the many magical, privileged moments that made up my childhood. Under the tree, there was a fire truck big enough for me to drive my brothers around the yard while they made siren noises in the backseat. A wooden slide for the playroom. Baby dolls and picture books and games my father would cheat at to let us win. In my grandfather's stable, my new pony whinnied in the dark. Or maybe that was the year before, or the year after. I can't remember. So I cannot tell you what it feels like to be scared, or hungry, or in danger as a child. What it's like when Dad is out of work or the baby is sick and there is no money for the doctor. But I can tell you how little it takes to make a six-year-old girl believe that she doesn't belong where she is. And I can tell you how achingly sweet it can be to stand on the sidewalk in the cold of December and feel yourself apart.

HOW WOULD YOU FEEL IF YOUR BOOK WAS SHELVED UNDER APPALACHIAN WRITERS?

During my defense, my MFA thesis director asked how I would feel if my books were shelved under Appalachian Writing.

"I'd feel great," I said, "but I'm not sure if Sarah Beth would be happy about it."

We all laughed. My friend Sarah Beth Childers writes excellent essays about growing up just a few miles from where I grew up, essays about her cigarette-smoking Granny, gospel singers in gravy-stained shirts, a father flicking cigarette butts into the community pool while his children swim, baby bottles full of Mountain Dew. Sarah's essays are lyrical and lovely and I admire them very much. But, although we grew up just a few miles from one another—walked the same streets, ate in the same restaurants, shopped at the same stores—these are essays I could never write. Her new book, *Shake Terribly the Earth,* is about a life lived both very near and very far from mine. The publisher says that she writes in a "thoughtful, humorous voice born of Appalachian storytelling." And she does.

No publisher will ever say that about my writing. But is the fond voice telling family stories in the past tense the only one an Appalachian writer is allowed?

IS THIS A STORY ABOUT LIVING IN APPALACHIA?

Of an evening, my husband and I might sit on the back porch of our house in Appalachian Ohio, smoking cigarettes and drinking beer. He'd have just put in a fourteen-hour day at work; I would have put in nine. There might be a deer nibbling the dogwood near our back fence, or the coyotes might be calling to one another across the narrow ravine on the other side of our road.

"I love our life," my husband would say. He says this when we sit outside of an evening, smoking cigarettes and drinking a beer.

This sounds Appalachian enough, but we work at Ohio University, not in coal mines or auto body shops. My husband is from Austria and laughs at me because I don't know how to waltz. He has clipped, European consonants, though a year in Athens has begun to smooth them out, and he wears good shoes. Ours is the poverty of graduate school, the purposeful sort that holds at its end a promise of tenure, retirement savings, and home ownership, and not the sort that grinds families down from generation to generation. The neighbors are college professors and high school teachers and retired professionals. The guy who mows our grass has a bachelor's degree in landscape architecture; the coffee at our favorite coffee shop is fair-trade and shade-grown. We live in the bubble of economic prosperity the university affords, and I'm not certain whether those of us in its boundaries live inside or outside of Appalachia.

Maybe Athens, too, is in but not of Appalachia.

CAN I EVEN WRITE "OF AN EVENING?"

My sister says *I don't care to* when she means *I don't mind*. My brother begins a fair number of his sentences with *Well, I reckon*, and if my father needs your screwdriver, he'll ask if he can *borry* it. But I spent years in childhood elocution classes—though we called it speech, so as not to sound too fancy—in order to smooth these markers of place out of my language. I don't know why my brother and sister didn't go. Perhaps the teacher retired and no one took her place, or maybe our parents just stopped worrying about our accents. Maybe those extra years of parenting gave them bigger things to worry about.

I know what folk mean when they say *up over yonder* and *the baby needs feeding* and *no I never*, but these are not things I myself would say. When I was a child, I thought they were wrong. Now, they just seem to belong to other people and not to me. I worry that to say—and even more to write—them is an appropriation. That I'm stealing the language of the men who worked for my grandfather. Mine is the language of universities, grammar books, and years spent in New York.

IS THIS AN APPALACHIAN HANUKKAH STORY?

I lived for most of my thirties in Manhattan, and for some of that time I dated a nice Jewish lawyer who took me out to his sister's house in Long Island for holidays. They were Jews of a sort I'd never seen; they didn't have Christmas trees or Easter eggs, they went to *shul* even when it wasn't the High Holy Days, their conversations were peppered with Yiddish. I was a little in awe of them because of it.

On our first Hanukkah together, I was invited to say the blessing over the candles. *Baruk atah Adonai* I began, and everyone started to giggle. *Eloheinu, melekh ha'olam.* The giggles became full-on laughter.

"I'm sorry," said my date's mother. "When you speak English, you don't have an accent at all. But listening to you say the blessing over the candles is like watching a *Beverly Hillbillies* Hanukkah special." She patted my arm, as if to say it was all right, and then her daughter took over the prayer.

And so maybe my speech isn't so unmarked after all.

Maybe I could be an Appalachian writer if I would just learn to write in Hebrew.

OUTLAW HEART

ANN PANCAKE
Tough

WE WERE RAISED tough in 1970s West Virginia. Boys, girls, all of us were, although I didn't recognize it until I left the place, and recognize it even more the further I leave the time. We got beat on regularly: at least, every kid I knew did. Got beat at school, got beat at home. I took the beatings so much for granted that the only thing I noted about them were the variations on the beating devices—kitchen ladles, hairbrushes, Hot Wheels tracks, Ping-Pong paddles. I collected these in my head when I visited friends and saw them or their siblings get it or get threatened. Then there was work. Lots of us in Hampshire County were farm kids or had families who used to be farmers or used to work for farmers. We were worked, and I don't mean dusting. We chopped wood; we put in and weeded and harvested enormous gardens; then we helped can; we made hay.

In the two-hundred-year-old house where I grew up, heat was spotty: wood and coal. We used our hands for our heat; we worked to get it. My brother and I were stoking the coal furnace before we hit sixth grade, the shovel big as us, and still, it was just always cold. At Romney Junior High, before the bell rang in the mornings and during lunch, they made us stand outside. In winter, we'd warm ourselves by crowding, eight or ten of us, into deep-set doorways, share body heat, then trade off and let others warm. That was us. Get resourceful. Don't complain. Tough. We did the same at our bus stop, which my five brothers and sisters and I reached by crossing an open railroad trestle. That trestle had no railings, and in those early winter mornings, an ice skiff would slick the ties, but we never fell, at least not off.

In the gravel turnaround along Route 50, we'd press into a little white bus shelter reeking of plywood pissed on some time ago. We'd huddle in there, my family, and little Petie and Tammy Chavez, if they were staying with their grandma, and retarded Billy, if his dad hadn't driven him in. We'd breathe our warmness into shared air, careful not to touch each other wrong because it was impossible not to touch some. We learned. To get by, to make do. The trouble was, it was the kind of tough that makes you put up with instead of grab when you're older. That's the kind of tough they made us. The durable kind, not the fighting kind.

Some of us took straightaway to the toughening. Others had less aptitude for it. I'm still not sure to which group I belonged, but I know Jamie was in the latter. Jamie Fout or Haines, his last name constantly shifted depending upon which father claimed him at any given time or else to which father his mother felt most sympathetic, I don't know. Jamie. I think of his scrawniness and his colorless hair. His ear operations and the way he blinked two seconds longer and tighter than everybody else. His pathetic gentleness. In sixth grade, he decided he was in love with me.

Toughness in much of West Virginia is not just an exhibition of masculinity. It's more deeply bound up with class, with poverty. It's hard to outline, much less make an outsider feel, the economics of back home, especially in the time I'm speaking of, the midseventies. So difficult to convey the pervasiveness of lack, a culture so saturated with lack that the absence turned inside out and became a presence, and the lack shaped all of us, even those of us, like me, who were middle-class by local standards. The easiest way to explain to a nonnative the class structure back home is this: anybody upper-class where I grew up would be considered middle-class in regular white America. The middle class where I grew up would be considered working class outside. Through a mainstream lens, the working class back home would be seen as poverty-stricken. And then there were our homegrown poor, who slip under all white categories in the ordinary American imagination, white people poorer than I'd see again in my life, a level of poverty I'd only see in Third World countries. What I'm saying is, the toughness, for many, wasn't bravado. Many of us were going to need it.

Jamie didn't have it easy, but he was better off than many boys who fell in love with me, some of whom I loved back. Johnny

Mulledy, special ed, a member of one of those families that just went on forever, a kid in every single grade, used to send me love letters written in stick figures. I never did figure out what the stick figures were doing. And Johnny's notes remind me of a time much later, in high school, when I had a casual boyfriend in a nearby town, a part black kid who lived with a white foster family. Once he sent me a picture of himself playing baseball, the back of the photo a dense web of surreal sentences. The handwriting was legible: that wasn't the problem. It was as if the sentences were a different species of mind working, and not until years afterward, when I was teaching English, did I realize he was illiterate. That boy was stunningly good-looking, the best kisser I'd ever know. He'd been placed with the foster family because his biological mother had raped him.

After Jamie, I had boyfriends whose families couldn't afford phones, so they'd call me from phone booths; boyfriends without plumbing, so they'd slather their adolescent odors with cologne. I had a boyfriend who was set between parked cars at the age of five and told to choose father's or mother's, and the decision stuck for life. Those boys had to be tough. Now I look back on what they had to squirm through and fight off and suffer on their way to becoming men, and I'm struck by several things. How as a kid I simply took their situations for granted, like I did our beatings, the cold, the lack. How I have never known since with any intimacy, nor will ever know again, people like them. How their circumstances made not only those boys, but made their love, and how the intersections of their love and mine went toward making me.

None of those boys really scared me. The boy who most frightened me never showed interest in me in a boyfriend way. Raymond Hays was the poorest of the poor, with wild rusted black hair textured like malnourished puppy fur, although there was nothing puppyish about Raymond. He was one of those kids who got old by age ten. He wore the free shoes the poor poor got in the principal's office—two-toned clodhoppers, bulbous toes—and those shoes marked them, the way their scalps marked them when they were shaved for lice. One day after lunch in fifth grade, I was passing the garbage incinerator on the way to the playground, and there Raymond stood, watching me. I accidentally walked close enough to hear him mutter something. I had to look back at him—and when I did, he stared at me unmoved, as though he hadn't spoken at all—and let the sentence replay in my head before I registered the words. He'd said: "Do you have hair on yours?"

That question terrifies me even now, in its understatement, its originality, the insidious indirection of the threat. How effortlessly he was able to violate a privacy so deep that until he spoke, I hadn't really known it was a privacy. When I heard the question that day, I felt my breath snatched down a narrow tube and snuffed. It wasn't terror that Raymond would harm me physically, but worse. The terror was of being sliced and spread open, exposed in the most intimate way, and my immediate impulse was to wrap my arms around myself, cover my insides and hide. My answer to Raymond's question was an unthought knowledge, an unarticulated premonition, that my life from there on would be a progressive hardening around my sexuality, which at that point I was barely even aware of. And although by that time I'd toughened in other ways, I'd not yet known how to toughen there.

IN THE winter of sixth grade, Jamie asked me to go with him. Of course, he didn't ask me to my face. He enlisted intermediaries. I don't know how many he asked to approach me for him—I can't imagine that it was more than one or two—but it turned into the whole pack of sixth-grade boy populars, getting a real rise out of this budding romance between nerdy little Jamie and weird reads-all-the-time me. These were boys at eleven, at twelve, already well hardened, at least in public, boys forever flexing and flaunting their little man-ness. Their favorite insult that year was "Woman." "Woman!" they'd spit at each other, the lowest of the low. Occasionally, they'd even fire it at us girls, and we'd accept it. As an insult. The pack descended on me on the playground, wearing jackets because the teachers made them, but the jackets unzipped, unbuttoned, flapping open in the brutal January wind, proof of their toughness. Prancing and feinting, they surrounded me, their legs spread, arms cocked off their sides. And the ringleader held out to me, always just beyond reach, a bracelet.

That was a year ID bracelets were big, ones with shiny thick links that folded into each other and a sturdy plate engraved with a name. I think this is how Jamie imagined the bracelet. But his had smaller links, an almost impossibly narrow mouth, no plate, no name, and was colored the opaque gray of used washing machine water. "He wants to give you this bracelet!" Scotty Combs jeered. "I don't know how you're supposed to wear it! Maybe on your nose!"

I wasn't self-conscious enough yet, hadn't hardened enough in that way, to reject the bracelet to save face. I took it from the pack and turned away.

I wore the bracelet for the rest of the school year. What did I feel for Jamie? I felt flattered. Appreciative that he perceived me as so much more than I knew I was. I felt friendliness, but not more. The boy I really "liked" was in that swarm of taunters. But Jamie paid attention to me, and I was famished for attention. I was the oldest of six children, the third-oldest of twenty cousins, and I was never made to feel like more than one of a crowd. Jamie would call me. He would walk with me and watch me and give me small presents. He was unfailingly kind and gentle, and he carried that tenderness right up front in his face. At first glance, the face just came off as slightly goofy, the way he'd flutter and squinch his eyes, the tubes in his ears and the cotton batting. Something about how his features were arranged gave the face a cartoon quality. But if you looked at it often enough, you saw how he reached with his face. His face extended an open invitation to come inside and sit with him, but at the same time, an invitation with more than a little consciousness that it would be rejected. That lay in the face too. Then, even beyond the anticipation of rejection, the face also, already, telling you, yes, the rejection would hurt, yes. But that would be all right. It was all right.

I knew later, and only a few years later, knew by the time I was in high school, that his gentleness was the main reason I couldn't love him back. I knew by the time I was sixteen that was the reason, but it took me another twenty years to understand why.

It was a strange cross-classedness that bred me. I was raised with a few middle-class opportunities and most middle-class expectations in a culture that was working-class, and now I realize how that hybridity served me after I left home. The toughening I learned as a kid meant that as an adult I had few fears about the physical world and took quiet risks. It meant I carried low expectations of others, high expectations of myself. Our work ethic helped me even more. We were brought up to expect absolutely nothing unless we worked to death for it, raised in a place where "he/she's a hard worker" was about the biggest compliment anyone received, and on that ethic I labored through graduate school. I muscled through my dissertation, which included research on class, and through that process, I became acutely conscious that the possibilities for the travel, for the advanced education, came only from the other part of my classedness: the middle-class strand. Still, like any virtue, the toughness cost me. A couple times it almost got me killed, literally, like the time a gynecologist didn't notice he'd perforated my intestine and I didn't go to the emergency room for three days because I figured I was just being a baby about the pain. More often, though, the deaths were emotional, I think.

Jamie's birthday was in March, and that year I was his girlfriend, I was invited to his party. At least I thought it was a party, until I got there and discovered I was the only guest. Nobody came except me, Jamie, his grandma, whom he lived with, and his mom, who didn't live there and had just come for the party. By this time in my life, a month after I turned twelve, I'd been in houses and trailers as destitute as any I'd ever enter again. Like so many homes of the poor or almost poor, Jamie's grandma's house was kept dark and felt crowded and close, as though the occupants have denned up against threats outside. I'd worn my good clothes, as far as those went. Not my Sunday clothes, but a pair of checked slacks and a sweater that I remember was a maroon of some sort. After the present opening, we ate slices of a bitter white cake, and because the birthday party had no games, and no food other than the cake, and no guests besides me, it didn't last long. After we finished our cake, Jamie asked me if I wanted to ride his bike in the empty parking lot across the street.

I couldn't love him back. It wasn't just my age, that's not what I mean. From the beginning, I only loved them tough. None of them ever hit me; it wasn't that kind of tough. It was quick anger and studied indifference and cockiness and control. It was him always forgetting whatever was important to you; it was a hand pressing your head toward his lap. It was motorcycles and hanging around during car repairs, it was watching violent movies and boring sports. It was not give in and do what he wants to do, but do what he wants to do so instinctively you never even recognize it as a giving in.

BY HIGH school, Jamie was cheerily sloshing about in a bath of drugs. This made him skinnier than ever and exaggerated the comical look on his face, but it didn't take the gentle. The reaching, the invitation, still spilled sloppy out his eyes, and I understand now it was in part the tenderness in him, his inability to toughen, that sent him to the drugs. I, on the other hand, have always been a fast learner. I'd roughened my soft spots. I fit in. While in sixth grade, Jamie and I had been on fairly equal social footing—geeky, shy—but by high school, I had a place in the popular crowd. A precarious place, in my opinion, but I was there. Jamie, although no one could possibly dislike him, was never cool enough, despite the drugs, to be included. Naturally it was in part his sensitivity that kept him out.

We had band together. I was first-chair trumpet while Jamie was with the other stoners in the percussion section. One afternoon we were rowdying around before practice when one of the boys back in percussion hollered up at me, "Hey, Ann, did you used to go with Jamie?"

And reflexive as a swallow, I hollered back, "Nuh-uh!"

A fast learner. At eleven, I wasn't self-conscious enough to turn down Jamie's bracelet from a hooting crowd. At seventeen, I'd so thoroughly internalized some adolescent self-preservation instinct that the lie came ten times more intuitively than the truth.

I see Jamie after I told this lie even though I know I didn't have the guts to turn around and look at him. Still, in my mind, I see his expression. I see him leaning forward in his metal folding chair, snare drumsticks dangling between his knees. His face a fresh wound already in motion with forgiving me.

That March afternoon of his birthday, we pushed his bike across the street. The lot was a small hill paved, good for coasting. We took turns riding. I was wearing the bracelet, the maroon sweater, the flare-legged checked dress pants; this was 1975. I was taking one of my turns, Jamie watching from across the asphalt, when that pants leg got caught in the bicycle chain.

I was a self-sufficient kid. It rarely occurred to me that someone else would take care of me. Typically, if I had a mishap like this one at home—or a mishap more serious—no one would care, or even notice, unless my brothers and sisters decided to laugh at me. So I stopped the bike, bent over, and got ready to work my pants free. I was disappointed that maybe I'd ruined my good pants, but I just reached down to get myself loose.

However, as I did this, Jamie, from the top of the lot where he was watching me, cried out, "Oh! Your pants got caught!"

I can hear now, almost four decades later, with absolute clarity the tone of Jamie's voice when he said this. The earnestness in it, the sincerity. A genuine concern verging on distress. I couldn't have been more taken by surprise. It was a tone that hadn't been directed toward me, except by one of my grandmothers, and never in a circumstance as insignificant as I perceived this one to be. But as clearly as I now hear the tone, I also recall my own reaction: first surprise, then bewilderment. And nothing beyond that. Standing there straddling Jamie's bike, looking at Jamie's figure small and tensed at the top of the hill, I was unable to feel anything beyond bewilderment.

A year ago, me far from home and another March, something in the smell of the before-thaw earth and air brought the bike ride back to me. The temperature, the texture, of that fleeting semiseason respoke Jamie's tone in my ear. And this time, after years of—what? has it been a softening? or simply a relenting? an erosion?—that tone entered me. Jamie's voice plunged past my hardness. And for the first time, his twelve-year-old tenderness touched the tenderness buried in me.

After he cried out, he rushed over, dropped to his knees on the blacktop, and gingerly freed my pants from the chain. A gesture, like his cry, spontaneous, and carrying with it no expectation of reciprocity.

PEOPLE BACK home don't raise their kids as tough anymore. There's more money in the county these days because the economic base has shifted from the death throes of agriculture I knew as a kid to agriculture's graveyard: subdivisions of vacation and retirement homes. The last time I saw Jamie was at our ten-year high school reunion in 1991. It was held at a county park under a picnic shelter. We all brought our own sandwiches. Jamie had with him a cute sullen teased-blonde girl at least a decade younger than us, and he told me he was working construction, commuting a hundred miles to northern Virginia every day. A lot of the boys at the reunion were doing something similar. Several members of the long-ago popular, the very ones who'd taunted me on the playground with the bracelet, were at the reunion, and even the ones who were absent, I knew what had become of most of them, too. I knew many of them had already used up their tough bodies, or their tough bodies had been used up for them, labor or accidents or drugs or all three. And the bodies that hadn't already busted, those bodies were cracking. They were leaking, you could see it in the bruised swaggers, the crippled grins. But they did grin, they did swagger, they kept on. The kind of tough they made us was the kind that makes you put up with instead of grab when you're older. The durable kind, not the fighting kind.

We were raised tough because a lot of us were going to need it; even if it broke by the time you were twenty-eight, you needed it to gut through until then. But how tough does the middle class need to be? Not very. I would have survived without the toughness, but I absorbed it anyway. It's where I'm from. I've been harder on myself than I've needed to be, put up with more hardness from others than I needed to do. As I've said, I know how my own toughness benefited me, and on good days, I'll think I got the best of both classes. Other days, I don't want the limitations or the guilt: the guilt of knowing I don't have to live like so many people I grew up with do because of what I've achieved through that combination of middle-class opportunity and Appalachian working-class ethics. The limitations my toughness has imposed on the way I have relationships. Because I've never stopped perceiving sensitive men like Jamie as weak, I've never been physically attracted to a "weak" man. Although my mind has learned better, my body has not. And it's one more hard thing to look very closely at how the toughness shaped the way I love and let myself be loved.

In 1991, Jamie's outsides looked pretty rough, but right under that crust, he carried the gentleness still. How his sensitivity might have contributed to that external ruin, I wonder. His face still reached to you, but it was battered and caved in around the bones and colored like dirty sky. His body was still thin, but a different kind of thin, a rigid kind, like boards tacked together, angled and flattish and stiff. And he had down one side of his face a corrugated scar as wide as my little finger and nearly as long as my hand. This is how I couldn't help but see Jamie: he looked like he'd been hit with a bicycle chain.

SHELDON LEE COMPTON

Dangerous Stories

WELL BEFORE PROFESSORS failed in coaxing me to clean up my twangdrawl accent, since, after all, I was studying English, I had started making up stories. Not about where I lived or the people who lived there, but about places like Alaska and people who flew airplanes and real estate agents with suitcases gripped in their hands and all the things as far away from where I sat with my pencil as my ten-year-old mind could conceive. Stories happened in other places, to other people. Eastern Kentucky was a tired brown of rolling breast-rounded hilly landscape, and the men at the gas stations and the women walking dogs and the other kids building bike ramps out of busted doors were individuals who populated the infomercials of my social insomnia.

I wrote stories about everything I didn't see or hear or know anything about at all, really. I was like hundreds of other writers— rejecting, replacing, or reworking my world at the beginning. But I felt my rebellion was unique, just like those hundreds of others. It gave me a sense of power I thought only I possessed, had mastered. I didn't feel ten feet tall and bulletproof. I felt ten thousand feet tall and smiteproof. I had no doubt I was making waves. Big waves. Nothing dull in my imagined world. It was all bright and flat and interesting and just sexy as anything. And when I wasn't elbow-deep at the kitchen table with my pencils and college-ruled paper, I could be found in the most sacred of places in Eastern Kentucky—my personal church, Pike County's Vesta Roberts Memorial Library, AD 1983.

Let's take a walk.

To get to the library, walking, as I did, you first come across Whetzel Damron. Now Whetzel's since passed on, but let's say he's there and coming at you bowlegged from his gas pumps, tucking his wallet swelled with ones and fives into his back pocket. He's going to smile so that his mustache lifts up into his nostrils, and the closer he gets, the more you smell the gasoline that has permanently fixed itself to his skin. He'll jab you between the ribs with his thumb and immediately throw his hands up like John Sullivan, then pat you on the arm and laugh and return to his pumps. Whetzel keeps you on your guard. A man can never know when he'll need to land a solid right hook. Whetzel's good for reminding you of important things like fighting and making money. Whetzel's interest in such things will become clearer as we go along.

Next you pass Trivette's Trucking, once owned by Dale Trivette who has also went on from this earth but whom we'll ask back for a time. His place is a massive brick garage with an office attached the size of most of the camp houses on High Street. Whetzel, you see, keeps a wallet big as a smallmouth bass because folks mostly pay with those ones and fives, but Dale is the richest man in the world. Dale's old man had owned coal mines and now Dale ran coal in his shortbed trucks. It's all about connections. Mostly you don't see Dale, though, for reasons we'll get into later. You see his drivers or mechanics— Spider, Torch, Bill Boy, Grape Ape, Wild Bill. You know them by their call names and you yell them out and they wave at you without smiling. They're not mean by a long stretch, unless provoked: just busy, and you'll understand that and keep moving.

Hamilton's Five and Dime is a sad place to pass by along the way. You're about at the halfway point here. Mind you, it wasn't sad then, though. That sadness would come later. As you keep on the worn path at the side of Route 461, made smooth from the kids in town walking to Virgie High School just up the way, you always, and that is always, stop here and look at the glass front door. It's a time machine. Go through that door and to your left are canisters of candy, each with a scoop. Butterscotch, peppermint, licorice, chocolate-covered peanuts in one and chocolate-covered raisins in another. The canisters are behind the counter and you ask Mary, the lady who doesn't own the store but who had worked there for an unknown number of years at that time and then decades afterward until its eventual closing, for a bag of this candy or that candy. She weighs it and then gives you the bag, my hand to God. But you don't go in, standing outside with the books for return curled under your arm, and there's no way to window-shop for peppermint candy at Hamilton's Five and Dime. You move on.

After the high school, an unknown place to you with an expansive parking lot great for riding bikes and ramp jumping, there's a quarter of the walk with nothing but a slender path next to the road where you need to watch for shortbeds blasting past. You walk this stretch thinking of the good-sized tributary of the Big Sandy River running behind the gymnasium at the high school, made perfect for taking your dogs for a swim and getting away from things. It keeps your mind off the speeding trucks two, three inches from you and your borrowed books. Besides, from here you can see the railroad tracks. And once you make it to the tracks, you'll see the library, not fifty yards away.

It's a short piece now from the tracks, warm to the touch from two trains a day. To the left is Stanley Johnson's old hardware store, now run by his son. Across the road is the clapboard building that is the even older old Johnson's hardware and feed store. Vesta Roberts was Stanley's kin, and the library named in her honor is now in sight. In seconds, you're home.

IT WAS my home, in any case. When the new location opened I was there and became the second person issued a library card. The first was my father, who promptly directed me to the juvenile biography section. I wouldn't truly emerge from this section for another three years. In that time, I read every book published in what collectively remain my favorite books of all time, the *Childhoods of Famous Americans* series. These books would both set ablaze my love of reading and writing and also act as the key factor in seeing me dream of being nearly everything except a storyteller.

I checked out *Pontiac: Boy Indian,* and took to the hills that same week, shirtless and carrying a spear made from a tree branch crooked as a dog's hind leg. Another week it was *John Paul Jones: Boy of the Sea* and the following task of dragging a broken door into the creek beside my house, a ship fit for a captain. *Eli Whitney: Boy Mechanic* saw me spend hours in my grandfather's workshop tinkering without any sense of direction or understanding, building tangles of metal hodge-podge with no earthly use or purpose.

The days went on in this routine, a different passion with each new biography. But after a time, reading the books wasn't enough. I wanted to write my own. And when I did, I wrote, as I said, about everything other than what I had experienced. That was at age twelve. It would be six years before I would place my heart firmly outside the safety of my chest and write from a place of burning, a place I knew had the potential to hurt and embarrass and confuse those who knew me well, or folks I knew better than they realized. Stories ready to be told.

This notion of embarrassing, hurting, or confusing, not to mention the very real chance of creating lifelong enemies of those around me, may need some explaining, as it applies to where I'm from in Appalachia.

Pike County, more specifically the town of Virgie, is a place where suspicion moves steadily through the buttermilk-thick blood of kin-folk and friend alike. You are met with this instantly if you spend any amount of time asking questions or trying to wrangle an opinion from anyone who might live here. And if they agree to talk, answer questions, or, say, pose for a picture, they change, right there on the spot. They stand a little straighter, they talk differently, they never take their eyes off you. The relaxed demeanor of mountain people each person from this area genuinely possesses without effort or no-tice will be stuffed beneath their hat as soon as you pull out a note-book, a pen, or a camera. You lose them and every unique quality each one gives off naturally without otherwise being aware it even exists. The subtle speech patterns, broken and beautiful, become hurriedly polished and as out of place on their tongues as patches of hair. That which replaces them is a blend of midwestern dialect, possibly mimicked from the trained anchor on the evening newscast, or, more likely, from a cousin or uncle who visits two or three times a year from Michigan or Indiana or Ohio. They become guarded and suspect the worse, arms crossed and as stiff as wood, and that's if they agree to take part at all. And it doesn't matter to them one single whit if you're a local. While your lips are moving, more often than not these fine people see you thinking the stereotype: the shoeless, the resident of the coal-era camp house perched on a hillside with a satellite dish nailed to a section of a roof with shingles peeling up like old scabs.

Better safe than sorry, they figure. And sometimes they're right. But the first time I focused my work on my people, my state, my region, I felt the pressure to tell stories honestly, and the fear that doing so would tear down everything.

I'VE NEVER thought much of the term "confessional writing." I feel all storytelling is confessional to an extent. I certainly had no real concept of this confessional sort of work when I sat down at eighteen during a study hall period in high school and decided to write what would become the first of hundreds of stories dealing with my father or the relationships between fathers and sons, stories filled with characters taken directly from the hills. I just sat down and opened a new document, intending to write my latest fantastical story set in some general locale, depicting nameless, faceless, bloodless characters. My stories were then the equivalent of the news anchor's midwestern accent, so widespread there appeared to be nothing of an accent to speak of, no semblance of a story, in my case, where anything other than plot was given consideration. But something happened this time. I wrote this sentence: "David Shannon gave his son, Paul, his life savings at his funeral." Where did that come from?

I look now at the sentence, nearly twenty years later, and see my clumsiness, the circus flips of pronouns no doubt forcing the reader to start at the beginning and begin again. But it had teeth, this sentence. I knew it. I felt it. And it had simply appeared, was just there on the computer screen, demanding and real. So I told myself this story in that hour and when I was done I called it "The Son." I felt like a true storyteller for the first time in my life. The reason was simple. I knew for certain I did not want anyone reading this story. It was mine, and it was honest.

But that was the pressure and fear sinking into my gut, mostly. I had killed the father and the narrator in this story, and thrown in Whetzel Damron and Stanley Johnson and a host for good measure. Other stories followed, all populated by a narrator clearly based on yours truly and a father or father figure whom anyone among family, friends, and acquaintances would have immediately recognized as my own father. Finally, I killed my father for the last time in a novel in my early twenties and shifted my interests to characters who had, until then, played supporting roles. But I needed to do something I rarely practice. I needed to do some research.

Living outside of Virgie by this time, I drove back one afternoon and parked my car at Whetzel's. It had been many years since I'd walked to the library, so I didn't waste much time. I passed the gas pumps and made it five or so feet before I heard Whetzel give a loud whistle. I turned and was met with a stiff finger to my ribs.

And so the walk begins again.

YOU SEE that fat wallet of Whetzel's and you know most of it came from selling drugs in between oil changes. Half the people working for him at the gas station sell them and use them.

You make a mental note.

Across the way, there's no Dale Trivette at Trivette's Trucking. He died a couple years back from a heart attack. Somebody said he ate two plates of chicken livers for lunch every day. His wife left him after sleeping with most of the guys who had call names and took paychecks from Dale. Could have been more than just chicken livers working on Dale's heart.

Mental note.

Now on the straight stretch of Route 461, you see Hamilton's Five and Dime ahead. Closed years ago, the windows are clouded with dust and grime. It's not candy you remember. Not now. You recall how Mary the cashier would follow you around the store, lagging behind about four or five feet, following you from one aisle to the next. Meant little to you at the time, but you know now she was watching for you to steal something. You figure, and figure you're right, that she saw your ragged clothes and dirty face and made her mind up about you soon as you walked through the door. Mary had the hint of a mustache and always smelled like cat litter.

Yep, you guessed it. Mental note.

You pick up the pace along the slim path leading to the railroad tracks, still worn down and still plagued by speeding coal trucks. It's surprising. Somehow you figured you'd be less afraid all these years later. Some things never change.

Across the tracks, it's Stanley Johnson's old hardware store, now a US Bank location. You're able to see how appropriate this is now. Stanley owned most of Virgie, held it hostage and asked the school board a war price when they came to him seeking a place to build a high school. Part of the deal was that the grade school be renamed George F. Johnson Elementary. Old George was Stanley's father, and also tight as a banjo string when it came to money. And giving up control.

No mental note needed at this point, because the Vesta Roberts Memorial Library is just ahead. You'll walk in, take a moment to breathe in the unique scent of hundreds and hundreds of books, then take a table near the back. With pen and paper you'll begin telling dangerous stories, writing truthfully in this holy place, writing as if in prayer, and protected in your reverence.

IDA STEWART

Between, Beneath, Beyond: Tunnel Vision in Coal Country

I HAVE A coal mine for a heart, and my heart is in my throat, and my heart is sinking because the ground, dark as a dream, deep as a dream, is being hollowed out beneath us while we sleep. So I can't sleep. I am wide-eyed in the dark. I mean, I can't sleep because it is too late, always too late. I mean, I am writing poems.

I mean, I am between the lines. In a tunnel. See a mantrip shuttle car carrying nine miners back up toward the surface at the end of their shift. Seven of them—and twenty-two others—will perish in the terrible explosion that has just been triggered over a mile deeper into the Upper Big Branch coal mine behind them. They are in the time between. Soon reporters will descend on the scene. Dateline, Comfort, West Virginia: "If you don't have tunnel vision, if you don't have the day-to-day, you will totally lose it," one woman will tell a reporter as she waits on the surface for news about the rescue and recovery. She lost her grandfather in a coal mining operation years before this disaster and has learned how to be a survivor. Tunnel vision, or else. Later this day, after the explosion, there will be a surge in sales of spray paint used to spell out the words "Pray for our miners and families" on bedsheets soon to be removed from linen closets and hung from front porches. There are cardboard boxes somewhere full of plain T-shirts about to be printed with the image of a miner in silhouette making his way through a tunnel so narrow that he must crawl on hands and knees toward the light that pours from his headlamp. Someone will design, purchase, and distribute these shirts, which will be worn like veils or uniforms in churches and community centers, where people will put their arms around one another, so that even the images on the shirts seem to embrace, and say, "There are no words," and from where I am currently caught, snagged, suspended in between the lines, looking back upon this upheaval from years and miles away, I have to agree. There are no words. Just the spaces in between, even the narrowest spaces between embracing bodies. See the lover pulling the dreaming beloved closer in the night, skin against skin: "You're still not close enough." Just the hollows, like the intervals in a suspended chord, and what forces weigh on those hollows, and how hard, and for how long.

I say there are no words as I dig into words—see words under my fingernails, staining the knees of my jeans, tracked inside the house with leaves and dirt. I'm trying to make some sense of the Upper Big Branch disaster and its aftermath—to get my mind, like hands, around it via poetry. I'm trying to find a way in through the cracks and crevices between voices, words, facts, and stories. I've been reading the interview transcripts from the state and federal governments' joint investigation of the explosion, as well as other narratives of the disaster, which are still even now unfolding in newspaper articles, photos, videos, blog posts, song lyrics, and so on. Thanks to the memory of the Internet, one can trace the evolution of these narratives the way investigators traced the source of the explosion back to the face of the mine's longwall, a thousand-foot-wide seam of coal that is mined using a "shearer," a massive machine that grinds back and forth across the seam. At roughly 3:00 p.m. on April 5, 2010, the shearer struck some sandstone and a spark was released, which ignited methane gas that had collected in the area. The explosion tore throughout the mine for miles, fed by highly flammable coal dust that, against the most basic of mine safety regulations, had not been rendered inert.

Upper Big Branch was owned by Performance Coal, a subsidiary of Richmond, Virginia-based Massey Energy. Massey's CEO, Don Blankenship, testified before a US Senate subcommittee that safety had been his number one priority at the company. "I felt that other safety programs were too reliant on slogans and signs. So I designated safety as S-1: Safety First," he said. (See the *sign* inside designated? Rhymes with excavated, devastated, desolated.) Countless safety violations and the testimony of numerous miners suggest that Blankenship doth protest too much, that Massey had an unofficial policy of sacrificing worker safety for increased production and profits. I write *countless* violations, for the investigation revealed that many went unrecorded, and the company would often notify miners using "code words" when an inspector appeared on the premises so they could quickly correct or hide deficiencies. As the Department of Labor and the Mine Safety and Health Administration wrote in their report to the president, "In short, this was a mine with a significant history of safety issues, a mine operated by a company with a history of violations, and a mine and company that MSHA was watching closely."

Stanley "Goose" Stewart, a miner who survived the blast, testified before the US House of Representatives Committee on Education and Labor that the mine was a "ticking time bomb." When he began to distrust the company's commitment to S-1, Stewart decided to keep a private record of the safety problems he observed. "I told my wife," he wrote in his prepared statement, "'If anything happens to me, get a lawyer and sue the [blankety blank] out of them! That place is a ticking time bomb.' Only I didn't say 'blankety blank' to her because I was so scared—and mad! She told me to write down things that were wrong because she wouldn't know specifics or the terminology to convey what was happening." See language as a wall, and a window. Hear the ticking blankety blanks.

Clay Mullins testified on behalf of his brother, Rex, who died in the explosion. I read Mullins's prepared testimony in his own handwriting on two pieces of notepaper that have been scanned and preserved in the House Committee's record of the hearing, and illuminate it with the *Charleston Daily Mail*'s account of the proceedings. During his testimony, Mullins went off script. He wore a T-shirt with Rex's photograph printed on it where you might expect to see a slogan, or logo, or nothing at all. At one point, he stood up and pointed to the photo. "This is my brother. I don't have him no more," he said. As the article describes, "He removed the shirt to reveal another beneath with the names of all 29 miners who were killed. 'This is my other family of brothers I lost,' he said, remaining standing before members of Congress." No words.

I watch a computer-simulated reenactment of the explosion, and I compare it to an interactive map that marks the bodies of the deceased. I hover my mouse over each little red X to reveal a picture of that miner and a few sentences about his life. At first so many of their stories seem the same—these men loved their families, loved to hunt and watch football—but the more time I spend with them by way of these maps and other artifacts, the closer I seem to be getting to something authentic, hard, and real. But then all I have to do is ask, *What is that something? What am I looking for?* and the sense of clarity blurs, escapes my grasp like a silvery minnow flipping out of the palm of my hand, or a mountain ridgeline gone to fog. I have no idea. I don't know yet. I don't know.

Again and again, I watch a CNN interview with Pam Napper, whose son Josh died in the explosion, along with her brother and nephew. Josh had been working at Upper Big Branch for only eight weeks. With incredible equanimity, Napper says that losses like this are commonplace in mining families, including her own. "It's their living; that's how they make a living," she explains. "That's just West Virginia, and when something bad happens we come together." Her words seem to keep her anchored in an expanding universe of grief, but on what ground do they rest?

I hear this saying—"That's just West Virginia"—again and again in response to the disaster, and I feel my head start to spin, nodding *yes* and *no* at the same time. "We come together," folks say, and I imagine a human chain in the form of the state's jagged borders. I feel a pulse in the first two letters of West: *we*. In the wake of Upper Big Branch, the grief I feel is not that of a coal miner's daughter, but rather that of a daughter of the state of West Virginia. Often when I tell a new acquaintance that I'm from West Virginia, he or she will mention having a friend from the state. My first impulse is always to ask, "Oh, where from? What's your friend's name?" assuming that I might know the person—or that the person I probably do not know is akin to family, part of that *we* to which I will always be bound. If our conversation lingers on the subject of West Virginia—the winding roads, good white-water rafting, history, politics, beautiful mountains, awful coal mining disasters—I'll inevitably end up saying something like "That's just West Virginia," claiming while displacing the bitter and the sweet. Later, I'll feel disappointed in myself for not being able to offer a truer, more complete defense or explanation of the place. And even later, I'll realize that minutiae about West Virginia is lousy cocktail party conversation in the first place; forget poems, I really need to work on my small talk. Most people don't go around acting like unofficial ambassadors for their homeland. I believe my impulse and struggle to sufficiently explain the place is a uniquely West Virginian trait, reflecting the value that this place puts on community and connection, a value which probably has a lot to do with why and how I write.

THE FIRST poem I ever wrote about West Virginia was in immediate response to the aftermath of another mining disaster, the explosion at the Sago mine in Upshur County on January 2, 2006. This explosion, which killed twelve of thirteen trapped miners, was exceptionally devastating, for during a brief bubble of time from around midnight to 3:00 a.m. on the morning of January 4, news outlets reported the opposite ratio of deceased to surviving miners. The ebullience of that time is preserved on the front pages of many major newspapers. A headline on the front page of the January 4 *New York Times* says, "12 Miners Found Alive 41 Hours After Explosion." I read the article now and feel a small unspoiled ember of joy flicker in my heart like the light from CNN that illuminated my dark living room in Ohio during the wee hours of that morning, years ago.

A correction ran later that day: "False Report of 12 Survivors Was Result of Miscommunications." The story transformed from the explosion to the "miscommunication." The International Coal Group's CEO, Bennett Hatfield, struggled to explain the false report. "In the jubilation of the moment, the rules didn't hold," he said, and apologized for having "allowed the jubilation to go on longer than we should have." The article uses the word "jubilation" no less than five times to describe that ecstatic time between. In the original article, an MSHA administrator described the protracted and disorienting experience of waiting for news: "every minute seems like an hour." One wonders how many minutes those three hours of false jubilation must have seemed like at the time, and what quality of space or time they still occupy in the grieving families' hearts. In a number of photographs accompanying the corrected article, women clasp their hands tightly over their mouths, as if something terrible and unknown might slip out of their bodies. A whole dream-life, a whole universe, might fill such a window.

My love for language and curiosity about what poems can do had never felt like a deep *need* to write until the vertiginous displacement of watching Sago unfold. Distance allowed me to truly understand the place I came from as "home" for the first time, yet I also felt like a voyeur, seeing its raggedy borders, its limits, as both an outsider and an insider. The message I heard in the miscommunication—through the tangle and transformation of signals between my living room in Ohio and the place where the men came to rest in the belly of that West Virginia mountain—offered clarity about what poetry does, clarity that I only felt in my gut at the time and have been refining ever since by writing and reading poems. For the first time I understood poetry as a tool (similar to, yet exceeding, a hammer, scalpel, microscope, magic word, lullaby, threaded needle, drum, explosive) that I wielded not in my hands but in my voice, between my mind and my heart. For the first time I saw the page as a kind of space beyond space where language, a material beyond material, could answer a phone I suddenly heard ringing off the hook.

I've found the first draft of that first West Virginia poem and I am glad to see that it is more interesting than I was capable of realizing when I wrote it years ago. The poem's central metaphor is about direction and orientation—the difference between using compass directions and using landmarks to navigate a landscape and, thus, through an *ars poetica* lens, the difference between the abstract and the concrete. Here are the first few lines:

> In West Virginia, we use landmarks
> instead of compass direction. Turn
>
> on the gravel road just past the barn.
> If you pass the church you've gone too far.

Despite that too-cute-by-half joke about religion, the poem recognizes its inability to comprehend the depth of the disaster. The poem lingers on the surface, and when I revised it and then eventually abandoned it years ago, I thought the poem's problem was its reliance on clichés, but that's a more complex problem than I realized at the time. The last line of the draft—"churches, pickup trucks, and gravel roads"—seems to suggest that although these "landmarks" may be cliché from the outsider's stereotype, they have real significance and meaning to the people who drive those roads in those trucks.

Regardless, I chickened out by pointing to the grain of the surface without digging beneath it. The poem reduces opacity to blindness, and it fails or refuses to try other senses or angles:

> Watching this
> from Ohio, I notice the hills
> and the way people from back home look
> on television, the familiar
> texture of the grass and the voices.

What is "the way," and can I account for what happens in the gap between the appearance and the real thing? Between the surface fiction/friction and the truth gasping for air miles beneath the coverage?

I read the final revised draft of the poem and see that I did try to push beyond that ambivalence. Instead of explanation, the revised poem begins with connection—an imperative and definite articles that attempt to break down the fourth wall of the page and sidle up to the reader. In the revised first line, I command the reader to "Take the gravel road next to the barn." And this version of the poem ends *inside* the mystery space between the surface and the unknown:

> They ask miners
> to explain how dark it is inside.
> I notice the hills, the familiar
>
> texture of the grass and the voices.
> *Just wave your hand in front of your face,*
> *ma'am, and you can't see nothing at all.*

I was getting there.

I SEE mines everywhere. I see poems everywhere. One of the essential challenges in coal mine engineering is preventing collapse of the roof of the mine. In "room and pillar" mining, the style used at Sago, up to sixty percent of the coal in a seam is left behind in the form of pillars that support the roof under the weight of the mountain. In "longwall" mining, the style used at Upper Big Branch, no pillars are used. The roof is allowed to fall into the expanding, unstable void that is left behind, called the "gob." The coal miners operating the shearer are sheltered from that collapse by an awning of hydraulic supports that jack up the roof above them. Another challenge in mine engineering is ventilation, to provide the miners with sufficient air to breathe and temperate working conditions, while dissipating the flammable gases that are released from the earth. Sago had a history of roof fall violations, evidence that the mine's support system was insufficient. And miner after miner testified about the terrible ventilation at Upper Big Branch and the company's chronic lack of concern. The mine was cited every month during 2009 for improper ventilation, including citations for redirecting airflow when men were working underground—a "cardinal sin" in mining. Gina Jones testified that her husband, Dean, who died at Upper Big Branch, would sometimes fall asleep at the dinner table after work, his body so exhausted from working in such low air.

One of my final revisions to the Sago poem involved breaking the first draft's single block of text into a series of three-line stanzas. Though the effect was similar to that of cutting more facets into an ersatz diamond, my intention must have been to put more air in the poem, to carve or engineer more room for movement, slippage, and breath, in its mine/mind-space. I can also see those breaks as a way to stabilize the poem—the white space like a skeleton undergirding the text. Over the years I've used different metaphors to account for how poems work, including the poem as a word-sculpture and the poem as a machine made of words. Those metaphors now seem too inert and cold. Poems, as I've come to understand them, are inhabited spaces. A poem is more like a house or a body or an embrace. A mine and a yours.

I see mines and poems everywhere. Mines as dark, volatile, and breathless as a word as it is being spoken. As ink. As Josh Napper's handwriting in the notes he left for his mother, fiancée, and baby girl before he went to work on April 5: "If anything happens to me . . ." As dark, volatile, and breathless as what he knew. As what happened. As dark, volatile, and breathless as the handwriting in Stewart's journal and Mullins's testimony. As dark, volatile, and breathless as the tunnel a word cuts into the infinite unspoken. As dark, volatile, and breathless as the space in which words are suspended. As the substance from which words are chiseled. As dark, volatile, and breathless as the silence that holds us in place. As the silence between the lines in all the poems ever written. All the silent and elided sounds and letters. All the darkness. All the breathlessness. All on the verge of collapse.

ROGER TONEY was headed out of the mine when the explosion happened. First he felt it in his ears. "Intense pressure," he told interviewers. "And instantly you couldn't see anything. It just—dust just blew overtop of us. And there was a lot of debris in the dust. . . . And you could hear signs—like in the mines there's signs that say like Plumley Switch this way and rescuer chamber this way. There's signs all through the mines, and it sounded like every one of them came overtop of our mantrip."

Not heard, but *felt* in the ears. *There's signs all through the mines.* Explosion as poststructural nightmare: sign unbolted from signified and whipped around in a narrow space overhead. Perilously literal and beyond comprehension. This is the poem the explosion wrote, which I read by writing other poems, the way a miner might feel his way back to the surface. Find the patterns that make the structure, inside and out. The poetry is in the process is in the body.

I'm surprised by how much of the "poetry" part of my mind I need to make sense of these interviews from the state and federal investigation. The transcripts are on the Internet for anyone to access, but I feel like I have my ear pressed to a door when reading them. The interview subjects are mostly Upper Big Branch miners and their family members. Their words vine through the rhythmic lattice of legalese. The attorneys and the miners are both fluent in the language of mining. I am not, but I do know the language of compression. I read along, mostly lost on the trail of Q&A, Q&A, Q&A, till I get snagged on pieces of language that connect me to the latent universal mystery. Mining terminology is rich with connotations; each word could be a poem unto itself. I imagine a book with one term per page: mouth, gob, rib, face, brow, vein, overcast, continuous miner, self-rescuer, black damp, mantrip, burden, break line. So many of these words attach the body to the mine, and as I read, I feel myself pulled in and under.

I'm between the lines. The signs fly over my head. I feel the danger in my ears before I know what it is. Michael Ferrell testified that he worked for Massey Energy for the whole of his thirteen-year mining career, and most of that time at Upper Big Branch, until he was let go in February 2010, just a couple of months before the April explosion. Some people might say that he was let go because he has a mouth on him, that he gets out of line, but of course that just depends on who's doing the drawing, how many miles deep, and how much value they've ascribed to the bottom line. Ferrell frequently received written reports from Performance Coal's president, Chris Blanchard, telling him it was "critical" for him to work faster. "And, you know, a lot of people can define critical in a lot of ways," Ferrell said, "but I knowed what that meant. That meant if I didn't get this stuff in to suit him, he was going to fire me. But I was not going to break rules or regulations to do it." Ferrell saw the writing on the wall. "I was not going to be the man that they wanted me to be," he said. "I mean, I made it abundantly clear in more than one instance that I was going to do whatever was right, it didn't matter what it cost me or this company."

"Massey speaks code," Ferrell said. "They will never come out black-and-white until you do something wrong. . . . But they speak their sign language to you. Anybody that's worked around the mines knows, you know, what's going on." Ferrell recalled a time Blanchard took him aside to express his disappointment in how long it had taken Ferrell's crew to do a job without cutting corners. "I think you use safety as a crutch here," Blanchard said. "I'm not going to lie to you."

I see the abstraction of safety nailed into a piece of wood and tucked under a man's arm. He gives it his weight, propels his body forward, out of the darkness. See him squint into the sun, exposed, like a piece of language decoded, turned out from between the lines and suddenly in the clear. Like a piece of coal, spent, exhausted to ash—that pallor, that light.

SOMETIMES WRITING feels like trying to tear the stars from the firmament, then finding dirt under your fingernails and realizing that it was really earth the whole time. Sometimes I sit down at the page with lead in my stomach. Sometimes light. Sometimes my heart chokes my throat. Sometimes I nearly write myself out of time and space—go so far in that I'm out. Sometimes I start so far out, that I can't get in past the surface. When I sit down at the page, I am making my life, my living. But no matter how strong these forces feel, I am not risking my life—"It's their living," Pam Napper said. And the feelings I have when "mining" language are simply not the same as what a miner feels when he goes underground. They're nothing like the weight that miner Gary Quarles carried to make his living. Quarles was a shearer operator on the longwall of Upper Big Branch. On Easter Sunday, the day before the explosion, Ferrell was working in his yard and noticed his best friend, Gary—"he was like my brother. . . . And I mean, his kids was like my kids"—driving back and forth on the road in front of his house. Ferrell could tell Quarles needed to say something. "And when you're around somebody enough, you kind of know something is wrong, you know." Ferrell signaled an opening by taking a break from his yard work, and Quarles finally stopped by. Ferrell recounted their conversation. "Man, he said, they got us up there mining and we ain't got no air. He said, You can't see nothing. Every day, he said, I just thank God when I get out of that coal mines that I ain't got to be here no more. He said, I just don't want to go back. He said, When I get up in the mornings, I don't want to put my shoes on. He said, I don't want to make myself go to work, because, he said, I'm just scared to death to go or, he said, something bad is going to happen."

Ferrell told Quarles that the conditions he'd found at his new mining job were vastly better than at the Massey mine. He offered to ask his new boss if there was an open position for Quarles. Sure enough, first thing the next morning, Ferrell got him a job. That day he must have felt in possession of the kind of news that begs to be printed in bold type on the front page of the *New York Times*. "Well, before I could make it home," Ferrell said, "I passed all the ambulances and fire trucks" coming from Upper Big Branch. Quarles was gone.

Writing is satisfying because it doesn't satisfy; it fills the writer only with the desire to write more, leaving resolution perpetually out of reach. The desire that keeps me coming back to the page is different from what motivated Quarles to overcome unspeakable dread and reenter the mine each day. But I imagine that the feeling of finally hitting upon some words that sing, closing the laptop, and saying "Enough. Done for the day" could be something like the satisfaction a miner might feel after a day's work—feeling that empty space inside the mine like a fullness inside his own body. Enough, yet never enough, to keep him coming back to that same mine, day after day, for decades. So much of poetry happens on its surface—rhythm, sound, structure. I remember the illusion I felt after finishing the first draft of my Sago poem—that my neat and tidy poem had righted some small part of the tremendous chaotic wrong. I imagine there might be a similar feeling in the body of a miner as he surveys how much of the mountain he has moved in a day's work. But, of course, that one poem was not enough. And as I toss and turn, unsettled by unfinished, unfinishable poems, I know that "Done for the day" is never "Done forever." See my imaginary miner climbing into the mantrip, riding to the surface, then washing up in the bathhouse. He heads home to dinner and sleep. See him wake the next morning to find coal dust in his bedsheets. Years later, coal dust in his lungs. You can't shake it.

I am not a miner. I am not a miner's daughter, wife, or mother. I am imagining all this from the comfort of great distance. I hope the distance can become a point of entry, but I worry about how I might mishandle, mishear, miscommunicate. And though I am suspicious of the news stories that seem to feed on the surface of this loss without ever getting close enough to feel the vacuum pulling not just on the heartstrings but on the actual body, I have an insatiable interest in such stories. I hope my interest is not voyeuristic, but rather rooted in the desire to dispel, puncture, expand, and complicate any false closure. But I confront those lines from my failed poem—"the way people from back home look / on television . . ."—and feel how hard it is to get to the real. You must allow yourself to become lost in a place that might collapse. You must feel the way out, which is only deeper in.

There are no words, but there are poems. The material of poetic language can, like a threadbare glove, put you in contact with the unknown while reminding you of the forgotten tenderness of your own skin. It is the threshold that enables empathy and understanding. *Under*standing, not *over*standing: standing under the same mountain as another person. Understanding requires the courage to come into contact with an unknown so real that it might take your whole being as you know it and never give it back. Understanding is immersing yourself, allowing yourself to be changed.

FIVE A.M., the lunar eclipse of dream. Sun, earth, moon. I'm a miner, I'm his grieving wife, I'm poet-me. Clutching a pillow, I'm clutching the space between the longwall face and the gob and a line break. Light sifts in, like earth, like ink blotting—*Hold this. Stay here,* poet-me thinks, trying to sleep the moment back together as it pulls itself apart. It slips away, like a balloon or a fireball or a heavenly body under earth. Too late. I'm back to my old senses again.

I dreamed a mineral line of questioning. I put my mind into the space between.

"Why," no one asked in the interviews, "do we do this?"

By this I mean bury our beauty alive. By this I mean breathe dirt.

I was in a mine, which was a poem, which was a problem, which was a heart, which was a bottomless hole, which was a closed loop pulsing, constantly, I suddenly realized, beneath my consciousness.

A spark touches combustible gas and becomes an explosion, leaving twenty-nine dead men in its wake. I write by, and try to do right by, the light and energy of such contact and connection. I strive to write poems that are as integral as the human chain of one hundred men who carried out the deceased from the belly of the mine. They didn't make anything resembling the shape of West Virginia; they made a line. That is a poem—one man, one lifeline, carrying a burden, and then turning it over to another. What is more simple, clear, and difficult to understand than that? That is how we recover, how we mine, how we mean.

RICHARD CURREY
Believer's Ride: Writing from the Mountains

SOME YEARS AGO, the literary magazine *Story* was revived after a twenty-two-year hiatus. Originally launched in 1931, *Story* was a magazine in whose pages appeared many if not most of the writers whose work shaped American literature in the twentieth century: Mc-Cullers, O'Connor, Hemingway, Fitzgerald, Salinger, Saroyan, Heller, Mailer, Algren, Capote, and many more. *Story* was a legendary piece of our literary history, and the editor behind the magazine's revival aimed to make the new *Story* the same touchstone it had once been.

My publisher called to tell me that the editor at *Story* had asked to look at any fiction he might have under contract. I was working on a collection of stories at the time, all set in West Virginia in the early years of the last century, and suggested we submit a piece called "Believer's Flood."

Told in the first person by a retired coal miner struggling with the disabling lung disease everybody in hill country knows as Black Lung, "Believer's Flood" recounts an episode in the bloody coal wars in southern West Virginia in the early 1920s. The story's narrator, Raymond Dance, was in the middle of that war and in the course of the story faces down violence and a moral choice in protecting his home and family.

After a few weeks, the editor at *Story* called to say that a member of the magazine's editorial board, one of those she had asked to read submissions and make recommendations about publication, had advised her to pass on "Believer's Flood." I knew the reviewer's name immediately, an eminent editor, critic, author—a literary Brahmin. His objection, I learned, was that he could not imagine a mountaineer coal miner bringing such introspective, insightful, and detailed thinking to a personal situation as Raymond Dance did in my story, nor would such a man as Dance communicate those thoughts so lyrically.

"He says it just doesn't work," the editor told me. "He doesn't think anybody will buy a miner from the hills talking the way yours does."

She was quick to tell me she disagreed with this opinion, but I understood her position was difficult: she had invited a celebrity of American letters to serve on the board of the magazine and to recommend what to publish and what not to. She needed such people to drive the success of the magazine, people who brought an imprimatur of both legacy and legitimacy, and there were inherent pressures to go the way the board members suggested she go.

I imagined the board member reading through my story once, quickly, then rendering his opinion like a judge speaking from the bench, remanding me back to my cell so he could move on in his busy day. He operated out of his own assumptions without a second thought, made his pronouncement, and I am sure he thought no more about it. I would love to recall that I delivered an impassioned speech on behalf of Appalachian writers everywhere. But what I did was stand there, phone to my ear, somewhere between confused and appalled, too much of either to speak. The opinion about my story carried the stagnant whiff of an imperious mindset I thought might have disappeared from the ranks of celebrated New York editors by the 1990s. Clearly not, since "Believer's Flood" was dismissed with a breezy discrimination that seemed to hold that Appalachians, all of us, lived free of such apparently high-born traits as introspection, insight, or emotional intelligence.

I WAS born in Wood County, West Virginia, in a place and time and into a family where one's potential was more or less limited by both reality and my family's prevailing assumptions about what was possible in any given life.

My father's family, going back to the 1830s in Appalachia, is a lineage committed to the primary and sometimes overwhelming task of survival on rocky land: every family story told was about this one thing. My mother's history is rooted in similar values but is even more stark. Born in 1927 in the front bedroom of her grandparents' four-room cabin on a West Virginia mountaintop, orphaned at three weeks of age, she grew up without electricity or running water. Her grandparents raised (or butchered) what they ate and traded for other goods at a general store they reached by horse-drawn wagon. My mother walked to a one-room school through a mile of deep forest, and never saw a town with a population greater than three hundred people before she was a teenager.

My parents' worlds cohered around rigor: physical labor, usually of the roughest sort, and an unadorned determination to stand the ground and persist and prevail, come what may. It was Americana writ small into one native territory, and creative or artistic callings were nothing that my people were privy to or would give way to; indeed, the creative arts, outside of a little barn dance music on Saturday night or making something useful like a chair or a piece of clothing, were deemed frivolous, trivial, hobbies at best and wastes of time at worst. This was the nature of things, written into the culture from the old days on.

So if one is a writer hailing from the Appalachia I came out of, the artistic challenge becomes twofold. There is the working bias delivered from the cultural mainstream—where a literary tastemaker cannot imagine a mountaineer with intelligence or insight. But there is also the internal prejudice rising from one's own community and within one's own family. If an Appalachian writer has made it far enough in his or her career to encounter the broader societal biases, that writer has also managed to renegade their way out of what my mother called "the old homeplace," against discrimination from within, the sort that rises out of one's own culture and is maintained and delivered by one's own people, the notion that we are forever barred from certain sorts of ambition or achievement. My mother called it "getting above your raisings," a common phrase in the mountains. And while my mother was not an unkind person, she was rigid about the rules of mountain life and society, exemplifying a kind of perverse pressure to fail that is alive and well in hill country today.

IT IS certainly not news that discriminatory attitudes toward Appalachia and Appalachians still work across the weave of American society. The fine writer from Kentucky, Silas House, has said that mountain folk "are the last people you can still publicly slur without people making a big stink about it."

John Fiske, a respected historian writing in the late nineteenth century, decided that mountain people were doomed to poverty and "backwardness" because, he believed, we are all descended from "convicts and indentured servants." Apparently Fiske viewed us as burdened with a kind of genetic curse, a deficiency born in the bloodlines. He would not be the last to opine that "internal deficiencies" drive a culture of poverty in Appalachia.

The broad currents of thought at work here are classic forms of discrimination, of peddling some loosely organized allegations of social cause and effect and then using those allegations to impose cultural isolation (with its various attendant evils, sadnesses, and squandered opportunities). In short order an entire population, and a large section of the United States, was and is still often reduced to Li'l Abner—a comic strip. A joke.

Indeed, one way of maintaining Appalachia's status as an impoverished sideshow of American life has been through humor. *Did you hear about the fire in the West Virginia governor's mansion? Took out the whole trailer park.* I laughed when I heard that one. And what's the harm in a joke? Not a lot, perhaps, and I do not believe Appalachians should be unnecessarily pompous or precious about lampooning our regional predicament, but, that said, it is of more than passing note that Appalachia continues to hold the lead for a demeaning brand of humor where incest, bestiality, sodomy, and single-digit IQs are the core (and, apparently, only) subjects of humor. Even former vice president Dick Cheney once cracked wise about West Virginia being a state prone to incest, at a public event at the National Press Club in Washington, D.C. Yes, Senator Robert Byrd took Cheney to task, and, yes, an apology was duly rendered, but the fact is: the joke was made. And a sitting vice president of the United States felt no particular qualms about making the joke in distinguished company at a televised event—another expression of the seam of ritualized bias that has, over time, leaked into the bloodstream not just of West Virginia but all of the mountain south. There is a strange sort of battered self-esteem that is institutionalized among Appalachians, a phenomenon not seen in residents of any other part of North America—but is it any wonder?

So what can any of this mean for Appalachian writers? We are often damned from within by both our families and our frequently sclerotic regional culture, and just as often damned from without by the mainstream of American culture. The (fallacious) unspoken question persists: Who is a mountaineer to imagine that he or she should be a writer? A maker of literature? The implied threat in this bullying question can provoke a kind of silence in the imagination that might come to afflict a writer's creative impulse, his or her voice—even the will to work.

It is all part of the broader disenfranchisement aimed at the mountain south, historically but even now, as the twenty-first century gets fully under way. It's a time-honored recipe: take the self-directed repression and fears that a group of people turn inward against themselves and their communities, add prejudices long inflicted by the "outside world," sharply reduce job options, personal income, and social support, shake well—and you have the classic makings of a ghettoized population. A "set-aside" group, as some sociologists have called Appalachians. And once one is a bona fide member of a set-aside place and people, the primacy of making any sort of art, written or otherwise, can slip quickly out of view.

THE FATE of my story "Believer's Flood" hung for a few weeks with the editor of *Story*, who in the end overruled her celebrity reviewer and published my story. Not long afterward, on a book tour for the collection the story appears in (*The Wars of Heaven*), I did a reading at a small college in West Virginia.

After the reading the crowd thinned out and a woman in her late eighties approached, small and slow, making her way carefully up the center aisle to the front of the room. She reached me and paused for breath and then said that her father was a man very much like my coal miner character Raymond Dance.

"Dad was there, you know. In the mine wars. And he fought. He marched and he fought and he stood up. And your story . . . well, it's perfect. I don't know how you did it but you got every detail right. Not just what happened, but how it felt. How it sounded. It's as if Dad came into you for a little while and told his story through you."

I was, of course, deeply touched, as any writer would be on receiving this sort of affirmation. That night, in my hotel room, I wondered at the fact that in another avenue of American writing, "Believer's Flood" had been quickly dismissed as a failure, unworthy of publication. But here, in the actual territory where the events of the story took place, it reached out in the very way that any of us who write always hope to connect with our readers.

The literary world has changed, of course, since "Believer's Flood" was first published and I spoke with an octogenarian daughter of a coal miner. Over the last thirty years many superb writers out of Appalachia have reinvented and reshaped the literature of the mountain south. Young writers hailing from the mountains are finding their voices at Appalachian universities and move on to MFA programs across the country. Appalachian literature has joined the larger reach of American culture, driven by formidable engines of talent and vision and voice.

But for some emerging Appalachian writers the battle is still being fought. I hear from these young writers, who tell me that there are places and families where the social and cultural permission to write is still denied in one way or another—if not actively derided, then simply ignored. Their writing is a secret, and it remains unclear to them how to take another step, how to find themselves as working writers, or how to locate the pathways cut for them by the generation of gifted writers who have gone ahead.

And, meanwhile, the wider stereotyping of mountain people seems to persist. We are, variously, benighted reality show characters unaware of our comic stupidity, or demonic brutes wandering the mountain nights, or even the innocent, unaware denizens of an Edenic pastoral landscape. Meanwhile, as actual mountain people hang on and battle the old threats (joblessness, poverty, disease, alcohol), and new ones (drugs and drug addiction of one kind or another), much of the mountain south remains a backwater, one of the nation's bad dreams, still widely cut off from hope and possibility. And who supposes anything like literary art might come out of that? But it will, and it must, because writing—storytelling, poetry, plays—has come to serve as a cardinal direction through the mountain culture's old legacies of loss and shame and self-imposed silences. Literature has always been a way to meet ourselves on the road forward, and the mountain south is a region that needs that crossroads of mind and soul and history as much and as urgently as it ever has.

RJ GIBSON

Outside the Fencelines of Eden

Therefore whatsoever ye have spoken in darkness shall be
heard in the light; and that which ye have spoken in the ear
in closets shall be proclaimed upon the housetops.

—Luke, chapter 12, verse 3

1.

I value dissent, marvel at the guerrilla assaults some artists manage. Part of my social role with friends is that I will say things others
will not. I write about sex and desire in as direct and candid a way as I
can. Not graphic, but matter-of-fact. Unsurprisingly, frank discussions
of various sodomies challenge a lot of people. And I think that's just
fine. But I recognize I'm a dissident. I've made myself unwelcome at
one local establishment that hosted a monthly reading series, insti-
gating a kerfuffle that led to the series relocating to a new locale after
being at the original site for more than six years. I know it has cost me
publications. That's fine, too. It's an aesthetic issue for me, a moral
issue for others (even if they won't admit it). I don't expect people to
realize that the erotic as a poetic tradition goes back to the Greeks,
that there's some awfully titillating stuff in the Bible. (The Book of
Ezekiel might be my favorite in terms of sheer range of sexual diversity: gold and silver dildos, foreigners with massive appendages, and
most importantly, copious ejaculate "similar unto horses'").

Art is a site for challenge; it is a practice that pushes my sense of
self. I like to say what I'm not supposed to say. I like to talk about what
I'm not supposed to talk about. For most people, that's sex. That's the

obvious forbidden in America. But that's not what I want to talk about, sex and desire. I'm obsessed with desire, how we live with and around its manifestations. I'm not merely prurient, but I'm fascinated by how prudish we are when it comes to talking about sex. Abstract discussions of desire are insufficient, though they may be lovely. I want representation in the canon. The queer body should be in poems, lovely or not.

My stance is not just about content, but poetry having a social function. Other queers might be served by seeing an unembarrassed representation of their desires and lives. Refusal has always been more beneficial than acceptance. And I seem to have an almost genetic resistance to doing things the easy way. But I'm here right now, forty, and I'm beginning to understand my work in different ways. I want more from it. I want different from it. I have made a specialty of a sort of *trompe l'oeil* where candor is a smoke screen for the emotional distance I maintain throughout the work. What I forbid myself, what I'm trying to embrace, is emotional vulnerability.

It's difficult, this reprogramming. Aesthetically, I admire a hyperborean eye. I love Flannery O'Connor's moral universe. There's no sense that she has any feeling at all for her characters. They're there to be worked upon. And the engines of her universe are delightful. The same goes for Hitchcock's films. I love that his vision was *the* vision. Everyone else was just there to make it happen.

From a purely practical aspect, in order to escape the bathetic, the best way to write about sex and desire is to work from a bit of rhetorical remove. It's the rhetorical angle of lyric poems that I find interesting—the personality and mind of the speaker. Not the floridness of the line or observation. A friend, a former teacher, gone now, would always comment on my poems' "coolness." It was just a "veneer" she said: underneath it was the heart, the heat. But that "veneer" was always problematic for her. We joked about blocked chakras. I can hear her saying it, in various rooms in different seasons. I didn't understand what she meant at the time. But I do now. The risks in my poems are all rhetorical or in terms of content. I wasn't ready to allow emotional risk into my work. Personal vulnerability did not flourish in my poems.

2.

I was raised in a family where "Because" was supposed to be a sufficient answer. I asked a lot of questions as a kid and I can't blame my family for eventually becoming exhausted. I was a sort of perpetual motion—I didn't sleep well, or long; I talked a lot; I craved hearing books read or stories told; I was and am the youngest son my family was ill-prepared for. My father was the worst about using "Because" as an answer. The understood finish was always, "I said so." That frustrated me and actually prolonged the questioning. Then, as now, I enjoyed testing the limits of what's permissible, and I took a sort of delight in pushing my father. I'd also take whatever punishment he brought my way. Every instance where he resorted to some abuse or violence, I knew I'd won that moment. The social dynamics surrounding my father were fascinating. He insisted that he was right in all things, and I chafed at those assertions. I felt sometimes that it was my duty to insist, to stand up to him.

Ex-military, he was rigid in terms of gender roles; he was the Dad, and the Dad was to be obeyed. But I knew somehow, early, that outside of our house, away from our family, he was not important. He didn't have much say in, or control of, anything. He was vexed and thwarted, considered himself too good to be a mail carrier, too special to be a father to *this* family, the smartest dude in the room. He could never admit mistake, regret, or vulnerability. He would lash out physically, but more often, he was verbally abusive. He specialized in threatening me with the denial of something I wanted, enjoyed, or valued. *No violin lesson if you don't. No trip to the mall, unless. You're gonna lose every one of those damned books if you won't.* He wanted me to cry, he wanted me upset, he wanted me timid and compliant. Over time I realized that. He could not control me, which he thought was his right. I was, and am, in any number of ways, a disappointment to and repudiation of my father. But to live with him, to share a home day after day, I had to somehow survive. My mother ran interference as best she could, but she was no physical match for him. She would beg me to give in, and I just couldn't. My own stubbornness, my own sense of entitlement to happiness, wouldn't allow it.

I can't remember when I realized that showing no reaction, no emotion, was the best strategy for dealing with my father. I wish I could remember the first time I didn't react. When I let him threaten and shout and bloviate and I just stood there.

And so, world, you have my father and his paternal failings, and my own stubbornness, to thank for my attitudes about men, authority, and the thrill of going as far as one can. The liberties of it are obvious. The limitations, less so, but somehow stronger.

3.

My first encounter with religious extremism came in second grade, in line for the water fountain. A nasty young Baptist named Angela stood on the other side of the fountain, proselytizing to each of us as we took our drinks. "Have you accepted Jesus into your heart?" "Are you saved?" "What will happen to your parents if they don't know Jesus?" She was a stout, potato-shaped thing with hair the color of an Irish Setter, and a small coffee-stain birthmark on her cheek. Aside from Bobby Bartlett, who had been held back twice, she was the biggest kid in the class. She loved Jesus and she resented almost every one of us who "had it better" than she did.

"Your mom thinks you're so great. You're just a little fairy." "You're not so special." "She doesn't know what you're really like." I heard that a lot from her, until I finally said, "It's your own fault that nobody likes you." She made great sport of hectoring Michael, the only Jehovah's Witness in the class, demanding the teacher explain why "he didn't have to stand for the Pledge," decrying him first for not believing in Jesus, so he wouldn't go to Heaven, then adding insult to the whole damnation thing by pointing out he never got presents. "Not birthday, not Christmas. Nothin'." She was adamant in the fire and brimstone theology of her church. She let us know of her devoted observance, the three services a week. Her idea of worship seemed correlated to her church's concept of baptism: one must be immersed totally, otherwise it doesn't take or count. If you only went to church once a week, you might as well not go at all.

She was astounding in her certainty. Seven years old, nearly five feet tall, she was like some offensive lineman for Christ, plowing through everything in her way, just waiting to spike it in that Heavenly End Zone. She loved the creation story from Genesis. Eden, the way she learned it, was just like West Virginia: mountains, and rivers, and wildlife. And in her cosmology, so was Heaven. One doesn't expect a second-grader to have a particularly sophisticated worldview. But even at the time, I was fascinated and perplexed by how unified Angela's was, how firmly entwined it was with her daily life. My experience of the creation story left me imagining Eden as some veldt from *Mutual of Omaha's Wild Kingdom*. Some *other* place, where the miraculous could live and happen. Even in kindergarten, I realized that my hometown wasn't a place that invited the wondrous. It was only what it was every day: dirt roads, pastures, unhappy families, and the sense that nothing was ever quite as good as it might be.

But for Angela, Rock Cave was her blueprint for the world entire and her unaffiliated Baptist upbringing was her lens. I went to the little local Methodist church regularly with my mom. I had perfect attendance for more years than I care to admit. Our sermons never made it to the outer reaches of crazy (we never learned that unicorns, Strawberry Shortcake, Rainbow Brite, and My Little Pony were tools of Satan and should be burned because they invited demonic notice, but at Revival, Angela did, and then told us about the bonfire of toys and unicorn posters held one night); the basic gist of our sermons was how to be Christian in this life, in this time and place. The Bible was there to guide us and teach us. There wasn't a hint on Sundays that the essential sinfulness of Man was insurmountable, that a corporeal legion of Satanic forces roamed the contemporary world. But that was Angela's world. "You know why it's rainin'? Jesus is sad. He's cryin'." It rains a lot here, so we heard it often. "So when it snows," I asked once, "does that mean God has dandruff?" I was told I shouldn't mock our Lord. Obviously, I wasn't a real Christian if I would say something like that.

Angela was another bully. Her righteousness wasn't the armor and shield of Acts, it was more like the cellophane on a Starlight Mint, another way she deflected her own disappointment, self-loathing, and jealousy. Once, she went to the pencil sharpener (this was first or second grade; we were using those ridiculously thick and long black pencils) and sharpened her pencil sharp as she could get it. On her way back to her desk, she passed this girl named Stephanie. The next thing we knew, Stephanie was shrieking, and blood was everywhere. Angela had driven her pencil into Stephanie's upturned palm. She stabbed the pencil in, left it standing straight up, and walked back to her seat. Later in her elementary school career she brawled during kick ball, and broke another girl's arm.

I was a particular target for her resentment and anger. She punched me, kicked me, tackled me, insulted me. I was afraid of her. She was impulsive. Worse than that was her meanness. We found out later she was abused, badly, by her father. Her anger, her volatility, and her religiosity were a frightening combination. Later in life, I saw the long-term damage such indoctrination had done to too many of my gay friends. I don't have that awful angry G*d to overcome, or the corrosive propaganda that accompanies their interpretation of the Gospel. I'm not one of those poor boys who ends up married and going to truck stops, suiciding before they even have to shave, going into decades of therapy so that they can somehow return to feeling they deserve love and happiness and respect. There are bits of the forbidden there, though: rejecting self-loathing, demanding some measure of happiness, accepting my queer self and finding pride and worth in that. All of those are worth talking about. And those are aspects of the forbidden I've dealt with. And I've heard the other stories so often that I could retell them as my own. My gayness wasn't something I had to deal with in that deep emotional way.

Angela was the first bully I encountered outside my family. Denying her the satisfaction of my upset by not reacting was my strategy with her, too. It was the strategy that I cultivated and perfected throughout the rest of my public school career. Every bully and peckerwood after her never got a reaction from me. Many of them interpreted it as a sort of weakness, a passivity. Eventually it became one. I was detached from my own feelings. I didn't realize the usefulness of anger, of outburst. I felt nothing particularly deeply. The unintentional consequence of self-protection.

4.

Like so many stories, it is not that this one is too close, too personal to share; it is the fact that it is complicated, and a lack of care in its telling would diminish it. So. My maternal grandparents died when I was in my midtwenties. They were the first deaths of any real import to me, the first that I genuinely grieved. My grandfather died first, at home. He was surrounded by family when he passed. I was there, my mother too. We embraced one another and stood there. And she asked if I was all right. I lied, "I'm okay."

I was so far from okay, it would be almost a decade before I truly was okay. I faced a crisis, and I was singularly ill prepared to deal with it. I had to accept that mortality is within us all. Death is around us, even in the midst of the ordinary. I watched my grandfather die on his couch as he reached for his coffee. He died, my grandmother would die, all of us. And my mother. One day my mother would die. And what I wanted to do was behave like a six- or eight-year-old and bury my face in her neck and beg, "Don't die, don't die, don't die, don't die, don't . . ." But I couldn't say that aloud. I could not admit that truth for years.

Eighteen months later, my grandmother passed. Her dying took nearly a month, a process that exhausted us and wore us to nubs. There was an air of drama to the whole affair that was so in line with my grandmother's demeanor and personality. Stubborn, temperamental, verbally scathing when she chose, my grandmother was elemental. Reasoning with her in some instances was like asking a hurricane to redirect its course. We dealt with surgeries, DNR orders (an agonizing debate in and of itself), bouts of pneumonia, delirium and mania from drug reactions and fatty embolisms, week-long refusals to eat, refusal to spend time in a facility where she would get care and PT. She wanted to be home. She wanted us to take care of her. And eventually, on a rainy winter night, she died in her hospital bed, my mother her sole companion. It took me over an hour to reach the hospital because of flooding. (It rains a lot here, like I said.) When I got there, my mother was near to destroyed. "I knew I'd be here," she said. "I knew I'd be the one." My mother and grandmother had a complicated relationship, and as I drove her home, through the dark, over those one-lane roads, I could not look at my mother. I knew she was suffering, that she felt somehow singled out for this because of her conflictions, that she loved her mother but resented her. And even though we were freed of our roles as caregivers and audience, we faced something more awful: unfinished business.

All of the grief for my grandfather and grandmother was fused with a huge, miasmal, fear for my mother. I was reckoning with her mortality. Reckoning with all of what I could understand, was beginning to understand, and ultimately, couldn't understand. I was still trying to go to school and teach and be at home as often as I could. This meant nearly a year of getting up and driving to Morgantown so I could be there in time to teach my eight o'clock writing composition class. I wasn't taking care of myself: I wasn't eating well, I didn't sleep enough, I thought I could just muscle through everything and I'd be fine.

I went out every weekend during this period. The goal wasn't to have a good time, it was to get fucked up. I drank too much; I took hallucinogens and amphetamines. This was not a conscious attempt to kill pain. I just wanted to cut loose for a few hours, to dance until I was a sweaty slick mess, to kiss men and women and maybe go home with someone. I wanted to feel powerful in my body. Of course, it all crashed and burned. My car was loaded up for the move to Morgantown. About fifteen minutes into the trip, I began itching, breaking out in hives, sweating. About twenty minutes after that, I had to pull off the interstate, get down on my hands and knees on the shoulder and vomit. And even after there was nothing left inside me, my body was still trying to purge. It was, I found out, my first full-blown panic attack.

There's no way for someone who's never had a panic attack to understand its particular awfulness. The throat constricts and the tongue becomes dry, like a stale biscuit in the mouth. You must concentrate to swallow. At the same time, hives burst into bloom, some the size of a quarter, others no bigger around than a pencil eraser. The adrenalin rushes, the heart beats so fast it thuds across the room, a full-body sweat breaks out. The torso feels like a soda can being crushed in a fierce grip. Lightheadedness amplifies the pulse in the ears. You're sure the heart *will* fail. That *this* is the middle of dying. The entire time, you experience an embodiedness you do not want, a hyperawareness of all the body's systems but with no way to soothe the self drowning in this biochemical fire. And then, you vomit. Like a cloud shadow in summer, it comes on quickly, and then passes. And you sit upright back where you are supposed to be, the proper distance from your innards' bits and pieces, but your muscles are rubber, your skin is clammy, your eyes dry and stinging. You are dehydrated, but wary of drinking anything too quickly, for fear of vomiting again. Your diaphragm is stressed and stretched and hyperreactive.

After my panic attack, I had my first serious experience with antidepressants and antianxiety medications. It took about two years before I felt like I could go out by myself. I was lucky to have friends who would take me places. I was fine with friends; alone, I was vulnerable, incapable, a raw nerve transmitting and transmitting. That period of depression and anxiety lasted about four years. During that time I developed a profound writer's block. I was unable to write more than a few sentences at one time. I stopped writing entirely at some point. I lost track of friends. I burrowed into myself, trying to figure out how I was going to live, if what I was currently doing even felt like living.

Slowly that sense of being alive returned, and in the decade since, the anxiety attacks have been sporadic and mild. But there's always that fear for myself. That I could go back there, back to that impotence and sense of just existing, not even living half a life. As my condition has improved, I've taught myself to write again, slowly. I began writing for five minutes at a time, like learning meditation. I practiced only as much as I could, and I wouldn't judge the quality of what I wrote. In the beginning, five minutes felt infinite. What I put down weren't even complete thoughts, just a few words, maybe an image. Over time, I upped my writing stint to ten minutes, then to fifteen, and so on. Now, with the habit thoroughly ingrained, I rarely write more than forty or forty-five minutes at a time. I hit a threshold and become antsy. I want to do something else, even the dishes. So I give in to that impulse and stop. Breaks are necessary for me, allowing me space to think, rethink, and understand. When I am seriously working on a writing project I go back to the desk three or four times a day. I am not someone who writes every day, though I read and think about poems daily.

5.

It was, and is, easy enough to overcome the criticism, pettiness, and bullying of those who disapprove of me, my life, or my poems. They're all the same thing, even though that's not a particularly popular thing to admit among other writers. It always says more about them than it does about me or what I do. And I'm fine with that. It was and is far harder to overcome the criticisms I place on myself. My pride, my anxieties, all those nasty little bits that are dangerous to ignore, as much as I want to. I'm not trying to dabble in some sort of romantic rot about the difficulty of being a poet, the tortured artiste clichés, the struggle. The writer part is pretty easy: I write what I want to write, relentlessly revise, and when I feel I can do no more good for the poems, I send them out in the world. I do nothing except what I believe other artists do. We have to overcome our own self-consciousness, -censoring, -doubt, and -sabotage. We have to cultivate confidence and humility. We have to strive to be better, but also generous enough to accept our limitations. I have to invite vulnerability into my poems, just as I've worked these last ten years on letting it into my daily life.

I come from people who cannot divorce worth from utility. A dog or cat must have a job—must mouse, or hunt, or guard—to be considered good. It must earn its affection, even though that is restrained. I come from people who were dirt farmers, skinners, who lost fingers in sawmills. People who drudged about and were exhausted. People who were old before they turned forty-five. I come from people who believe in scarcity economies: there's only so much luck, happiness, or love in the universe and it doesn't come to people like us. I come from people who keep secrets: bastard children, institutionalization, alcoholism, thievery. People who don't understand how they're their own worst problem. People who can't conceive of a future as something hopeful; it's only going to be the revisitation of past disappointments. I come from people who appreciate beauty but who don't think they deserve it. "That's really pretty," my mom says when we're out. But before I even entertain the idea of her having it she says, "I don't need it, though."

I'm of my family, but unlike my family. I understand their reticence to speak. I understand their refusals to take vacations. Their universe was one of adversity and labor. And what I will never be able to explain is that mine is, too. That I have spent the last few years dedicated to the idea of bringing the personal to my writing. That I spent the decade before that trying to understand my own feelings. During the worst part of my depression, when I was a human-shaped null, I would identify an emotion each day. I would try to remember that feeling, how it happened, how it felt, where it happened, how long that feeling lasted. Despair and desire I knew; they're the polestars of my life. But I learned how to be angry, how to flash toward protecting myself and others. I learned how to be afraid in a useful way, how to take that rush, that uncertain tingle, and channel it. I learned the benefits of trying and failing. The specific reward of that experience. Each day, I give myself permission to fail. And when it happens, I go on. No recrimination, no self-chastisement.

At some point, I have to be as kind to myself as we are to our poems.

JAYNE ANNE PHILLIPS
Outlaw Heart

THE WRITING LIFE is a secret life, whether we admit it or not. Writers focus perpetually on the half seen, and we live in the dim or glorious shadows of partially apprehended shapes. We could bill ourselves as perceptually challenged—given that we live two lives at once, segueing from one to the other with some distress—but we accept, long before we publish, the outlaw's mantle. We occupy a kind of border country, focused on the details that speak to us. Ask those who marry us, or those who don't: we're too intensely involved, yet never quite present. Perhaps we're difficult to live with as adults, but often we were precocious, overly responsible children—not in what we accomplished, necessarily, but in what we remembered, in the emotional burdens we took on. Many of us were our mothers' confidantes, the special children with whom hopes and betrayals were discussed. Our mothers were often women who lived alone, in reality or in spirit, women whose passionate beliefs and perceptions knew little outlet but this blood tie, this receptive listener who would take it all to heart. We listened out of love, and because we felt in ourselves a reservoir of longing: we were unfailingly attracted to the secrets of others, and to secrets shrouded in the phenomena of the world. We knew too much: in this we were outlaws. Early on, we were awarded possession of a set of truths, enlisted to protect someone's version, yet we lived in the context of those stories and we understood the truth to shift. The truth was agile as a dream. Only language could match its permutations or approach its complexity.

So it is that we children who become writers evolve into a particular genus of angelic spy, absorbing information, bargaining with ourselves, banking on the possibility that we might one day intervene in the dynamics of loss, insist that sorrow not be meaningless. In this way we might speak, yet not betray a trust. Those whose voices first blessed us with an ambivalent power still stride through our heads, their luminous forms breaking down. They are lost, finally, as we know ourselves to be lost. Yet literature insists on history—the story of a life, intimately known—and writers gamble with redemption. Surely our hope in holding a world still between the covers of a book is to make that world known, to save it from vanishing. We may be agnostics or furious atheists, but we are all religious, and we practice a faith. We probably don't pray: prayer is always a veiled request, and writers avoid asking for directions. Writing as practice is more similar to meditation, which requests nothing. There is the same silence and the waiting, but writers are notoriously failed seekers. We watch our thoughts arise and practice attachment, fascinated by the dance of the flames. There's a mystery to penetrate within that heat, one that defies boundaries. Writers grow up with permeable selves, and the very process of secrecy feels familiar.

Writers begin as readers, and words become a means of survival. At some juncture deep within family life, the child sees in written language a way to embrace her own burden. When I was young, words themselves seemed secret because I read them in my mind and no one else could hear. Knowledge was often secret; the most interesting things were repeated in low tones. And late at night the life of the house was magnified. My father was an insomniac who walked the long hallway; he'd camp out in the bathroom while everyone else was asleep, smoking and reading. What did he read? Those books were stacked on the top shelf of the bathroom cabinet, behind closed doors, out of reach. They were all paperbacks, detective stories with guns on their covers, or couples, half-undressed, or maybe a woman in defiant high heels and clothes that clung. We kids weren't allowed to lock doors, but we got around that rule in the bathroom by shutting the door and pulling out a drawer that in effect barred any entrance. I had to climb up on the counter and hang perilously to the shelves themselves in order to look at my father's books, to page through them looking for the most secret, forbidden lines, and so it was that

I discovered, at age eight or nine, Updike's *Rabbit, Run*. I opened the book to find Janice on her knees beside the bathtub, drunk and panic-stricken, trying to find her baby in the deep water. I read the scene once, I read it twice: I felt myself flung inside Janice and I couldn't get out. I couldn't stop reading, maintaining my cramped balance by holding to the frame of the narrow window, only letting go to turn pages. Outside a drowsy bank of lilacs nodded in the heat, bulbous and densely fragrant, shaded in foliage, and suddenly it really was night, I was in my bed, seeing the image of the book, its cover illustration so like the others, shut away. There were layers of secrets. Adults failed miserably, parents killed their children: I knew this already, having heard the women talk about a fourteen-year-old girl out our road who gave birth alone in a field and left the baby there. That girl was a stranger. But I recognized Janice from my own nightmares; she was like me in dreams I couldn't stop having that summer; partially blind, on her knees in a room that tilted, and she'd done something that could never be undone; it was too late. I woke from the dreams terrified, relieved to discover nothing was wrong—nothing visible, nothing real. I said the word in the dark, banishing last fears after every startled awakening: nothing. Janice was nothing like Marlo Thomas or Mary Tyler Moore, plucky icons of my childhood sitcoms, and nothing like my own mother, who would never, never lose her baby in a bathtub. Who was Janice then, and why did I know her? I saw that the trick within the world of the book was like the trick in dreams: it had been too late always, even before the book began. The water in the tub was too deep, the baby was slippery, she was blind drunk and lost her grip, then forgot for an instant she'd lost it. Everything beyond that moment was drenched with shadow; everything before it was lit up. Now when I woke at night and saw a sliver of light cast across the dark hallway, spilled out from under the closed bathroom door, I knew Janice was in there. All my dark dreams had flown to her: I didn't have them anymore.

This, then, was how language worked. And if it could save me, it could save us all.

Contributors

DOROTHY ALLISON grew up in Greenville, South Carolina, the first child of a fifteen-year-old unwed mother who worked as a waitress. Now living in Northern California with her partner Alix and her son Wolf Michael, she describes herself as a feminist, a working-class storyteller, a Southern expatriate, a sometime poet, and a happily born-again Californian. An award-winning editor for *Quest, Conditions,* and *Outlook*—early feminist and Lesbian & Gay journals—Allison published a chapbook of poetry, *The Women Who Hate Me,* with Long Haul Press in 1983. Her short story collection, *Trash* (1988), was published by Firebrand Books. *Trash* won two Lambda Literary Awards and the American Library Association Prize for Lesbian and Gay Writing. Allison says that the early feminist movement changed her life. "It was like opening your eyes under water. It hurt, but suddenly everything that had been dark and mysterious became visible and open to change." However, she admits, she would never have begun to publish her stories if she hadn't gotten over her prejudices and started talking to her mother and sisters again. Allison received mainstream recognition with her novel *Bastard Out of Carolina* (1992), a finalist for the 1992 National Book Award. The novel won the Ferro Grumley prize, an ALA Award for Lesbian and Gay Writing, became a best seller, and was the inspiration for an award-winning movie. It has been translated into more than a dozen languages. *Cavedweller* (1998) became a national best seller, a *New York Times* Notable Book of the Year, a finalist for the Lillian Smith prize, and an American Library Association prizewinner. Adapted for the stage by Kate Moira Ryan, the play was directed by Michael Greif and featured music by *Hedwig* composer Stephen Trask. In 2003, Lisa Cholendenko directed a movie version featuring Kyra Sedgwick. Awarded the 2007 Robert Penn Warren Award for Fiction, Allison is a member of the board of the Fellowship of Southern Writers. A novel, *She Who*, is forthcoming.

ROB AMBERG was born in Washington, D.C., in 1947. He moved to Madison County, North Carolina, in 1973 and began what has become his lifetime project—writing about and photographing the evolving culture and environment of his adopted county. His first book, *Sodom Laurel Album*, was published in 2002 by the Center for Documentary Studies at Duke and the University of North Carolina Press. His second book from Madison County, *The New Road: I-26 and the Footprints of Progress in Appalachia*, was published in 2009 by the Center for American Places at Columbia College Chicago and the University of Georgia Press. A third book, tentatively titled *Shatterzone*, is in progress. Throughout his career Amberg has been on staff or done assignment work for nonprofit organizations and philanthropic foundations. His work has largely focused on rural communities, family farms, and the environment. His photographs are regularly published and exhibited internationally. He is the recipient of awards from the John Simon Guggenheim Memorial Foundation, the National Endowment for the Humanities, the North Carolina Humanities Council, the Center for Documentary Studies, and others. In 2004, he had the honor of presenting *Sodom Laurel Album* at the Library of Congress. Amberg lives on a small farm in western North Carolina.

PINCKNEY BENEDICT grew up on his family's dairy farm in Greenbrier County, West Virginia. He has published three collections of short fiction—*Town Smokes, The Wrecking Yard*, and *Miracle Boy*—and a novel, *Dogs of God*. His stories have appeared in *Esquire, Zoetrope: All-Story, Tin House, StoryQuarterly*, and *Ontario Review*, as well as a number of other magazines. His work has appeared in the O. Henry Prize series, the Pushcart Prize series, the New Stories from the South series, *The Ecco Anthology of American Contemporary Short Fiction*, and *The Oxford Book of American Short Stories*, as well as a number of other anthologies. He is the recipient, among other prizes, of a literature fellowship from the National Endowment for the Arts, a literary fellowship from the West Virginia Commission on the Arts, the Plattner Award for fiction from *Appalachian Heritage Magazine*, a fiction fellowship from the Illinois Arts Council, a Michener Fellowship from the Writers' Workshop at the University of Iowa, the *Chicago Tribune*'s Nelson Algren Literary Award, and Britain's Steinbeck Award. He has taught on the creative writing faculties at Oberlin College, Ohio State University, Princeton University, and Hollins University. He serves as a professor in the English Department at Southern Illinois University Carbondale and on the core faculty of the low-residency MFA program at Queens University in Charlotte, North Carolina.

KATHRYN STRIPLING BYER lives in the Blue Ridge Mountains of North Carolina, where she served as North Carolina's first woman Poet Laureate. Her work has appeared in numerous anthologies and journals, including *Atlantic Monthly, Poetry, Georgia Review, American Scholar,* and *Cortland Review,* and her essays and political commentary in *Shenandoah, Boston Globe,* and *Raleigh News-Observer,* as well as other North Carolina newspapers. Her first book, *The Girl in the Midst of the Harvest,* was an Associated Writing Programs Finalist, chosen by John F. Nims, and published by Texas Tech University Press. Louisiana State University Press has published subsequent books, including *Wildwood Flower,* an Academy of American Poets Lamont (now Laughlin) Selection; *Black Shawl,* chosen by Billy Collins for the Brockman-Campbell Award; and *Catching Light,* the winner of the Southern Independent Booksellers Alliance award for poetry for 2002. *Coming to Rest* received the Hanes Poetry Award from the Fellowship of Southern Writers in 2007. *Descent,* her most recent collection (LSU Press, 2012), received the Southern Independent Booksellers Alliance award for poetry. Her first collection was reprinted in the spring of 2012 by Press 53 in Winston-Salem, North Carolina.

SHELDON LEE COMPTON is the author of the collection *The Same Terrible Storm,* recently nominated for the Thomas and Lillie D. Chaffin Award. His work has been published widely and been four times nominated for the Pushcart Prize, and was a finalist in 2012 for the Still Fiction Award as well as a finalist for the Gertrude Stein Award in Fiction the following year. He survives in Eastern Kentucky and edits *Revolution John.*

MICHAEL CROLEY was born in the foothills of the Appalachian Mountains in Corbin, Kentucky. A graduate of the creative writing programs at Florida State and the University of Memphis, Croley's work has won awards from the Kentucky Arts Council, the Key West Literary Seminars, and the Sewanee Writers' Conference. His stories have regularly appeared in *Narrative,* where he was named to their list of Best New Writers in 2011. His other fiction and criticism has been published in *The Paris Review Daily, Blackbird, The Louisville Review, The Southern Review, Fourth Genre,* and the *Cleveland Plain-Dealer.* His first novel, *After the Sun Fell,* is forthcoming. He teaches creative writing at Denison University in Granville, Ohio.

RICHARD CURREY was born in Parkersburg, West Virginia, and is the author of *Crossing Over: The Vietnam Stories, Fatal Light, The Wars of Heaven,* and *Lost Highway.* His stories have been widely anthologized, including in the O. Henry, Pushcart, and Best American Short Story collections, adapted for the stage and performed at Symphony Space in New York, and aired on both NPR's *Selected Shorts* and Sirius-XM Satellite Radio. Currey has received many awards, prizes, and fellowships, including two National Endowment for the Arts Fellowships and the Daugherty Award in the Humanities from the State of West Virginia.

JOYCE DYER grew up in Akron, Ohio, in a company town built by Harvey S. Firestone for his rubber workers. She is the author of three memoirs, *In a Tangled Wood, Gum-Dipped,* and *Goosetown,* and the editor of *Bloodroot: Reflections on Place by Appalachian Women Writers,* winner of the Appalachian Book of the Year Award. She has published essays in newspapers and magazines such as *North American Review,* the *New York Times,* and *Writer's Chronicle.* Dyer teaches creative writing at Hiram College and lives in Hudson, Ohio, where she is working on a book about her town's most famous citizen—John Brown.

SARAH EINSTEIN grew up in Huntington, West Virginia. Her memoir, *Mot: A Memoir,* won the Association of Writers and Writing Programs' Award for Creative Nonfiction in 2014 and is forthcoming from the University of Georgia Press. She currently lives with her husband, Dominik, in Chattanooga, Tennessee, where she is an assistant professor of creative writing at the University of Tennessee at Chattanooga. Her work has appeared in *Ninth Letter, PANK, Fringe,* and other journals and has been awarded a Pushcart Prize. She is the managing editor of *Brevity*.

CONNIE MAY FOWLER is the author of seven books, including the novels *How Clarissa Burden Learned to Fly* and *Before Women Had Wings*, which received the 1996 Southern Book Critics Circle Award and was a New York Times best seller. Her lauded memoir, *When Katie Wakes*, tracks her descent into and escape from an abusive relationship. She is the author of numerous essays that have appeared in the *New York Times, London Times, Japan Times, Oxford American,* and elsewhere. She wrote an Oprah Winfrey–produced award-winning teleplay, which she adapted from *Before Women Had Wings*. Her work has been translated into seventeen languages. Her mother hailed from Grundy, Virginia. Her family traces their roots to Appalachia several generations back to at least the early 1800s. She teaches at the Vermont College of Fine Arts, where she is core faculty and directs their annual Novel Retreat. She is founder and director of The St. Augustine Writers Conference and is editor-in-chief of *Tambourine: The Literary Journal of Social Protest. A Million Fragile Bones*, a memoir, is forthcoming.

RJ GIBSON was raised, and still lives, in Buckhannon, West Virginia. He is the author of the chapbooks *Scavenge* (co-winner of the 2009 Robin Becker Prize) and *You Could Learn a Lot*, both from Seven Kitchens Press. He holds an MFA in Poetry from the Program for Writers at Warren Wilson College. His work has appeared in *Court Green, Columbia Poetry Review, Kenyon Review Online,* the *Cortland Review,* and the anthologies *My Diva: 65 Gay Men on the Women Who Inspire Them* and *Collective Brightness: LGBTIQ Poets on Faith, Religion & Spirituality.* In 2008, he was a Lambda Literary Foundation Poetry Fellow.

MARY CROCKETT HILL's debut young adult novel *Dream Boy*, coauthored with Madelyn Rosenberg, was published in 2014 by Sourcebooks Fire. In her other life as a poet, Mary is author of *A Theory of Everything* (winner of the Autumn House Poetry Prize) and *If You Return Home with Food* (winner of the Bluestem Poetry Award). Her poems have appeared in numerous journals and anthologies, as well as on *Poetry Daily* and in *American Poetry: The Next Generation*. Mary's work has been nominated for a half dozen Pushcart Awards and recognized as

Best of the Net. In her *other* other life as a person trying to eke out a living in the valleys of southwestern Virginia, Mary has worked as a factory slug, a staggeringly bad waitress, an incompetent secretary, and the person who irons name tags into industrial uniforms. She has also served as the director of a history museum, a college English teacher, and a higher education fundraising spy. Mary currently works as a freelance writer, creative director, and novelist. She tweets poetry nonsense @marycrocketthil and kidlit nonsense @marylovesbooks. For more about her writing for children and teens, see www.marycrockett.com.

BELL HOOKS is Distinguished Professor in Residence in Appalachian Studies at Berea College. Born Gloria Jean Watkins in Hopkinsville, Kentucky, she has chosen the lowercase pen name bell hooks, based on the names of her mother and grandmother, to emphasize the importance of the substance of her writing as opposed to who she is. She is the author of over thirty books, many of which have focused on issues of social class, race, and gender. Her latest book is titled *Belonging: A Culture of Place.*

SILAS HOUSE is the best-selling author of five novels, three plays, and a work of creative nonfiction. House's writing has appeared in the *New York Times, Oxford American, Newsday, Paste,* the *Southeast Review,* and many other publications. A former contributor to NPR's *All Things Considered,* House is the winner of the E. B. White Award, the Intellectual Freedom Award, the Audie, the Nautilus Award, and many other prizes. He serves on the fiction faculty of the MFA program in creative writing at Spalding University and as the National Endowment for the Humanities Chair at Berea College.

JASON HOWARD is the author of *A Few Honest Words: The Kentucky Roots of Popular Music,* a collection of profiles of contemporary roots musicians that explores how the land and culture of Kentucky have shaped American music through the years and continue to do so today. He is the coauthor of *Something's Rising: Appalachians Fighting Mountaintop Removal,* which was hailed by the late historian Studs Terkel as "a revelatory work," and the editor of the environmental anthology *We All Live Downstream.* His features, essays, and reviews have been featured in the *New York Times*, the *Nation, Sojourners, Equal Justice Magazine, Paste*, the *Louisville Review*, and on NPR. In recognition of artistic excellence, Howard received the 2013 Al Smith Individual Artist Fellowship in Creative Nonfiction from the Kentucky Arts Council. From 2010 to 2012 he served as a James Still Fellow at the University of Kentucky. Howard holds an MFA in creative nonfiction from Vermont College of Fine Arts. He lives in Berea, Kentucky, and edits *Appalachian Heritage*.

DAVID HUDDLE holds degrees from the University of Virginia, Hollins College, and Columbia University. Originally from Ivanhoe, Virginia, he taught for thirty-eight years at the University of Vermont, then served three years as Distinguished Visiting Professor of Creative Writing at Hollins University. He also held the 2012–2013 Roy Acuff Chair of Excellence in the Creative Arts at Austin Peay State University in Clarksville, Tennessee. Huddle has continued to teach at the Bread Loaf School of English in Ripton, Vermont, and the Rainier Writing Workshop in Tacoma, Washington. In 2014 he joined the faculty of the Sewanee School of Letters. Huddle's work has appeared in the *American Scholar, Esquire, Appalachian Heritage*, the *New Yorker, Harper's, Shenandoah, Agni*, and the *Georgia Review*. His novel *The Story of a Million Years* (Houghton Mifflin, 1999) was named a Distinguished Book of the Year by *Esquire* and a Best Book of the Year by the *Los Angeles Times Book Review*. His novel *Nothing Can Make Me Do This* won the 2012 Library of Virginia Award for Fiction, and his collection, *Black Snake at the Family Reunion*, was a finalist for the 2013 Library of Virginia Award for Poetry and won the 2013 Pen New England Award for Poetry. His new poetry collection, *Dream Sender*, will appear in September 2015.

TENNESSEE JONES is the author of the short story collection *Deliver Me from Nowhere*. He is the recipient of several fellowships, including awards from the Jacob K. Javits Foundation, Christopher Isherwood Foundation, and Phillips Exeter Academy. He was the Philip Roth Writer in Residence at Bucknell University in 2013, where he continued work on a novel about a small Appalachian town notorious for two brutal incidents: the hanging of an elephant and the expulsion of its entire black population. He was raised in the mountains of East Tennessee and currently lives in Brooklyn, New York.

LISA LEWIS's new book of poetry, *The Body Double,* is forthcoming in 2015 from Georgetown Review Press. Her other books include *The Unbeliever* (Brittingham Prize), *Silent Treatment* (National Poetry Series), *Vivisect* (New Issues Press), and *Burned House with Swimming Pool* (American Poetry Journal Prize, Dream Horse Press). A chapbook titled *Story Box* was also published as winner of the Poetry West Chapbook Contest. Her work has appeared in numerous literary magazines and anthologies, including *Kenyon Review, Washington Square, Third Coast, American Literary Review, Fence, Seattle Review, Rattle,* and *Best American Poetry.* She has also won awards from the *American Poetry Review* and the *Missouri Review,* a Pushcart Prize, and a fellowship from the National Endowment for the Arts. She directs the creative writing program at Oklahoma State University and serves as poetry editor for the *Cimarron Review.*

JEFF MANN grew up in Covington, Virginia, and Hinton, West Virginia, receiving degrees in English and forestry from West Virginia University. His poetry, fiction, and essays have appeared in many publications, including *Arts and Letters, Prairie Schooner, Shenandoah, Willow Springs,* the *Gay and Lesbian Review Worldwide, Crab Orchard Review,* and *Appalachian Heritage.* He has published three award-winning poetry chapbooks, *Bliss, Mountain Fireflies,* and *Flint Shards from Sussex;* four full-length books of poetry, *Bones Washed with Wine, On the Tongue, Ash: Poems from Norse Mythology,* and *A Romantic Mann;* two collections of personal essays, *Edge: Travels of an Appalachian Leather Bear* and *Binding the God: Ursine Essays from the Mountain South;* two novellas, *Devoured,* included in *Masters of Midnight: Erotic Tales of the Vampire,* and *Camp Allegheny,* included in *History's Passion: Stories of Sex Before Stonewall;* two novels, *Fog: A Novel of Desire and Reprisal* and *Purgatory: A Novel of the Civil War;* a book of poetry and memoir, *Loving Mountains, Loving Men;* and two volumes of short fiction, *Desire and Devour: Stories of Blood and Sweat* and *A History of Barbed Wire,* which won a Lambda Literary Award. He teaches creative writing at Virginia Tech in Blacksburg, Virginia.

CHRIS OFFUTT grew up in Haldeman, Kentucky, a former mining town of two hundred people in the Daniel Boone National Forest. The dirt roads were recently blacktopped and the post office shut down.

He attended grade school, high school, and college within a ten-mile radius of his home, graduating from Morehead State University with a BA in theatre and a minor in art. He is the author of *Kentucky Straight, Out of the Woods, The Same River Twice, No Heroes,* and *The Good Brother.* A novel and a collection of stories are forthcoming. He has written screenplays for HBO's *True Blood* and *Treme,* Showtime's *Weeds,* and TV pilots for Lionsgate and CBS. His TV work was nominated for an Emmy. Chris has published over seventy stories and essays, including appearances in the *New York Times, Esquire, GQ,* and on National Public Radio. His work has been anthologized in *Best American Short Stories, Best of the South,* and *Classic American Memoirs,* among others. His prose has received awards from the Guggenheim Foundation, the Whiting Foundation, the Lannan Foundation, the National Endowment for the Arts, and the American Academy of Arts and Letters. *Granta Magazine* included him in their list of the "Top 20 Young American Writers." He is currently teaching at the University of Mississippi.

ANN PANCAKE is a native of West Virginia. Her first novel, *Strange As This Weather Has Been* (Counterpoint, 2007), features a southern West Virginia family devastated by mountaintop removal mining. The novel was one of *Kirkus Review'*s Top Ten Fiction Books of 2007, won the 2007 Weatherford Prize, and was a finalist for the 2008 Orion Book Award and the 2008 Washington State Book Award. Her collection of short stories, *Given Ground* (University Press of New England, 2001), won the 2000 Bakeless award, and a new collection of stories, *Me and My Daddy Listen to Bob Marley,* was released in 2015. Pancake has also received a Whiting Award, a National Endowment for the Arts grant, a Pushcart Prize, and grants from the states of West Virginia, Pennsylvania, and Washington. Her fiction and essays have appeared in journals and anthologies like *Orion,* the *Georgia Review, Poets and Writers,* and *New Stories from the South: The Year's Best.* She earned her BA in English at West Virginia University and a PhD in English literature from the University of Washington. Currently, she teaches in the low-residency MFA program at Pacific Lutheran University in Tacoma, Washington.

JAYNE ANNE PHILLIPS was born in Buckhannon, West Virginia. She is the author of five novels, *Quiet Dell* (2013), *Lark and Termite* (2009),

MotherKind (2000), *Shelter* (1994), and *Machine Dreams* (1984), and two collections of widely anthologized stories, *Fast Lanes* (1987) and *Black Tickets* (1979). She is the recipient of a Guggenheim Fellowship, two National Endowment for the Arts Fellowships, the Heartland Prize, and a Bunting Fellowship. A National Book Award finalist and twice a National Book Critic's Circle Award finalist, she was awarded the Sue Kaufman Prize for First Fiction (1980) and an Academy Award in Literature (1997) by the American Academy of Arts and Letters. Her work has been translated into twelve languages and has appeared in *Granta, Harper's, DoubleTake,* and *The Norton Anthology of Contemporary Fiction.* She is currently Distinguished Professor of English and director of the MFA program at Rutgers-Newark, the State University of New Jersey. Essays, reviews, and text source images are available at www.JayneAnnePhillips.com.

MELISSA RANGE's first book of poems, *Horse and Rider* (Texas Tech University Press, 2010), won the 2010 Walt McDonald Prize in Poetry. Her poems have appeared in *32 Poems,* the *Hudson Review, Image, New England Review,* the *Paris Review,* and other journals. She is the recipient of a Rona Jaffe Foundation Writers' Award, a Discovery / The Nation award, and fellowships from the American Antiquarian Society, the Fine Arts Work Center in Provincetown, the Virginia Center for the Creative Arts, the Sewanee Writers' Conference, and the National Endowment for the Arts. Originally from East Tennessee, she lives in Wisconsin and teaches at Lawrence University.

CARTER SICKELS is the author of the novel *The Evening Hour* (Bloomsbury USA), a finalist for the 2013 Oregon Book Award, the Lambda Literary Debut Fiction Award, and the Publishing Triangle Edmund White Debut Fiction Award. Carter is winner of the 2013 Lambda Literary Emerging Writer Award and the recipient of a 2013 project grant from the Regional Arts & Culture Council. He has been awarded scholarships to Bread Loaf Writers' Conference, the Sewanee Writers' Conference, the MacDowell Colony, and Virginia Center for the Creative Arts. Carter earned his MFA in fiction at Penn State University and his MA in folklore at the University of North Carolina at Chapel Hill. He currently teaches in the low-residency MFA programs at West Virginia Wesleyan University and Eastern Oregon

University. Carter grew up in Ohio and has roots in the southeastern part of the state, in the foothills of the Appalachian Mountains, where he spent some of the best times of his childhood and lived in his early twenties.

AARON SMITH is the author of two full-length collections of poetry, both published by the University of Pittsburgh Press: *Appetite*, a finalist for the Paterson Poetry Prize, the Lambda Literary Award, and the Thom Gunn Award; and *Blue on Blue Ground*, winner of the Agnes Lynch Starrett Prize. His chapbooks include *Men in Groups* and *What's Required*, winner of the Frank O'Hara Award. His work has appeared in numerous publications, including *Court Green*, *Ploughshares, Prairie Schooner*, and *The Best American Poetry 2013*. He is an assistant professor in creative writing at Lesley University in Cambridge, Massachusetts.

JANE SPRINGER is the author of two collections of poetry, *Dear Blackbird* (Agha Shahid Ali Prize, 2007), and *Murder Ballad* (Beatrice Hawley Award, 2012). Her honors include a Pushcart Prize, a National Endowment for the Arts fellowship, and a Whiting Writers' Award, among others. She currently teaches English and creative writing at Hamilton College, in upstate New York, where she lives with her husband, kid, and dog.

IDA STEWART is the author of *Gloss*, winner of the 2011 Perugia Press Prize for a first or second book of poetry by a woman. Her poems can also be found in journals including *Field*, the *Laurel Review*, the *Tusculum Review*, and *Connotation Press*. She holds an MFA in creative writing from the Ohio State University and a PhD in English from the University of Georgia. A native of West Virginia, she currently lives in Philadelphia and teaches writing at the University of Delaware.

JACINDA TOWNSEND grew up in Bowling Green, Kentucky. She studied creative writing at Harvard, Duke, and the University of Iowa, where she received her MFA. Her debut novel, *Saint Monkey*, was published in 2014 by W. W. Norton. She teaches at Indiana University and lives in Bloomington with two beautiful children.

A West Virginia native, JESSIE VAN EERDEN holds an MFA in non-fiction writing from the University of Iowa. She was selected as the 2007–8 Milton Fellow at *Image* and Seattle Pacific University for work on her first novel, *Glorybound* (WordFarm, 2012), winner of *ForeWord Reviews'* 2012 Editor's Choice Fiction Prize. Her essays, short stories, and poems have appeared in the *Oxford American, Bellingham Review, Rock & Sling, Memorious, Waccamaw,* and other publications. Her essays have been selected for inclusion in *Best American Spiritual Writing* (2006), *The River Teeth Reader* (2009), and *Red Holler: An Anthology of Contemporary Appalachian Literature* (2013). Jessie has taught for over twelve years in adult literacy programs and college classrooms. She lives in West Virginia, where she directs the low-residency MFA writing program of West Virginia Wesleyan College.

A native of Southeastern Kentucky, JULIA WATTS is the author of the Lambda Literary Award–winning young adult novel *Finding H. F.,* the Lambda Literary Award finalist *The Kind of Girl I Am,* and several other novels for adults and young readers. She teaches at South College and in Murray State University's low-residency MFA program. She has lived in Appalachia her whole life. Her new novel is *Secret City.*

CHARLES DODD WHITE is the author of the novels *A Shelter of Others* (2014) and *Lambs of Men* (2010) and the short story collection *Sinners of Sanction County,* and is coeditor of the contemporary Appalachian short story anthology *Degrees of Elevation.* He is the recipient of the Jean Ritchie Fellowship and an individual grant in prose by the North Carolina Arts Council. His work has appeared in *Appalachian Heritage,* the *Collagist, Fugue,* the *Louisville Review, North Carolina Literary Review, PANK,* the *Rumpus,* and several other journals. He is an assistant professor at Pellissippi State Community College in Knoxville, Tennessee.

CRYSTAL WILKINSON is the author of *Birds of Opulence; Blackberries, Blackberries,* winner of the 2002 Chaffin Award for Appalachian Literature; and *Water Street,* a finalist for both the UK's Orange Prize for Fiction and the Hurston/Wright Legacy Award. Wilkinson is the recipient of awards and fellowships from the Kentucky Foundation for Women, the Kentucky Arts Council, the Mary Anderson Center for the Arts, and the Archie D. and Bertha H. Walker Scholarship at the Fine Arts Work Center in Provincetown. She is the winner of the 2008 Denny Plattner Award in Poetry from *Appalachian Heritage Magazine* and the Sallie Bingham Award from the Kentucky Foundation for Women for the promotion of activism and feminist artist expression. Wilkinson is currently the Appalachian writer-in-residence at Berea College. She and her partner, artist Ron Davis, are founders and editors of *Mythium: A Journal of Contemporary Literature Celebrating Writers of Color and the Cultural Voice.* They own The Wild Fig Bookstore in Lexington, Kentucky.

Editors

ADRIAN BLEVINS was born in Abingdon, Virginia, in 1964 and educated at Virginia Intermont College, Hollins University, and Warren Wilson College's MFA Program for Writers. She is the author of *Live from the Homesick Jamboree* (Wesleyan University Press, 2009), *The Brass Girl Brouhaha* (Ausable Press, 2003), and two chapbooks, *The Man Who Went Out for Cigarettes* (Bright Hill Press, 1996) and *Bloodline* (Hollyridge Press, 2012). Blevins is the recipient of many awards and honors, including a Kate Tufts Discovery Award for *The Brass Girl Brouhaha,* a Rona Jaffe Writer's Foundation Award, a Bright Hill Press Chapbook Award, the Lamar York Prize for Nonfiction, and, more recently, a Pushcart Prize, a Cohen Award from *Ploughshares,* and the 2012 *Zone 3* Poetry Award. She teaches at Colby College in Waterville, Maine.

KAREN SALYER MCELMURRAY'S *Surrendered Child: A Birth Mother's Journey,* was an AWP Award Winner for Creative Nonfiction and a National Book Critics Circle Notable Book. Her novels are The Motel of the Stars, *Editor's Pick by* Oxford American, *and* Strange Birds in the Tree of Heaven, winner of the Chaffin Award for Appalachian Writing. Other stories and essays have appeared in *Iron Horse, Kenyon Review, Alaska Quarterly Review,* and *Riverteeth,* and in the anthologies *An Angle of Vision; To Tell the Truth; Fearless Confessions; Listen Here; Dirt; Family Trouble; Red Holler; Women and Their Machines.* Her writing has been supported by grants from the National Endowment for the Arts, the North Carolina Arts Council, and the Kentucky Foundation for Women. Her essay "Strange Tongues" was the recipient of the Annie Dillard Award from *The Bellingham Review.* During 2015–16, she will be Visiting Professor at Gettysburg College.

Acknowledgments

BLEVINS

Thanks to each of the amazing writers in this collection for the gifts of your experience, insight, knowledge, and nerve. Thanks to Karen McElmurray for her experience, insight, knowledge, nerve, and fortitude. Thanks to Gillian Berchowitz for gathering us together and seeing us through, and to Nate and August Rudy for their patience and assistance with all the technology-related confusion and ineptitude. Thanks to Colby College for the sabbatical, and, finally, thanks to my paternal grandparents Banner and Elizabeth Nina Howell Blevins, buried in McCall's Gap, Virginia, not very far from their North Carolina mountain birthplaces: though you guys would not approve of every sentence in this book, I think you would get the need for it and, given your pioneer hearts, maybe even sort of like its feistiness.

MCELMURRAY

For these essays, I thank back roads and highways out. I thank leaving and staying put and wanting both, all at once. I thank skyways and lightning bugs, Mason jars and fluted glasses, quilting rings and embroidered pillowcases from Rajasthan. I thank ways old, ways new. I thank what is forbidden, and what is not, and riding down the cusp of both on a hot summer night in Johnson County, Kentucky. I thank Hager Hill, the house that is gone forever, the only home I really loved, before now. I thank my teachers of ways Appalachian— Loyal Jones, Bill Best. I thank my grandmothers, Fannie May and Beck, Pearlie and Ida May. I thank all the authors of these essays, their chances taken, their risks and truths. I thank Adrian Blevins, Gillian Berchowitz, and Ohio University Press for fostering these words along the way.

Credits

"Preface: Deciding to Live" by Dorothy Allison from *Trash* (Plume, 2002) reprinted by permission of the author and The Frances Goldin Literary Agency.

"ORGO vs the FLATLANDERS" by Pinckney Benedict reprinted by permission of the author.

"Introduction to *Appalachian Elegy*" by bell hooks from *Appalachian Elegy* reprinted by permission of University of Kentucky.

"Someone Else," by Chris Offutt, was first published in *River Teeth* and is forthcoming as well in *Best American Essays 2015*.

"Outlaw Heart" by Jane Anne Phillips reprinted by permission of the author and John Wiley & Sons, Ltd.

"Homage to Hazel Dickens" by Irene McKinney from *Have You Seen Enough Darkness Yet?*, West Virginia Wesleyan College Press, 2013.